W9-BVE-981

HOW TO DEVELOP AND PROMOTE SUCCESSFUL SEMINARS AND WORKSHOPS

The Definitive Guide to Creating and Marketing Seminars, Workshops, Classes, and Conferences

HOWARD L. SHENSON, CMC

John Wiley & Sons, Inc.
New York • Chichester • Brisbane • Toronto • Singapore

Recognizing the importance of preserving what has been written, it is a policy of John Wiley & Sons, Inc. to have books of enduring value published in the United States printed on acid-free paper, and we exert our best efforts to that end.

Copyright © 1990 by Howard L. Shenson.

Published by John Wiley & Sons, Inc.

All rights reserved. Published simultaneously in Canada. Reproduction or translation of any part of this work beyond that permitted by Section 107 or 108 of the 1976 United States Copyright Act without the permission of the copyright owner is unlawful. Requests for permission or further information should be addressed to the Permissions Department, John Wiley & Sons, Inc.

This publication is designed to provide accurate and authoritative information in regard to the subject matter covered. It is sold with the understanding that the publisher is not engaged in rendering legal, accounting, or other professional service. If legal advice or other expert assistance is required, the services of a competent professional person should be sought. *From a Declaration of Principles jointly adopted by a Committee of the American Bar Association and a Committee of Publishers*.

Library of Congress Cataloging in Publication Data

Shenson, Howard L.
    How to develop and promote successful seminars and workshops : the definitive guide to creating and marketing seminars, workshops, classes, and conferences / Howard L. Shenson.
        p.   cm.
    Includes index.
    ISBN 0-471-52708-4
    ISBN 0-471-52709-2 (pbk.)
    1. Seminars—Handbooks, manuals, etc.   I. Title.
    AS6.S49   1990
    658.4'56—dc20   90-12104

Printed in the United States of America

10   9   8   7   6   5   4

47/45

To my father-in-law,
Harold Seligmann,
who has always been supportive,
enthusiastic, and interested.

85562

INTRODUCTION

The adult education business—seminars, workshops, classes, conferences—is one of the fastest growing industries in North America and can be extremely profitable. State-of-the-art knowledge and information have become vital and meaningful economic assets of the postindustrial, information-driven society. While there are numerous ways to obtain information, seminars are particularly attractive because they communicate desired knowledge quickly and in an organized and strategically capsulated form. Seminars are an important aspect of the pervasive information revolution.

This book is designed to ensure that those who offer seminars, workshops, classes, conferences, and training programs are maximally successful. A substantial body of research information has replaced hunches and guesses in the promotion of adult learning programs, and the potential for success in the seminar and workshop business has become tremendous. The need and demand for continuing adult education and training are already considerable and will continue to grow as our society's technology, economy, and daily life become increasingly specialized, technical, and complex. Seminars, workshops, and other programs meet this need.

As evidence of the important and growing role of seminars, enrollment in both public programs and contract training programs is high and is on the increase. The following enrollment statistics resulted from combining sample data obtained from surveys of program participants and managers with actual reports by various providers:

Year	Public Seminar Enrollments			Contract Training Enrollments		
	Low	–	High	Low	–	High
1989	6,300,000	–	8,950,000	7,650,000	–	12,900,000
1988	5,825,000	–	8,350,000	7,225,000	–	12,100,000
1987	5,450,000	–	8,025,000	7,100,000	–	11,850,000
1986	5,050,000	–	7,825,000	6,725,000	–	11,300,000

Fees for public seminars range widely. The following data reflect the percentage of program offerings at different price levels:

Year	Under $100	$100–$200	$200–$500	Above $500
1989	18%	30%	35%	17%
1988	19	29	36	16
1987	17	34	35	14
1986	13	40	37	10

Some observers of the seminar business have predicted that, by the year 2010, some 80 percent of the nation's adult population will have attended one or more public seminars or workshops. At the present time, only 32 percent have had this experience. Thus, several million first-time participants will be candidates for the seminars and workshops provided each year. A large proportion of these new attendees will find that seminars are a viable learning approach and will attend two to five or even more public programs annually. Conservatively, enrollments in public seminars can be expected to continue to grow at a 5 to 9 percent annual rate over the next five years and enrollments in contract training, at a 4 to 7 percent annual increase. Enrollments are impacted, of course, by economic conditions; growth rates are higher in a growing economy and lower during a recession. Contract training is more adversely impacted by an economic decline than are public seminars.

I have stated that the seminar and workshop business can be profitable; estimated annual seminar industry revenues will give you some idea of the lucrative overall profitability of the field. Annual revenues are best determined by multiplying the number of enrolled participants by the average fee charged for programs. Based on the sources described above, average fees paid per person trained were:

Year	Public Seminars	Contract Training
1989	$233	$208
1988	221	193
1987	205	184
1986	197	178

Using reliable estimates of the numbers of participants during 1988, total estimated revenues for public programs were $1,287,325,000 to $1,845,350,000, and for contract training programs, $1,413,725,000 to $2,335,300,000. Combining these totals, the 1988 estimated industry revenues reached between $2.7 billion and $4.1 billion.

Estimated average operating ratios can help to give a slightly more detailed insight into the expenses and profits of seminar and workshop providers:

Operating Ratios,	*Public Seminar Providers:*
Sales	1.00
Marketing expense	0.37
Program delivery	0.22
Overhead	0.21
Profit	0.20

A 20 percent return on sales is a handsome profit, particularly since no meaningful capital investment is required to enter the business. Many providers have built highly profitable public seminar and contract training businesses with an initial capital investment of less than $3,000.

Not all entries are profitable. The very low capital investment and ease of entry into the business invite providers who see a high profit potential but lack the precise knowledge and information that would result in their being successful. This book is intended to enable those new to the business, as well as experienced seminar providers, to make and implement decisions that ensure success. To make a seminar or workshop personally and financially rewarding, providers need to research their subject and their target market, develop a program and program materials, determine a promotional strategy and design promotional materials, carry out the promotion, conduct the program, and *test everything.*

This book helps with all of those tasks. The primary focus is on open-to-the-public programs but the information is easily applicable to captive or contract training programs. The topics covered are: selecting seminar topics, target marketing, evaluating and selecting appropriate promotional strategies and media, evaluating and choosing sites and times, selecting hotel and conference facilities, pricing a program, developing or obtaining program materials, adding to profits through back-of-the-room sales, hiring outside presenters, making the most of the promoter/presenter–participant relationship, conducting a winning program, and much more. Particular emphasis is placed on marketing and promotion, especially through direct mail, which often determine the success or failure of the enterprise. Practical problems that confront seminar developers and promoters are emphasized, and realistic, cost-effective solutions are offered.

Not all who offer seminars seek profit from registration receipts. One of the fastest growing segments of the adult education business is seminars conducted without charge and designed to persuade the participants to buy the products or services of the provider. Commercial entities—banks, computer manufacturers, insurance companies, and professional practitioners, for example—regularly hold seminars for showcase purposes. This book will be of vital importance for these providers because, with numerous similar offerings and competition from television seminars and lectures, providers must utilize sophisticated marketing strategies to be successful. Simply posting notice of a free seminar no longer fills the house.

Some readers may determine that sponsoring seminars entails more work and activity than they bargained for. If they elect not to become seminar providers but their desire to develop and conduct successful programs remains strong, they have another option to consider: working with a sponsor. Colleges, universities, professional, trade, and civic associations, commercial entities, and other organizations unable to develop and conduct their own programs are often excellent sponsors. Unfortunately, too many sponsors lack sophisticated knowledge about seminar promotion, pricing, packaging, and related issues. A seminar developer with knowledge of seminar marketing becomes essential in guiding and directing their programs and will then share handsomely in their success.

Do you have a great idea for a seminar and do you want to reap the benefits of the seminar and workshop business? Then forge ahead: carefully, thoroughly, and optimistically.

ACKNOWLEDGMENTS

I am indebted to Tiffany Jordan for her expert) editing of the manuscript and to my many clients who have been sufficiently visionary to authorize the expenditure of valuable time and money to experiment. I am sure that they often thought that being more conventional would have been less risky, but the greatest successes have always resulted from a willingness to take controlled and calculated risks.

HOWARD L. SHENSON

Woodland Hills, California
July 1990

CONTENTS

NOTE TO THE READER

Masculine pronouns and possessives are used throughout this book to simplify communication, but the information is of equal value to men and women. Additionally, although the words *seminar* and *workshop* have distinct meanings, they are often used herein to convey information about seminars, workshops, lectures, classes, conferences, and similar convocations that may be given different names. Where the information does not apply uniformly to other delivery mechanisms it is noted, but the use of *seminar* or *workshop* alone has been chosen to simplify communication.

1

HOW TO SELECT SEMINAR TOPICS THAT SELL

The adult education business made up of seminars, workshops, conferences, and classes is one of the fastest growing and most profitable industries: billions of dollars are expended annually in both open-to-the-public (open enrollment) seminars and workshops, and captive (contracted for) programs. Yet the field is riddled with unsuccessful enterprise. To ensure that your program will be a worthwhile and lucrative undertaking, not a failing venture, you can take measures that begin with the very conception of the seminar topic and end at the completion of the seminar presentation.

CHOOSING A SALABLE TOPIC

A key factor in determining one's success in the seminar and workshop business is the ability to select salable program topics. The choice of a topic is the result of a synthesis between your interests and expertise and the needs and interests of your target market. Your objective is to achieve a good match between these two sets of variables, keeping in mind that your primary focus should be on marketing what will sell and not on your personal interests.

Topic selection is a complex process involving a number of factors—market identification, development and presentation costs, topic longevity, overall economic conditions, and the potential for future marketing opportunities and expansion of seminar activities. A decision matrix for topic selection has been developed that provides a sophisticated, highly reliable basis for evaluating and comparing seminar topics under consideration. The factors used in the evaluation are discussed below; the decision matrix itself is presented on pages 13 and 14.

THE TARGET MARKET AND TOPIC SELECTION

Successful seminar promoters begin their quest for a viable, profitable program by identifying a target market. Starting out with a market orientation spares them from wasting time and money becoming "hapless inventors." Rather than dreaming up topics that seem like good ideas but that no one really needs or wants, successful promoters tailor their ideas to fit a clearly identifiable market or market segment. When the topic finally chosen for presentation at the seminar is of sufficient interest to this market, a profitable outcome for the promoters is ensured.

The long-term success of your seminar depends on your ability to choose a topic in which your market exhibits a sustained interest. Does the topic depend on temporary economic conditions—some "glitch" that may disappear in a few months, leaving you high and dry with a seminar in which no one is interested? Is the interest level time-sensitive—that is, at any given time is your market too limited to support a seminar? For example, seminars on selling your house without a broker, which some promoters felt would do well during a recent real estate boom, were not successful, primarily because the market window was so narrow. People had no interest in that topic prior to a decision to sell their homes or after they had sold (or turned to a broker). Thus, the total universe of people interested in selling their homes themselves at any given time was very limited.

The same principle applies to "faddish" topics. Interest in fads and trendy ideas, while intense for a short period, is not likely to be sustained. Long-term profitability is found in the basic, "bread-and-butter" information related to success and personal development, which never seems to become passé or go out of vogue. Of course, a quick market penetration of a short-term trend can be highly profitable, though it will not offer the roll-out potential (the ability of a program to adapt to changing locations and circumstances) of the bread-and-butter topics.

Nor should topics that respond to pressing current needs and issues be excluded from consideration. New legislation and mandates issued by regulatory agencies may generate a number of viable, salable seminar ideas, provided they mesh with the target market and can be readily adapted to reflect future developments.

There are two ways to gauge the target market and the potential for success: conduct market research, and test market the program.

Conducting Market Research

Market research allows you to assess the viability of an idea or a topic without committing yourself, your time, and your money to its development. One possible and frequently fruitful way to conduct market research is to design a questionnaire that measures potential seminar participants' likely responses to a specified situation. You might ask questions such as:

1. Would you attend a seminar on [the chosen topic]?
2. How much would you be willing to pay to attend the seminar?
3. What kinds of activities do you think should be included?

Market surveys are most effective in captive training programs—those under contract to organizational clients. Market research can be a particularly useful and efficient means of analyzing the needs, desires, and moods of a target market and evaluating a topic's potential, especially if the information requested is specific and factual. A typical request might be: In what areas would you like further training to do your job more effectively?

Test Marketing

Market surveys measure potential participants' *expectations* of a seminar; test marketing measures actual participants' *responses* to the seminar and its results. Ideally, test marketing can take place with low financial investment and little risk, while replicating the conditions in which the seminar will eventually take place. If your test sessions are inexpensive and simply designed, you will be able to:

1. Change various elements of the program quickly and inexpensively in response to feedback and changing circumstances, and
2. Conserve capital so that the marketing approach can be changed and tested again if the initial sessions do not result in the expected and/or necessary number of participants.

If a seminar succeeds in a good test market, it will probably roll out successfully on a national level. While most seminars are tested through direct mail promotion, it is sometimes effective to test a program by making use of other promotional media such as newspaper advertising or radio commercials. When using these mass media to test your choice of a market, there are important factors to consider:

1. *Media Availability.* Noncompounding of media is the ideal situation for a test market city. This means that media in larger, adjacent cities will not interfere with your test of local media. For example, if you are testing with a newspaper ad in the Los Angeles area, Santa Barbara is an excellent test market because few households in Santa Barbara read the *Los Angeles Times* and those that do are very likely to read the local Santa Barbara paper as well. If radio or television commercials are promoting your test seminar, Santa Barbara would not be as good a choice, since many Santa Barbara residents listen to and watch Los Angeles broadcasts.
2. *Demographics.* The population characteristics of a small-city test market should be about the same as those of populations in your ultimate target cities.
3. *Cost of the Media.* Again, if the local media are relatively isolated from nearby big-city media, you can save substantially on media costs.

4. *Availability of Facilities.* Be sure the small cities you select have the facilities you will require to give your presentation. You should be able to rent a suitable meeting room with the needed equipment, and the hotel must be convenient to transportation and restaurants for the participants.

5. *Regionalism* If your program has greater appeal in some regions of the country than in others, your test results may be misleading. Inexplicable regional variations are often very real and impossible to predict without testing the waters. Therefore, it is useful to test in a place where you are unsure about market conditions, as well as on your own turf.

When testing with mass media, the cost of promotional media (newspaper space, air time, and so on) is generally less in smaller markets. However, when testing with direct mail, a smaller market usually has no meaningful advantage. It costs you no more to mail across the country than to mail next door.

According to a survey of 212 seminar providers, conducted by the author, the 10 best test markets for mass-media-promoted seminars are:

1. Bergen County, New Jersey
2. Santa Barbara, California
3. Albuquerque, New Mexico
4. Madison, Wisconsin
5. Spokane, Washington
6. Columbus, Ohio
7. Manchester, New Hampshire
8. Austin, Texas
9. Salt Lake City, Utah
10. Richmond, Virginia

Pay close attention to test market characteristics. One promoter did not and suffered as a result. To keep test cost low, he tested a seminar for the Los Angeles area by promoting it in a suburban community of greater Los Angeles, using a suburban newspaper. His test did not produce the desired results. Later testing revealed that the readership of the suburban newspaper was demographically different from the readership of the *Los Angeles Times*. It was only when he tested his program in San Jose that this became apparent.

A successful ongoing seminar has a net worth of between three and five times its annual profit—for most programs, between $150,000 and $400,000. Investing effort may thus produce an asset valued at between $450,000–$2,000,000. By staying responsive to the currents of change, your program can only become better and more profitable, a natural growth process fueled by assiduous testing and fine-tuning of the many elements of a program's promotion and conduct.

Many variables contribute to the success and quality of a seminar. Among them are:

1. *The Topic Itself.* Is there a readily identifiable population with a sustained interest in the topic you have chosen? Is that population large enough?

2. *Geographic and Regional Variations.* Will your seminar do better in some regions of the country than in others, and will it have the greatest appeal to people in rural areas, suburbs, or cities within a given region? Is your seminar limited to the interests of a specific group, location, or time frame? For instance, if you are going to conduct a seminar on real estate syndications in Los Angeles, ascertain whether you can take that same seminar to Denver and New York without the need for unreasonable expense to research the specific laws and relevance for each area.

3. *Price Sensitivity.* Will your fee be regarded as too high in some places and not high enough to instill credibility in others? To maximize profitability in a program open to the public, the price should be set at the highest level people are willing to pay to attend. Through testing or experience, promoters try to determine what price sensitivity, if any, exists for a particular program. They then set the price just under the amount that would result in a decision not to attend.

4. *Location.* To what degree will the location and facility in which you hold your sessions affect the way the public perceives the program? The image you want your program to convey should be substantiated by the meeting site. First-class hotels are important to many programs, and you should never skimp on such details as location, quality of materials and advertising, or refreshments. They can be critical to the marketing success of the program or subsequent marketing objectives you may have established.

5. *Time of Day, Week, and Month.* Should you schedule your session in the evening so that people can attend after work, or during the day so that they must miss work to attend? Should you schedule on weekdays or weekends? At one time of the year rather than another?

6. *Length of the Program.* A few hours, or a few days? How does its length affect the way your program is received and the fee you can charge?

You can and should test all of these variables, and others, by introducing changes from session to session, one at a time (don't confuse the effects by analyzing too many variables at once), and comparing the results. These and other issues will be discussed at length in later chapters.

Is It Worth the Effort?   Research conducted by the author indicated that, of 87 academic and proprietary seminar providers, those who insisted on test marketing all or almost all promotions experienced a program profit that was, on the average, 26.7 percent higher than those who did not test or tested very infrequently. Many providers think that they are testing, but are they? Test marketing involves much more than merely counting the registrations received from the first marketing campaign in order to make a decision to continue or abandon. Legitimate testing also requires appropriate controls to ensure that the result obtained is isolated from other factors.

Testing enhances decision making in three ways:

1. It prevents potentially successful programs from being abandoned;
2. It prevents unsuccessful programs from being maintained; and
3. It fine-tunes marketing to enhance program success.

Test for What?   Providers have a seemingly endless number of variables to test because scores of factors determine whether a program will be a marketing success. In theory, you could test all of them; in practice, successful promoters test the following most often: fee charged, mailing list/advertising medium used, promotional copy, direct mail piece/ad size, impact of follow-up promotion, and use of color. If you think that testing is an unnecessary expenditure or is likely to produce too little information for the investment of time, consider the following.

□ A proprietary seminar firm discovered that a fee reduction on a sales seminar, from $245 to $149, resulted in an 18 percent increase in enrollments but a 55 percent decline in profitability. It also learned that a fee increase, from $245 to $345, resulted in an 11 percent decline in registrations and a 27 percent increase in profit.

□ A community college found that the use of a three-color brochure increased registrations by 22 percent over the response to a one-color brochure previously used for a time management program.

□ A proprietary provider discovered that shifting from an 11″ × 17″ self-mailer to a package of an 11″ × 14″ brochure, three-page sales letter, response card, and publisher's letter resulted in a 42 percent increase in response for a computer training workshop.

□ A university continuing-education dean learned that running three newspaper ads for a two-day annual conference, rather than six ads, produced only a 12 percent decline in registrations, but a 44 percent decrease in promotion expense.

□ A professional association found that sending out two follow-up mailings to members rather than one produced a 17 percent increase in program participation, which returned additional profit equal to three times the marketing expense differential.

Must It Be Expensive to Produce Results?   Many providers avoid testing because they believe the cost or effort required for reliable testing is too great. Valuable data can be obtained from easy-to-implement, low-cost testing; successful marketers test something every time they promote. Some providers claim a preference for market research rather than testing. In the seminar business, however, market testing is usually far less expensive than good marketing research and certainly far more reliable. Marketing research is a powerful tool. It should be used in those situations where the cost of start-up (tooling) is very high. But, when start-up costs are low, as is the case for most seminars, market testing makes better sense.

The details of three test cases reveal the impact on the bottom line of inexpensive but carefully executed market testing.

Case 1.   A promoter planned on offering a seminar in 12 major markets and wanted to test the impact of color in a newspaper ad. The total averaged cost of adding color to advertising in the 12 markets was in excess of $4,200. To test the impact of color on sales, a controlled test of color in a smaller, less expensive market was implemented. Using a perfect A/B split run in the market's only major daily newspaper, 50 percent of the circulation received copies of the paper with the color ad and 50 percent received papers with only a black and white ad. The total cost of the advertising test was $1,432. The black and white ad (cost: $581) produced 35 registrations—a marketing cost of $16.60 per registrant. The color ad (cost: $851) yielded 42 registrations, $20.26 per registration. Fearful that the result was a fluke, the promoter replicated the test two more times with similar results.

Case 2.   A provider wanted to test three different promotional appeals (copy) for a direct mail promotion of a two-day management program conducted quarterly. A total mailing list (in-house and rented) of 66,451 names was merged and purged and divided into three random, promotionally identical lists. The promoter found that the yield per 1,000 pieces of mail was 3.2 registrations for copy A, 2.4 for B, and 4.1 for C. The cost of the test was $846, including added printing and mail service expense. Had the sponsor used copy C on the entire mailing as opposed to B, the registration would have been 271 rather than 159. With a program fee of $89, the $846 investment translated into additional revenue equal to almost $10,000.

Case 3.   A program sponsor wanted to test the impact on marketing of using the back page of an 11″ × 17″ seminar brochure to sell books and tapes on a topic related to the seminar being marketed. Would seminar registrations suffer? Would product sales be sufficiently significant to balance any loss in seminar registrations? The mailing to a 42,000-name rented list of magazine subscribers made use of a perfectly random split (*n*th name selection). Seventy-five percent of the list received the seminar promotion sans product offer and 25 percent received the seminar promotion with product offer. All other elements of the campaign remained constant. What happened?

Factor/1,000	*Seminar Only*	*Seminar and Product*
Total number of sales	2.4	2.9
Seminar registrations	2.7	2.3
Product orders	0.0	0.8
Revenue	$661.50	$732.20

Registrations received were lower, but total revenue was higher and profits increased by 7.7 percent.

To be effective, market testing, like any field research project, must employ carefully planned field research controls. Since small changes in price, copy, color, and similar components can spell the difference between success and failure, testing pays. Most sponsors know that it makes sense to test mailing lists, but successful promoters know that a dedication to test marketing on all promotional variables pays off handsomely.

COMPETITION

The extent of competition from other sources must be considered when choosing a topic. The presence of some competition may serve as a healthy stimulant to developing a marketable program in which there is an existing high level of interest. Entry into a market that is saturated or approaching full maturity will be more difficult (though by no means impossible) and the profit margin is apt to be diminished.

Success under competitive conditions depends to a large degree on the promoter's ability to create successful marketing strategies—for example, identifying a market segment that is not being adequately served by the competition. Market segmentation and a well-designed promotion campaign may enable you to create a market niche and earn a healthy profit margin on your seminars.

A complete lack of competition may indicate the absence of a market for your topic, or it may suggest a profitable, undiscovered opportunity. The seminar field abounds with cases of overnight success in an untapped market—and with many instances of failure. Again, the key to success is development of appropriate marketing strategies. An initial outlay for a market test is a worthwhile investment because it will help you to determine the extent of interest in your topic.

Nonseminar materials—books, audio cassettes, videotapes, and low-cost continuing education classes—are another source of competition for your program. If these alternate sources of information are plentiful and adequately cover the topic, people will not be as apt to pay to attend a seminar. On the other hand, these materials may stimulate interest in the types of knowledge that are best suited to the seminar format. When selecting a topic, you should survey these sources to evaluate their quality and perhaps find new ways of approaching your subject.

COST AND PRICING

In evaluating the cost effectiveness of your topic, you should ask the following questions:

1. Will developing the program require significant expenditures to bring it to market?
2. Is the program dependent on high-cost staff or outside consultants?
3. Will a significant expenditure for hospitality and support services be required?
4. Will reaching the target market require using high-cost media?

High cost, per se, is not adequate reason to abandon your idea, provided the market will support a sufficiently high price to ensure a reasonable profit margin. But in the absence of market support, your idea should be reformulated so that costs can be kept within acceptable limits.

Pricing is another important consideration in topic selection. The elasticity of demand for your seminar—that is, the degree to which the seminar fee affects the consumer's buying decision—can be influenced by your choice of topic. If the market perceives that the seminar will help them to become more successful or make more money, price will be less of a factor in their decision. Further, if professional development, recognition, and status are important to people in this market, their demand will be less price-sensitive, provided the topic chosen will enhance their professional image.

Economic conditions also affect the price sensitivity of the market. In a strong economy, people will exhibit little or no sensitivity to the price of seminars; during a recession, or when people perceive that a downturn is imminent, price becomes an important variable. Thus, it is important to be aware of current and projected economic conditions when selecting a seminar topic.

PROMOTION

The marketing of seminars is highly promotion-intensive; you must thoroughly understand the target market and how to access specific and highly cost-effective media, most often mailing lists. Are inexpensive mailing lists, which you can use in a direct mail campaign, available for your target market? Is relatively low-cost ad space available in newspapers and magazines that are read by your target market? A low readership base among your target market may necessitate advertising on radio or television, which can be very costly.

Public relations can provide a cost-effective avenue for promoting your seminar. The nature of the program, the reputation and capabilities of the presenter, and the abilities of support personnel will determine the effectiveness of public relations in increasing your exposure and generating valuable free publicity. The salability of your topic is influenced in part by whether it lends itself readily to a quality, cost-effective public relations campaign in conjunction with paid promotion.

SEMINAR DEVELOPMENT AND EXPANSION

Topics that lend themselves to further marketing opportunities deserve serious attention. You should examine your topic's potential in three areas:

1. *Frequency of Presentation.* Can this material be presented a number of times, with minor modifications, to your target market, or is it a one-time-only topic?
2. *Secondary Markets.* In addition to the primary market, are there any viable secondary groups who would be attracted to your seminar?
3. *Spinoff Products.* Is your topic able to generate a wide range of spinoff products, such as books, tapes, newsletters, and other seminars, that could be readily developed and marketed?

When shaping your topic, you should be aware of these additional marketing opportunities.

THE PRESENTER/PROMOTER

Focusing on the market in selecting a seminar topic, while critical to success, does not mean that the interests and expertise of the presenter should be ignored, particularly if the promoter is also the presenter. If the subject is one in which the presenter is extremely knowledgeable and interested, the presentation will be lively and interesting, enhancing the future market potential of the seminar. On the other hand, if the presenter finds the subject tedious, the program will quickly become time-consuming drudgery for both the presenter and the audience. If the presenter/promoter is genuinely interested both in the topic and in making money on the seminar, he will spend more time and energy researching the subject and developing materials that are sophisticated, up-to-date, and entertaining for both presenter and participants. It is important to remember that successful programs need to be much more than instructional. They need to be entertaining as well. It has been said that a good seminar is 60 percent education and 40 percent entertainment. Seminars and workshops are not required university courses. To a certain extent you are in competition with the entertainment media.

If you are the presenter as well as the promoter, you should choose a topic on which you can expound intelligently for several days on a moment's notice. Breadth and depth of knowledge of a topic that you find intrinsically interesting puts you in control of your material—and of your audience. If you are widely acknowledged as a prominent authority on the subject being presented, so much the better. Expectations will be higher, but so will attendance and the price you can charge.

If you retain an outside consultant to do the actual presentation, you naturally will want to choose someone who is knowledgeable on the topic you have chosen and has a proven track record in giving successful presentations. Thus, availability of skilled presenters at a reasonable fee should be considered when you are selecting a topic. The long-term promotional success of your seminar (the roll-out potential) depends, to an extent, on word-of-mouth endorsements about the program. Your presenter, therefore, must be skilled in answering participants' questions and satisfying their special needs for information. The presenter must be knowledgeable, up-to-date, and enthusiastically interested in the subject.

SOURCE OF SEMINAR PAYMENT— OUT-OF-POCKET VS. BENEFACTOR

In selecting a seminar topic, consider whether the attendees will be paying for the program out of their own pockets or the costs will be absorbed by an employer or other benefactor. If the participants are paying for it themselves, the type of topic selected should fall into one of the following categories:

1. Provides information that enables the participants to make more money—for example, investing in the stock market or starting a direct mail business.

2. Provides information that enables the participants to keep the money they have—for example, tax avoidance strategies.

3. Appeals to avocational or recreational interests—for example, cooking, travel, or photography.

4. Offers techniques and strategies for personal growth, self-awareness, and dealing effectively with others on a personal and professional level. Communication workshops and assertiveness training programs are two examples of this type of topic.

Common to each of these categories is the fact that they appeal to personal interests and provide a direct, perceptible economic option of the market.

DECISION MATRIX

The decision matrix on the following pages has been designed to assist the user in selecting the most viable or profitable topic for a seminar or workshop from among two or more different topics being considered for promotion and conduct.

1. Review carefully each factor in column 1 and the instructions on how to rank the factor in column 2.

2. Based on the instructions in column 2, assign each factor a rank from 1 to 10. Enter the rank assigned in column 3 for each topic being considered. It is best not to compare more than four programs at a time. If you want to compare a greater number of programs, analyze four at a time until you have completed the analysis of all the programs.

3. The decision on which program to conduct and promote is made up of a total of 100 points. In column 4, indicate the total number of points, out of 100, which you will assign to each factor in making a decision. The total of column 4 must equal 100.

4. Multiply column 3 by column 4 to determine the score on each factor for each seminar topic listed in column 5.

5. Sum the totals in column 5. The highest total is the expected determination of the most viable or profitable seminar. If your "hunch" suggests that this is not the best seminar to conduct, you have incorrectly assigned values in columns 3 and 4 and you should alter the values assigned in these columns until the mathematical analysis is the same as your "hunch."

(1) Factor	(2) How to Rank	(3) Rank/ Each	(4) Weight	(5) Weighted Average Topics			
				A	B	C	D
The program is previously developed to a level of quality which makes significant expenditures of time and money unnecessary to bring it to market	Disagree, very strongly = 1 Agree, very strongly = 10	A B C D					
The market for which the topic is appropriate and the nature of the program is such that a significantly large expenditure will be required to provide hospitality/supporting services	Agree, very strongly = 1 Disagree, very strongly = 10	A B C D					
There exists a wide range of needed, useful spin-off products such as books, tapes, newsletters and other seminars which could be developed or obtained to sell to the market	Agree strongly and such spin-offs are available for sale now = 10 Disagree strongly = 1	A B C D					
The topic is new and unique	Agree, very strongly = 10 Disagree, very strongly = 1	A B C D					
The group to which this topic will be marketed will regard the fee to be paid for the program as being of very little or no consequence in their decision to participate	Agree, very strongly = 10 Disagree, very strongly = 1	A B C D					
The group to which this topic will be marketed is very easily identifiable and served by relatively low cost and specific media (mailing lists/publications)	Agree, very strongly = 10 Disagree, very strongly = 1	A B C D					
In addition to the basic group for which it is planned to market this program, there are a number of viable, secondary groups likely to attend if marketed	There exists a large number of such other markets which could be inexpensively reached = 10 There are few, if any, secondary markets which could be reached on a cost effective basis = 1	A B C D					
Professional development, professional recognition and status are of great importance to the groups who are likely to attend this program	Agree, very strongly = 10 Disagree, very strongly = 1	A B C D					
Frequency with which seminar or workshop could be held in the market(s) which you serve	Very often, say monthly/weekly = 10 Very infrequently, say once every year or two years = 1	A B C D					

Figure 1–1. Decision matrix for selecting seminar topics. Copyright © 1989 by Howard L. Shenson.

13

(1) Factor	(2) How to Rank	(3) Rank/ Each	(4) Weight	(5) Weighted Average Topics			
				A	B	C	D
Dependency on high cost staff or external consultants and trainers to conduct the seminar or workshop	Very dependent on several such persons = 1 No dependency on such persons = 10	A B C D					
Extent of competition from other seminars and workshops on the same or quite similar topic	No competition = 10 Significant and meaningful competition = 1	A B C D					
Degree of competition from non seminar and workshop sources such as books, tapes, low cost classes and lectures, etc.	None, very little = 10 Great and regular = 1	A B C D					
Longevity of program: Topic fundamental process technology or information for which there exists a long-term, recurrent demand and not just a short-term need or fad	Significant longevity = 10 Very poor prospects for longevity = 1	A B C D					
Program responds meaningfully and obviously to pressing current needs, issues or mandates of legislative and/or regulatory agencies	Agree, very strongly = 10 Disagree, very strongly = 1	A B C D					
Those individuals who will conduct the program are recognized widely as known, prominent authorities on the subject by those who will attend the program	Agree, very strongly = 10 Disagree, very strongly = 1	A B C D					
Extent to which persons who will conduct the program are currently highly interested in, motivated about, and engaged in continuing research and study on the topic	Highly interested in, motivated about = 10 Very low interest, motivation and little continuing research and study = 1	A B C D					
The market for this program is large and growing rapidly	Agree, very strongly = 10 Disagree, very strongly = 1	A B C D					
The nature of the program, the personnel involved and/or the capabilities/reputation of the sponsor/presenter enables obtaining highly cost effective quality public relations support for the program	Agree, very strongly = 10 Disagree, very strongly = 1	A B C D					
TOTALS			100				

Figure 1–1. (*continued*). Copyright © 1989 by Howard L. Shenson.

14

2

MARKETING AND PROMOTION

Approximately one-half to two-thirds of the total cost of presenting a seminar is spent on the deceptively simple enterprise of generating interest and trying to exercise a positive influence on people's decision to attend. Moreover, success in the seminar and workshop business is much more a function of marketing and promotion than it is the result of program design, materials development, and instructional competency. Thus, to ensure the success and profitability of your enterprise, it is essential that you understand the range of promotional options open to you and the techniques of enhancing the effectiveness of whatever promotions you choose to use.

Since promotional dollars must be spent in advance, with no guarantee of effectiveness, thorough advance planning is necessary. In order to plan well, you should understand all of your promotional options and explore all of the available promotional media.

Many solid, salable programs have failed because the promoter continued to invest in marketing strategies that were clearly unprofitable. Do not expect all of your promotions to succeed, especially if you are taking risks reaching for new business; some of your efforts will almost invariably fail. However, you can increase your chances of success by exploring all of your options and putting out the best promotion possible for your seminar or workshop.

DEVELOPING A MARKETING PLAN

A good marketing plan should start with a purpose and should answer very specific questions.

1. What is the service/product to be provided?
2. What is the primary market for the service/product?
3. What evidence exists that the service/product meets a meaningful demand which exists for those in the primary market?
4. Are there secondary markets for the service/product?
5. What evidence exists that the service/product meets demands for those who comprise the secondary markets?

Question	Sources of Information/ Data to Be Tapped	Sufficient Data Collected (Yes/No)	Answer
1. What is the service/product to be provided?			
2. What is the primary market for the service/product?			
3. What evidence exists that the service/product meets a meaningful demand which exists for those in the primary market?			
4. Are there secondary markets for the service/product?			
5. What evidence exists that the service/product meets demands for those who comprise the secondary markets?			
6. What is the nature of competition in the market and in what unique ways will this plan respond to the competition?			

7.	What is the potential for this service/product?			
8.	What marketing strategies will be employed to sell the service/product?			
9.	How will the market be tested?			
10.	What is the roll-out plan?			
11.	What test-market results will be considered sufficient to implement the roll-out plan?			
12.	If test-market results are insufficient to implement the roll-out plan, but sufficient to maintain continued test marketing, what further test marketing will be undertaken?			
13.	What level of funding is necessary and how will funds be expended?			
14.	What additional products and/or services are planned for the primary market?			

Figure 2–1. Seminar marketing plan worksheet.

17

6. What is the nature of competition in the market, and in what unique ways will this plan respond to the competition?

7. What is the potential for this service/product?

8. What marketing strategies will be employed to sell the service/product?

9. How will the market be tested?

10. What is the roll-out plan?

11. What test-market results will be considered sufficient to implement the roll-out plan?

12. If test-market results are insufficient to implement the roll-out plan, but sufficient to maintain continued test marketing, what further test marketing will be undertaken?

13. What level of funding is necessary and how will funds be expended?

14. What additional products and/or services are planned for the primary market?

Use the worksheet in Figure 2–1 to organize your answers to these questions. By carefully considering the questions and filling out the worksheet, you should be able to develop a marketing approach that will successfully promote your program.

PROMOTIONAL OPTIONS

Whichever promotional model you select, keep it simple and direct. If a promotional piece is too complicated or offers too many options (too many decisions to be made), your prospective participants will become confused and will simply ignore it. Group rates, discount schedules, and registration deadlines carry the risk of overwhelming the potential participant, as well as complicating your task as promoter, with extra administrative details. Some complexity is necessary, to appeal to the different motives that make people decide to attend a seminar or workshop and to include the many factors that influence their decisions; however, there is a point of diminishing returns in providing these options. In general, the more straightforward the offer, the better it is for both the potential participant and the promoter. Four promotional options are described here.

The One-Step Promotional Cycle

This is the type of promotion most commonly used for public seminars and almost always used for contract programs. The promoter has one chance to convince a prospective participant or client that his program is needed. For contract training, the promoter outlines the costs and benefits of the program and attempts to elicit the prospective client's support in the form of a contract. In the case of a public seminar, a direct mail brochure or one space advertisement in a newspaper typifies the one-step promotional cycle.

The Two-Step Promotional Technique

This option provides for at least one follow-up promotional treatment, perhaps the mailing of a promotional brochure five weeks in advance of the seminar, with a follow-up post card or telephone reminder two weeks in advance. Some potential participants are encouraged to register as a result of the first promotion treatment and others are encouraged by the second. While the promotion yield will not be doubled, it can often be increased by as much as 40 to 60 percent with an appropriate follow-up. Two-step promotions often provide the option of registering for a program in advance, while enabling a last-minute decision as well: "Act now and get a bonus. Save money and register now, before you put this brochure down. But if you forget it today, don't worry. You can still come, at a slightly higher price."

The Presale/Sale Technique

This technique is commonly used in investment and real estate seminars open to the general public. The public is first invited to attend a free lecture. If the topic is interesting and the program is offered at a convenient time, people will be drawn to it. At the lecture, the participants are often subjected to an intensive sales pitch to sign up for a longer and more comprehensive seminar or workshop.

The success of this method depends on two key elements—the ability of the presenters to sell effectively and the nature of the prospective audience. Because some presenters in the seminar business are not the most adept salespeople, many programs that use this type of promotion hire outside professionals to conduct the initial session. Moreover, the nature of the prospective audience should suit the seminar topic and format. Are the people who will be drawn by a free lecture on your chosen topic good candidates for the longer sessions? Are they likely to be able to afford the fee? A topic such as commodity investing may be a good choice for this type of promotion because it attracts people who have capital to invest and who are willing to spend some time and money to maximize their profit potential. In addition, the complexities of the subject warrant a longer program for complete understanding.

Last-Minute Fever

"First come, first served. No advance registration. Come early if you want to get a seat." This method works with many programs; however, the promoter has no way of knowing how many people will show up, how large a room to get, and so on. A major reason for using this option is to create a promotional environment of mild hysteria. The promoter attempts to communicate that the program is so good and in such demand that he only has to announce its availability and open the gate, to receive a flood of participants. While such marketing psychology is not suitable for all seminars, it will boost the promotional effectiveness of many for which it is acceptable.

PROMOTIONAL MEDIA

You have several different options to choose from when deciding what type of medium to use to promote your seminar or workshop. Understanding a little about the various types of promotional media will help you to choose the most appropriate and most cost-effective ones for your needs.

1. *Direct Mail Marketing.* Direct mail is the most frequently utilized advertising medium in the seminar and workshop business. The inherent advantage to direct mail marketing is that you can target your promotion to the specific population that is most likely to be interested in your program. Once you have identified the typical characteristics of your likely participants—occupation, common interests, income level, trade or profession, licensing, academic degree, or almost any other criterion you can think of—you can rent mailing lists that have a high probability of successfully reaching people with those characteristics. Although direct mail marketing costs more per contact than any other kind of marketing (except phone and personal contact), it is often both the most efficient and effective medium.

2. *Newspaper Advertising.* Placing an ad in a newspaper can be a highly effective way to promote your seminar or workshop, particularly when the target population is not easily recognizable and/or the topic is of extremely broad interest.

3. *Advertising in Journals and Magazines.* Consumer magazines (general-interest publications) and trade publications for special-interest groups can be viable means of promotion. By thoroughly assessing and understanding the distribution and readership of a magazine, a target population can be identified according to region or interests; thus, though the cost may be high, a large percentage of the readers may be good prospects for your program.

4. *Television and Radio.* Because of the high cost of having commercials professionally produced (a requirement in television and advisable in radio) and the often high price of air time, very few seminars

and workshops are advertised via television and radio. A 30- or 60-second commercial rarely provides sufficient time to communicate all of the information necessary to motivate someone to attend a seminar or workshop. However, as television continues to become more specialized, through cable services and the increased use of UHF channels, it will become more feasible as a cost-effective advertising avenue. This is especially true for seminars that are promoted to the consumer and nonprofessional community. A number of providers have enjoyed strong success by advertising on the financial/stock market stations and/or networks and in developing full 30- or 60-minute informationals (commercials that give the appearance of being talk shows or news broadcasts).

5. *Telephone Marketing.* Telephone marketing works particularly well with the business community and sophisticated "upwardly mobile" groups, especially when it is used to prescreen interest for subsequent direct mail, when it delivers a follow-up or reminder device to reinforce prior promotion (often direct mail or newspaper or magazine advertising), and/or when the program deals with personal rather than professional interests. The high cost of telephone marketing generally requires a relatively expensive seminar to be a profitable promotional device.

6. *Public Relations and the Help of Others.* There are many ways to work with other people to keep your promotional cost low and extend the reach of your advertising efforts. Most newspapers and radio stations have a "calendar" or "weekly schedule" section that will list your seminar or workshop at no charge. Appearing on radio and television talk shows to discuss your program is an excellent way to increase your exposure, while stirring wide general interest in your topic. Hosts of these shows will usually ask for all the pertinent details of your operation without any prompting on your part. Also, local newspapers often run feature articles on businesses that offer unique services likely to interest their readers. Making the effort to keep informed about local resources and public relations opportunities has the desirable effect of developing a network of contacts within the business and media communities. Good public relations can help increase your exposure and spur word-of-mouth referrals, engendering participation in your program. However, publicity alone never suffices; it must be used as an adjunct to paid promotion. (See Figure 2–2.)

7. *Direct Selling.* Salespeople traveling to homes or businesses trying to sell a program is a seldom used promotional practice. It works best for long-term courses of several weeks' duration. The cost of direct selling necessitates an expensive program or a sale to several people simultaneously. Direct selling has worked well, for example, for a sales seminar sold to real estate brokers at $75 per participant, on behalf of their agents. One provider found that a cost of $175 was incurred for each

SMALL BUSINESS / Jane Applegate

Consultants Need Some Advice, Too

Most people think that consultants are too busy helping others to need help themselves, but Howard Shenson has built a small business around counseling consultants since 1971.

Through books, seminars and lectures, Shenson of Woodland Hills helps consultants build their practices while coping with the changing business climate. Here are a few of his "101 Proven Strategies for Building a Successful Practice." The copyrighted booklet is available by mail for $3 plus tax by writing to Shenson at 20750 Ventura Blvd., Suite 206, Woodland Hills, CA. 91364. Information on his Nov. 1 seminar is also available by mail.

■ Write a separate brochure for each target market you serve. Concentrate on the benefits that you provide to each type of client.

■ Never use a resume to promote your services. You may have to develop a resume to satisfy the files of an existing client, but it is a disastrous first marketing piece.

■ Do not promote your services to the personnel department. Always promote your services to the executive or manager.

■ Devote about 15% to 25% of your working hours—each and every week—to marketing and selling. The time to market is not when you have run out of clients.

■ Don't bad mouth your competition. Explain why your services are better and the unique advantages you offer. If you are really better than the competition, it will be obvious to your clients and prospects.

■ Dress the way your client or prospect dresses, within reason. Don't be overly formal or informal.

■ Don't look upon having to write a proposal as unnecessary drudgery for getting the business. Research clearly shows that those who write proposals (even when they don't have to) wind up getting bigger and better assignments.

■ When writing letters, increase impact with a handwritten P.S. It will result in your letter being read first and it will instantly grab the reader's attention.

■ Be listed in all trade and professional directories that reach your target market. More than half of all directories will allow you to be listed free of charge.

■ Charge for travel expenses on a per-diem basis rather than a direct reimbursement basis. Most clients prefer the simplicity of per diems, and it avoids any criticism of how you spend expense dollars.

Figure 2–2. Example of newspaper public relations. Copyright © 1989 by the *Los Angeles Times*. Reproduced by permission.

sales call, but the average unit of sale was nine participants at $75, or $675.

The following list shows the results of the author's survey, in which 212 seminar providers and promoters were asked which promotional media they used for their most recent seminar. Direct mail was the primary medium; many made use of space advertising and public relations as well. Because these media, alone or in conjunction with each other, are the most effective means of marketing and promoting seminars and workshops, they are discussed in the remaining sections of this chapter.

Promotional Media	*Percent Using This Medium*
Direct mail	86.3
Newspapers	18.1
Public relations	14.2
Business/trade/professional magazines	13.3
Direct sales	8.8
Telephone	8.4
Consumer magazines	5.6
Television	4.9
Radio	4.1
Postering	2.6

DIRECT MAIL VS. SPACE ADVERTISING

The issue of which type of promotion is most effective for a given seminar involves the basic, often stressful decision of where to spend one's promotional dollars. The most frequently used advertising medium for seminars and workshops is direct mail marketing. Space advertising in newspapers, magazines, and journals can also be an effective form of promotion for certain seminars. Because these are the two most commonly used and primarily the most effective media for promoting seminars and workshops, the advantages and disadvantages of direct mail and advertising are compared and contrasted here.

As with any question relating to seminar promotion and presentation, deciding whether to use direct mail, space ads, or some combination of both is a difficult, complex process requiring adequate information and careful, sophisticated analysis. In evaluating which method will result in the highest profitability for their programs, seminar promoters must consider a number of interrelated factors: type of market, nature of the seminar topic, the seminar fee, promotional costs, and so on. Successful seminar promoters base their decision on a thorough knowledge of the target market, an understanding of available options, and past experience with various types of promotional campaigns.

Direct Mail

There are certain advantages inherent to direct mail promotion. It generally costs more per contact than other types of advertising, but direct mail is the most frequently used medium by seminar sponsors and promoters. In general, any promotion is more effective when it can be targeted to a specific, readily identifiable population. Direct mail reaches populations identified by any number of characteristics.

Mailing lists are available by every conceivable characterization. There are subscriber lists from journals and magazines; buyer lists (for example, people who spent more than $xxx on training in a given year); lists of people with shared characteristics, such as scientists listed by discipline, or business executives listed by industry. Information on over 55,000 direct mail marketing lists that can be rented or purchased is available in *Direct Mail List Rates and Data,* published by Standard Rate and Data Service.

Direct mail costs can be controlled by buying or renting lists as a mailing list broker, since brokers are, in many cases, entitled to a 20 percent commission. A similar discount also is normally available to advertising agencies. A promoter can take advantage of these savings by establishing a list brokerage or ad agency operation (see Chapter 8).

Space Advertising

Space advertising in newspapers, magazines, and journals also has certain inherent advantages. If the seminar is intended for the general public, or for a specialized group that is more readily reached through this medium than through direct mail, space advertising may prove to be the more effective promotion. Seminars that have been promoted effectively through space ads include programs on speed reading, investment opportunities, and memory improvement.

A complete overview of the print media, including editorial profile, circulation, advertising rates, deadlines for submitting copy, and ad sizes is provided by the following publications, all published by Standard Rate and Data Service:

1. *Newspaper Rates and Data*
2. *Consumer Magazine and Farm Publication Rates and Data*
3. *Business Publication Rates and Data*
4. *Newspaper Circulation Analysis*

Circulation alone is not adequate to determine the best newspaper or combination of media for a given metropolitan area. Reader demographics such as income level should also be carefully considered so that the ads are reaching the most likely seminar participants. For example, a seminar promoter might decide that for a seminar in the New York metropolitan area, the *New York Daily News* would be the most effective advertising vehicle because of its higher circulation in that area. However, an examination of the demographics of newspaper readerships in that area would probably reveal that the likely participants for most seminars read the *New York Times.* Of course, for a particular seminar, the *Daily News* may well be the most appropriate choice, but the promoter should reach this conclusion only after carefully weighing all the factors involved, not by focusing on a single variable such as circulation.

Costs for space ads can be controlled by running them in regional editions of national newspapers and magazines. For example, it costs much less to advertise in the Southwestern edition of *The Wall Street Journal* than in the national edition and may be equally effective for reaching your target market. Check to be certain that your identification of a region is the same as the publication's—a state or region that you consider to be part of the Midwest may be considered the East by the publication.

"Tickler ads," designed to stimulate curiosity so that readers call for follow-up information, can be an effective, low-cost means of gauging interest in a seminar topic. Those who call in response to the ad are sent a brochure with more information. One successful promoter ran a tickler ad reading simply, "Grantsmanship—How to Get Government Grants," followed by a phone number. A recorded message described the seminar to callers, who were asked to leave their name and address if they wanted to receive a brochure. About 40 percent of all callers left their names, of which 60 percent registered for the seminar. The tickler ad generated a respectable response rate at a fraction of the cost of a larger display ad.

Even the lowly classified ad, often overlooked by seminar promoters, may be an effective form of promotion for a particular market. Some people carefully peruse the classified looking for business or employment opportunities, real estate investments, and other types of information. An ad for a workshop on writing an effective résumé or making money on foreclosures might do very well in the classified section. The reader should remember, however, that the classified section of most newspapers is read on any given day by only a small percentage of the newspaper's audience and, thus, advertising in the display sections of the papers is much more likely to be noticed by the readership in general.

COMPARATIVE EFFECTIVENESS: A MARKET STUDY

A study conducted by the Center for Entrepreneurial Management (CEM) compared the effectiveness of space advertising and direct mail promotion for the following seminars:

"How to Become a Master Negotiator," conducted by Somers White

"How to Build and Maintain a Full-Time/Part-Time Consulting Practice," conducted by Howard L. Shenson

"Financing Business Growth," conducted by Joseph Mancuso

Each seminar was held in three cities: New York, Houston, and Los Angeles. Each full-day (six-hour) program was priced at $95, with a special $75 fee for CEM members.

Two-color direct mail pieces were sent to a total of 75,000 names, 50,000 of which were from house lists; the balance were from rented lists, mainly magazine subscriber lists. For the New York programs, lists covering the tri-state area (New York, New Jersey, and Connecticut) were used. Mailings were sent out in Texas for the Houston seminars, and in California, Nevada, and Arizona for the Los Angeles programs.

Direct Mail/Promotion Costs

The direct mail costs reported by CEM in the *Entrepreneurial Manager's* newsletter have been adjusted here to reflect actual list rental and mailing costs. CEM figures, when they differ from the adjusted figures, are shown in boldface.

	Per Unit Standard Cost	Total Standard Cost	Adjusted Cost
Printing	$0.053	$ 4,000	**$ 4,500**
Mailing list rental (based on a cost of $60/ 1,000 names)	0.060	4,500	**4,000**
Postage (based on a for-profit rate)	0.109	8,175	**4,500**
Art/design/typesetting	0.007	500	
Mailing cost (printing/ stuffing envelopes, addressing, bulk sorting)	0.030	2,220	**1,000**
Miscellaneous	0.007	500	**1,000**
Totals	$0.266	$19,895	**$15,000**

Newspaper Advertising Costs

Two newspaper ads were run in the Sunday editions of the newspapers listed below, two weeks prior to the seminars and on the Sunday immediately preceding the seminars. For the Houston program, one ad was run in the Southwestern edition of *The Wall Street Journal*. The costs of newspaper ad space, shown below, have also been adjusted, based on an analysis of typical advertising rates and production costs.

New York City: A total of 900 lines of advertising in the Sunday *New York Times* at net ad rates, excluding agency commissions/cash discount.	$ 7,688
Houston: A total of 900 lines in the *Houston Chronicle* and 882 lines in the *Houston Post* at net advertising rates, excluding agency commissions/cash discounts ($5,160)	$ 6,097
A total of 346 lines in the Southwestern edition of *The Wall Street Journal*, excluding agency commissions/cash discounts ($937)	
Los Angeles: A total of 882 lines in the *Los Angeles Times* at net retail rates.	$ 4,680
Preparation of advertising mechanicals/delivery	$ 275
Total Newspaper Advertising Expense	$18,740

Findings

The two sets of data on page 28 represent findings reported by CEM, and adjusted figures. The Houston direct mail figures were modified in the CEM report to allow for "an unusually low mailing in that area based upon the lists selected." The actual attendance figures for Houston are shown in the second set of data. The reasons for this adjustment are twofold: first, under normal circumstances a promoter would not select lists that would yield an unusually low number of participants in one of the market areas; second, because the mailing was concentrated in three market areas, it would be necessary to adjust the New York and Los Angeles figures to reflect a higher-than-average yield from the direct mailings.

It is reasonable to assert that certain imbalances may exist in a particular market area when one is doing a national mailing. However, the issue of imbalance does not apply in this test because the mailing lists were selected for certain market areas.

Based on its analysis of the data, CEM concluded that direct mail is a more effective form of promotion than space advertising. The recom-

Figures from the CEM Study

	Negotiating (White)	Consulting (Shenson)	Financing (Mancuso)	Totals
New York:				
Space ads	17	34	22	73
Direct mail	35	48	25	108
Total	52	82	47	181
Houston: °				
Space ads	16	27	9	52
Direct mail	22	25	17	64
Total	38	52	26	116
Los Angeles:				
Space ads	15	27	21	63
Direct mail	30	30	22	82
Total	45	57	43	145
Totals:				
Space ads	48	88	52	188
Direct mail	87	103	64	254
Total	135	191	116	442

° Houston direct mail numbers have been adjusted to reflect an unusually low mailing in that area based on the lists selected.

Adjusted Figures from the CEM Study

	Negotiating (White)	Consulting (Shenson)	Financing (Mancuso)	Totals
New York:				
Space ads	17	36	22	75
Direct mail	35	48	25	108
Total	52	84	47	183
Houston:				
Space ads	16	27	9	52
Direct mail	8	8	6	22
Total	24	35	15	74
Los Angeles:				
Space ads	15	31	21	67
Direct mail	30	30	22	82
Total	45	61	43	149
Totals:				
Space ads	48	94	52	194
Direct mail	73	86	53	212
Total	121	180	105	406

mendation to promote via direct mail, while applicable in some cases, may not be appropriate for all seminars in all markets. The effectiveness of a particular form of promotion should be evaluated based on cost effectiveness and overall profitability.

Consider, for example, the seminar on negotiating. Direct mail was more cost-effective in obtaining participants in all three cities, but the seminar was unprofitable at all three locations for the fee charged and the promotion used. For the consulting seminar, space advertising was more effective and the program was profitable at all three locations.

The results of the financing seminar were mixed. In terms of return on space advertising, the program was profitable in Los Angeles. Space advertising was also more effective than direct mail in New York, but not in Houston. Overall the seminar was unprofitable in all three locations.

Thus, it is not possible to draw a definitive conclusion about the relative effectiveness of space advertising and direct mail based on these findings. The decision of which type of promotion to use for a particular seminar must be evaluated on a case-by-case basis, taking all relevant variables into account.

The target market and seminar topic emerged as important variables in this study. A general subject such as consulting, which targets an educated, upwardly mobile market, may be promoted more effectively through space advertising. A more specialized topic such as negotiating may do better through direct mail to specific lists of people who are likely to need training in management skills.

A SECOND MARKET STUDY

Another study, less complex and more controlled than the first, involved the promotion of a two-day real estate financing seminar conducted in San Francisco. Designed for sophisticated private investors as well as real estate professionals, the seminar was promoted using both direct mail and space advertising in the *San Francisco Chronicle/Examiner.*

The direct mail campaign used rented lists of 8,543 real estate professionals and private investors within a four-county area (including San Francisco County) who had purchased real estate at a price of $200,000 or more in the previous year. Space advertising consisted of two ads in the Sunday *Chronicle/Examiner.* The costs were as follows:

Direct mail (8,543 × $0.34)	$2,904.62
Newspaper advertising	1,877.09
Other seminar costs	967.30
Total	$5,749.01

At a fee of $225 per participant, a total of 26 participants was needed in order for the seminar to break even. A total of 44 enrolled and attended—17 from the newspaper ads, and 27 from the direct mail. The cost of obtaining a registration from the newspaper ad was $110.42, and from direct mail, $107.58. The two costs are virtually the same, without even a statistically significant difference.

The promoter of this seminar conducted two other comparative studies for a seminar on real estate financing—one in Portland, Oregon, and one in Phoenix, Arizona. The Portland seminar, a one-day program, was priced at $125. The cost of obtaining a registrant from newspaper advertising was $48.34, and from direct mail, $66.23.

The three-day Phoenix program was priced at $450. For this seminar, the costs of obtaining a registrant were $367.02 from the newspaper and only $227.19 from direct mail.

For the higher-priced program, direct mail was relatively more cost-effective than newspaper advertising. For the lower-priced program, space ads proved more effective. Thus, the fee charged for a seminar may have an impact on the relative effectiveness of promotion.

While generalizations are always dangerous in the seminar field, it is possible to draw certain broad conclusions about the relative effectiveness of direct mail and space ads, always with the proviso "all other things being equal."

In general, direct mail is a more effective promotional medium when:

1. The program is intended for a specialized group for which mailing lists can be obtained.
2. The group being targeted is easily identifiable.

Space advertising generally is more effective when:

1. The seminar is moderately priced.
2. The program is intended for the general public.
3. The program is intended for a specialized group that cannot be effectively reached via direct mail.
4. The target group is likely to be reading the newspaper.

These are merely guidelines, not truisms that will apply in all cases. The successful seminar promoter avoids simplistic answers to complex questions such as which form of promotion is more effective, and instead bases these decisions on experience, insight, and sophisticated analysis.

PUBLIC RELATIONS

The National Association of Mutual Savings Banks includes a list of do's and don'ts in a booklet on publicity. These hints should help you to utilize public relations as an economical and highly productive means of promoting your seminar or workshop.

Publicity Do's and Don'ts

Do:

Mark your release with date of issue and release date.

Use standard 8 ½″ × 11″ sheets for your releases—smaller or larger sizes are a headache for an editor—and use only one side of the paper.

Double-space your releases, leaving three inches at the top of the first page for editors' use and margins on each side wide enough for editing.

Give a source for additional information (name, address, phone number) and make sure your source knows all the details and does not have to check with someone else for answers if a reporter calls for more information.

Be certain that your release is really news, not just a rehash of something you've sent the editor before.

Get the facts in your release correct the first time. If it is necessary to send a correction, send a fresh copy of the entire news release with any changes clearly indicated.

Avoid superlatives. If they're warranted, the editor will add them.

Keep your releases to the minimum length necessary to present the facts of interest to the editor.

Keep your news release mailing list up to date. You cannot make a good impression on an editor when your releases are addressed to one of his or her predecessors.

Include a sample copy of literature with all releases that mention or describe such literature.

Know the editorial deadlines of your local newspapers, especially those of columnists if you are trying to get them to use your material.

Keep in mind the deadlines of weekly and monthly magazines and see that they receive your news releases far enough in advance to permit them to compete with daily newspapers.

Let editors know in advance if a news release will not reach them until they are "on deadline."

Give background information when necessary to amplify news releases.

Check your news release copy against what ultimately is in the press. This will provide a guide to the acceptability of your material and to what your local editors consider solid news.

Send your news releases to the editor, not the advertising director or publisher.

Lead off with the names of the people involved, not the name of the person making the announcement, when making a personnel change announcement.

Follow accepted news style in all releases—remember who, what, when, where, why, and how.

Remember that it is an editor's prerogative to arrive at a different evaluation or interpretation of news.

Remember that just one attempt to "pull the wool" over an editor's eyes will make him or her skeptical of your releases for a long time.

Completely identify everyone mentioned in news releases.

Avoid dating your releases ("Today, John Doe announced . . ." or "Last week, the Jones Co. . . .") when sending to monthly magazines. Better yet, send in advance of the event if possible.

Be prepared to give prompt attention to requests for additional information, special photographs, and so on.

Don't:

Distribute carbon copies of new releases.

Photocopy releases unless you are sure that your machine will turn copies which are as clear as the original typing.

Use onionskin paper for releases.

Ask the editor to send you tear sheets if the material is used. If this is the publication's policy, you'll get them anyway.

Use highly technical language unless your release goes only to technical publications.

Try to get too much into a single news release. If you have several subjects, send separate releases.

Try to get tricky in your releases. Stick to the facts and present them clearly.

Give a far-in-advance release date and expect the editor to hold your material until the date.

Expect the editor to use your release just because you are an advertiser or a potential advertiser. Nothing will alienate an editor quicker than this kind of pressure.

Use press releases in lieu of advertising. If this is the case, it is usually obvious to the editor, and your release will get a quick rejection.

Try to pass off something as an exclusive if it really isn't. If the editor ever catches you doing this one, you've had it.

Criticize competitors in releases.

Try to pass off the same releases to business publications, consumer magazines, and newspapers. The readers of each deserve your special attention and treatment.

Release a story to a favored publication at one time and then send a general release to competing publications at a later date. If it's an exclusive, keep it that way!

Release news after it has appeared in your advertising.

Expect the editor to be able to recall—or even see—every release received by his or her publication.

Invite inquiries for more information unless you're fully prepared to provide it promptly.

Accuse an editor of being unfair or negligent if he or she doesn't use your release, and don't remind him or her that he or she has used "less important items about your competitors," etc.

Tell the editor that his or her readers will be interested in your story. If they will, no one knows better than the editor, who is paid to know his or her audience.

Send additional copies of a release just because the editor didn't use the first one.

Ask to check galley or page proofs on a story. This is a sure death warrant for any story.

Call the editor to complain about how your release was handled or about its position or placement in the paper.

IMPACT OF PUBLICITY ON REGISTRATIONS

Most seminar, workshop, class, and conference providers believe that getting publicity for their programs will have a favorable impact on enrollments. But getting good publicity is time-consuming and not inexpensive. Knowing the impact of publicity on program success would enable the provider to determine how much money and time to invest in the effort. Let's look at some research data.

A major provider of one- and two-day seminars for the business market selected five of its 14 programs for extensive public relations (PR) and publicity treatment over a nine-month period, September through May. The provider budgeted $40,000 for publicity on the five programs and was able to secure numerous announcements, feature articles, talk show interviews, and related publicity support. Although the source of *all* registrations is difficult to determine, the provider found that $31,205 of actual dollars of revenue received tracked to PR.

Was the Expenditure a Waste?

Does this mean that the campaign was an unproductive investment? No. Those experienced in the public relations field know that publicity, at least in the short run, is unlikely to produce a dollar-for-dollar return. Most realize that PR supports, augments, and intensifies the effectiveness of other marketing. And this seemed to be the case here.

The provider found that the return on marketing investment was significantly higher for the programs supported by publicity. The five programs receiving PR support returned $3.87 in revenue for each dollar expended on marketing. The nine programs not supported by PR produced $3.23 in revenue for each dollar invested in marketing. Of course, the PR-supported programs may have been better sellers to begin with. To control for this factor, the provider looked at marketing expense for the September–May period of the prior year. The PR-supported programs in that year returned $3.44 in revenue for each dollar of marketing. The eight non-supported (one was new) programs produced $3.35 in revenue during the prior year. The data strongly suggested that PR had a favorable impact. Since the provider invested in excess of $250,000 in marketing the five PR-supported programs, the dollar return from PR would seem to be well worth the investment.

Lack of Predictability

Providers often avoid using PR because of uncertainty that they will be able to secure coverage. Direct mail and advertising are far more predictable: You pay, you get. PR is much more like a fishing expedition: Sometimes you get coverage, but often you don't. And even if you do, you can't be sure that it will produce registrations. Let me give you three examples involving my own seminars.

I was scheduled to give an open-enrollment, public seminar in a major eastern city on a Tuesday. The Friday before, I received a call from the producer for a major morning television talk show, asking if I would be willing to be a guest the day before the seminar (Monday). It was the highest audience show in its time slot. It even had a studio audience, and telephone call-ins. I did all the right things. I mentioned the location, price, registration procedure, and other details. I even gave a local phone number for personal answers to viewers' questions, and later that day I spoke with 45 callers. Few asked questions of substance. They wanted specifics: what freeway exit to take, how long the lunch break would be, could they pay by credit card. I anticipated that the publicity might result in an additional 50 to 60 registrations. On Tuesday, not one of these callers showed. But, before you conclude that PR isn't viable, let me share two other experiences.

In a major western city where a Thursday seminar was scheduled, the "Meetings and Events This Week," column in the business section of the Sunday edition of the dominant metropolitan daily newspaper gave about 20 words of copy mentioning the name of the seminar, its location, and the fee. No phone or address was given. Thirty-six registrants walked in as a result. In another western city, a 45-minute appearance on a network affiliate radio talk show at 3:00 P.M. the day before the seminar produced 57 walk-in registrations.

Few are willing to rely on public relations and publicity as the sole source of registrations because of its unpredictability, but experienced promoters know that PR can and often does produce substantial results. A major university continuing education department, for example, reported that 1 ½ inches of ink in a major metropolitan daily (circulation 900,000) produced 387 registrations for a seminar on money management for women at a fee of $25.

BE CREATIVE

Those who generate the best results are creative in approaching the media. They recognize that the media are not a tool of promotion. Often, the media are unwilling to use their editorial position to foster publicity likely to create a greater economic benefit for the provider than the public. An indirect approach often works better.

3

HOW TO DESIGN AND WRITE PROMOTIONAL MATERIALS THAT GET RESULTS

A variety of different strategies are available for securing the number of registrations needed to produce a comfortable level of profit from a seminar, workshop, or class. Yet, in a recent survey of major seminar providers, direct mail marketing was identified by 86.3 percent as their primary strategy and by more than 70 percent as their exclusive means for obtaining registrations. Even though direct mail marketing costs more per contact than almost any other form of promotion, its numerous advantages in the promotion of seminars result in its continued use by experienced seminar promoters.

The two advantages of direct mail most often mentioned by experienced promoters are that it enables tight targeting of the prospects most likely to attend a program and that the promoter/provider can control the total expenditure on promotion at a budget level equivalent to the degree of risk the promoter is willing to accept.

Historically, the seminar business has been populated by relatively small providers who have limited capital and engage in niche marketing—they identify pockets in the market that are not adequately served by seminars, workshops, and classes pertinent to target-market needs. Direct mail has permitted small providers to isolate these niches while simultaneously controlling the total dollar expenditure committed to their campaigns.

IS DIRECT MAIL MARKETING RIGHT FOR YOUR SEMINAR?

To answer this question you must first ask yourself: How well do I know my intended audience? Direct mail marketing is most effective when the target population is identifiable by some "reachable" criteria—occupation, common interest, income level, geography, reading preferences, buying habits, academic degrees, licensure, and so on. Mailing lists derived from these and similar criteria are generally available for rental, often on the basis of several criteria simultaneously.

If lists that tightly target your intended population are available, direct mail is likely to be a viable strategy. Of course, you need not limit your promotional campaign to direct mail. You may determine that other marketing media—newspaper or magazine ads, radio commercials, telephone marketing, or other alternatives—are more effective or that the best marketing strategy involves the use of direct mail combined with other media choices.

Just as there are many media available for the promotion of a seminar or workshop, there is a seemingly infinite number of reasons why a particular promotion campaign may fail to produce the number of desired participants. Among the most common reasons are:

- The market is not interested in your topic/subject.
- The price for your program is either too high or too low to create a price/volume relationship that will produce an acceptable profit.
- The mailing lists selected or the media used are not sufficiently responsive.
- The geographic location, date, time, conduct facility, or similar factors produced a negative impact on the decision to enroll.
- The design and copy of the promotional piece prepared to promote the seminar did not sufficiently motivate prospective participants; the level of demand created for the program was inadequate.

A SUCCESSFUL SEMINAR PROMOTION IS NOT PURE LUCK

Seminar providers often blame external variables for a lack of success, but preventing failure or limiting losses is usually within our control. We need to avail ourselves of all of the pertinent information and data that will enable us to make the best decisions. Of equal importance is a healthy respect for risk. We must avoid expending funds in excess of the amount absolutely necessary to provide an adequate test. Some promoters are so sure that they will have a "hit" that they plunge—they invest more money than is absolutely necessary for a test because they are impatient and feel that the extra expenditure will let them capture the profits this month instead of next. If they have made all of the right decisions, a plunge will turn out to be the best strategy and their success story will be retold for years. But, the first time out, they are likely to have made some mistakes and hence it is in their interest to be cautious.

In that regard, the design and copy of your seminar promotional materials will likely benefit from the information in this chapter, which is based on formal and informal field research in the promotion of more than 500 seminars, workshops, conferences, and classes. Sample seminar and workshop brochures are reproduced at the end of the chapter. Examples of the myriad of brochure styles in use probably arrive every day in your mail. Looking at different styles, formats, and approaches can help you design your own brochure to be effective and dynamic.

TESTING, TESTING, TESTING

Even the most successful seminar promoters make mistakes. The successful are distinguished by the fact that they are willing to test before investing large sums in their promotional concept. Here are 45 elements that can be tested in direct mail campaigns:

1. Mailing list
2. Price
3. Timing of the mailing
4. Headline
5. Title of the program
6. Guarantee
7. Free gift or bonus or absence thereof
8. Self-mailer vs. envelope
9. "Telegram" or "mailgram" vs. traditional mail
10. Letter vs. brochure vs. letter and brochure
11. Length of letter
12. Illustrated letter
13. Formal letter vs. brochure-style letter
14. Use of postscript
15. "Handwritten" note on letter or brochure
16. Computer letter vs. nonpersonalized form letter
17. Typed, printed, ink-jet or laser printed
18. Color and quality of paper (and envelope)
19. Polybag (plastic) vs. paper envelope
20. Window envelope
21. Copy on outer envelope vs. plain outer envelope
22. First class vs. bulk mail
23. Metered or stamped postage
24. Use of business reply envelope or postcard and toll-free phone response
25. Prepaid vs. unstamped business reply envelope
26. Stickers, punch-out tokens, and other response devices
27. "Bill me" vs. payment with registration only
28. Discount for payment with registration
29. Installment payment option

30. Impact of credit card as a device for paying fee
31. Use of discount coupons
32. Multiple registrations discounts
33. Limited time offers
34. Toll-free numbers for information and/or registration
35. Telephone follow-up to mailing
36. Coordination with newspaper, magazine, radio, or television promotion
37. Sale of subscription or membership vs. one-time sale
38. Brochure size and format
39. One-color, two-color, or four-color printing
40. Copy written in first person vs. copy in second or third person
41. Hard-sell vs. soft-sell copy
42. Use of self-test to stimulate interest
43. Use of underlines, boldface, or italics
44. Separate $8\frac{1}{2}'' \times 11''$ sheets or $11'' \times 17''$ folded
45. Photographs vs. line drawings vs. no illustrations

WHAT SIZE SHOULD YOUR BROCHURE BE?

Beyond the obvious answer—no larger than necessary to secure the maximum number of registrations or highest dollar profit (which can be different)—you should be aware that some prospective participants tend to associate certain prices of seminars with particular sizes of promotional brochures. Before these prospective participants will part with several hundred dollars for a seminar learning experience, they expect you to provide them with at least an $11'' \times 17''$ (four $8\frac{1}{2}'' \times 11''$ pages) promotional piece. They have been educated by other providers to expect that a more costly seminar requires more information on which to base their decision. You might successfully buck this trend, but most providers reason that it is generally in their interest to spend a little more to meet prospective participants' information expectations.

These guidelines form a good rule of thumb:

- Fee of $150 or less: Provide one sheet ($8\frac{1}{2}'' \times 11''$), two sides
- Fee of $151–$695: Provide two sheets ($8\frac{1}{2}'' \times 11''$), two sides (i.e., $11'' \times 17''$)
- Fee of $700 or more: Provide three sheets ($8\frac{1}{2}'' \times 11''$), two sides (i.e., $11'' \times 25\frac{1}{2}''$)

Most promoters have so much they would like to say about their program that finding enough words to fill two or three pages on both sides is generally not a problem. However, you should never adopt a size simply because it is expected. Many expensive programs have been promoted with a quantity of words no greater than a half-page, and some inexpensive programs are better promoted with an entire booklet of information.

You should never write only to fill space, nor should you ever cut essential selling copy to force a promotion to fit some preconceived smaller size.

A more important and vital rule is that you should say no more than is necessary to secure the required registrations/profits and you should be willing to eliminate any copy that is not producing enrollments.

The size of your promotional piece will have an impact on your cost of promotion and hence on your profitability. But the impact is not linear. That is, a brochure that is $11'' \times 25\frac{1}{2}''$ (folds down to create six $8\frac{1}{2}'' \times 11''$ panels) will not result in a promotion expense that is $33\frac{1}{3}$ percent greater than a promotion piece that measures $11'' \times 17''$ (four $8\frac{1}{2}'' \times 11''$ panels). The cost, all things considered, of the larger piece will probably be about 13 percent higher and certainly worth the investment if it boosts direct mail yield by any amount greater than the cost.

One provider tested a larger brochure against the $11'' \times 17''$ size in a controlled market test. The costs per 1,000 units mailed were $297 ($0.297 per unit) for the smaller piece and $341 ($0.341 per unit) for the larger piece. The larger piece, however, resulted in higher registrations. Specifically, the smaller piece produced $774 in revenue for each 1,000 units mailed but the larger piece produced $853. The extra $79 in revenue per 1,000 units made the additional cost of $44 a smart investment.

GETTING THE READER'S ATTENTION

Once you have decided upon the best size for your direct mail seminar promotion, you must deal with the all-important question, How do I get the reader's attention? It does not matter what you say about your seminar, its price, or anything else if you cannot capture the reader's attention and get him to read about the program.

The people you are trying to persuade to attend your seminar are likely being flooded by direct mail promotions of every description. Their reading time is limited and you must literally grab their eyeball and get it to pay attention to your message.

People new to the business of direct mail marketing of seminars are often scared by the low response to direct mailings reported by their competitors. They simply cannot understand how they could live with the reality of mailing out 1,000 brochures and securing only two or three registrations. Were they to stop and think about the economics of that response, however, it would be acceptable. If it costs $300 per 1,000 pieces ($0.30 each) to reach prospective participants and the fee for the seminar is $500, a response of three per 1,000 will produce $1,500 in revenue against a marketing cost of only 20 percent of revenue—a ratio that is quite acceptable to most promoters. Obviously, the lower the price of the seminar, the higher the yield must be.

The important point for our purposes here, however, is that the more you can do to create attention and obtain readership, the higher your response is likely to be. When the daily stack of mail arrives, you generally have less than three seconds to grasp the attention of the reader and cause him to "get involved" with your mailing piece. Failure to get the prospect involved results in the greatest loss of potential business. Awareness of these facts allows you to truly understand how a sharp promoter can produce only a few registrations per 1,000 units mailed.

On the surface, to a nonexperienced promoter, the following does seem absurd:

> You carefully select a mailing list of 1,000 dentists who are in need of more business, schedule a relatively low cost/high impact seminar which promises them mastery of marketing and selling techniques which should increase their billings by a minimum of 30 percent (more than 150 times the cost of the seminar), hold the program at a first class, convenient location, and find that only four of 1,000 register.

What happened to the other 996? Let's give them some excuses.

> Less than the best mailing list, deduct 75 dentists. Less than the best promotional copy, deduct 125 dentists. Do not believe the pitch and are unwilling to take a chance, even at odds of 150 to 1, deduct 200 dentists. Inconvenient time, location, and so on, deduct 150 dentists. Other causes, deduct 300 dentists.

We are still missing 146 registrations. The single largest explanation of the lack of higher enrollment is that the prospects did not see, did not notice, or did not bother to read the promotional piece.

ATTENTION . . . ATTENTION . . . ATTENTION!

Start by doing everything possible to get the prospects' attention:

- What compelling words can you use in the brochure headline to increase the chances that your prospect will start to read your brochure?
- What colors can you use to cause your piece to be noticed?
- What graphic designs, photographs, interesting layouts, shapes, folds, and other presentation features can you use to make your piece stand out from "the crowd"—today's stack of mail?

The unfortunate reality is that many people in the seminar promotion business will spend more time figuring out what they should wear to a cocktail party (to be noticed, to look their best) than they will spend on gaining attention for their direct mail piece. Why? The majority of the promoters are educators, not marketing people. Deep down, even if they will not admit it, they believe that a good message will get through. It will, of course, but not unless it is noticed and read. The impact from gaining better attention translates into increased profitability and is exponential.

Do not think that when all of this "get attention cleverness" produces 5 percent more readership of your piece, you will have a 5 percent increase in sales. The sales increase will be much greater. For example, for one of my clients I did a controlled test on two brochures for the same seminar on time management. The pieces were identical, except that the headlines on the cover were changed. One piece was tightly target-marketed to a specific buyer group and stressed personal benefits to the members of that group. The other piece was generic and stressed more the intellectual and technical benefits associated with attending a seminar on time management. The results of a follow-up readership survey were quite interesting.

	Generic/Technical Brochure	Targeted/Benefit Brochure
Noticed	11.2%	15.5%
Read	3.7	5.1
Read and remembered	1.2	2.2

Out of 1,000 brochures mailed to each group, 12 read and remembered the generic/technical brochure, but 22 read and remembered the targeted/benefit-oriented brochure. Not much of a difference? Look at the impact on sales:

	Generic/Technical Brochure	Targeted/Benefit Brochure
Registered for the seminar	2	5
Phoned/wrote to request more information	3	7
Unable to attend/ordered the materials	1	2

While only 1 percent more of those surveyed read and remembered the targeted/benefit-oriented brochure, total revenue rose from $489 to $1,173 per 1,000 units of mail.

Anything you can do to attract attention is likely to have a significant bottom-line impact on your promotional profitability. "Getting attention" is not something to which you pay lip service; it is something you spend hours on.

Approach your promotional brochure with a commitment to get more readership. Do something meaningful, even outlandish. In the "outlandish" department, consider the following.

A client of mine, promoting a seminar on a subject which can best be described as dull and relatively uninteresting in a competitively crowded market, was not obtaining the results he needed to be profitable. He believed that the seminar would be of great value to the participants, if he could only persuade them to attend. Persuading them, however, necessitated that they at least read the promotional brochure.

The headline for the brochure read:

"I will pay you $5 if you can pass this test!"

The first paragraph explained his problem:

> Here is a dynamite seminar of great value to you and your company, but I am a lousy brochure writer. I can't get people to read the brochure and if they don't read it they can't learn about the benefits of this seminar. So, if you will read the brochure and answer my seven-question test at the end of the brochure and return it in the postage-paid envelope enclosed, I will send you $5.

He was convinced that everyone who received this in the mail would jump at the chance to make a quick five bucks. I told him most would not bother but that he should expect a higher level of registrations. He limited me to mailing out 1,000 pieces; he was willing to take a $5,000 risk.

We did a 2,000-piece controlled mailing to a split mailing list. Half received his usual brochure, 1,000 received the $5 "read the brochure" offer.

The $5 offer did get attention. Thirty-four respondents mailed in their test and requested $5; four of them registered for the seminar. Three additional persons also registered. The total of seven attendees at $245 each yielded revenue of $1,715, less $170 to pay the 34 $5 promises, or net sales of $1,545. The control brochure produced only three registrations for a total of $735.

Dare to be different!

TARGET MARKETING

Even for those who do not feel overly creative, one sure way to increase reader attention is to target market. Suppose that I am able to obtain a mailing list of 1,400 university deans of continuing education and I wish to send them a promotional brochure designed to cause them to register for my seminar on marketing and promoting seminars and workshops. Consider the following three headlines for the brochure:

1. How to Increase Profits in Direct Mail Marketing
2. How to Increase Profits in Direct Mail Marketing of Seminars and Workshops
3. How University Continuing Education Departments Can Increase Profits in Direct Mail Marketing of Seminars and Workshops

These headlines are successively more targeted. University continuing-education deans should respond with interest to headline 1, but I am willing to bet that they will be even more attracted to headline 2, and will pay a great deal more attention to headline 3. Admittedly, target marketing is a bit more expensive. You must research the needs and motivations of the specific targets more deeply, spend extra time writing copy that specifically addresses them, and incur the added costs of printing specialized brochures and other extras. Is it worth it? Probably yes, but you will have to test for your specific program.

"UGLY DIRECT MAIL"

As a part of the effort to grab and hold the reader's attention, you should be aware that a great deal of evidence suggests that "ugly direct mail" works better than "beautiful direct mail." Beautiful designs, use of extensive white space, and commanding and tasteful graphics may win advertising awards, but the garish, often ugly, borax brochures generally do a better job of producing sales. For evidence, you need only look at the highly effective seminar brochures placed in the mail by those who purport to be direct marketing gurus. You do not have to go out of your way to make your promotional piece intentionally ugly (though some suggest that this is a good idea), and you do need to pay attention to your audience and their concern, if any, for esthetics. But, remember, this is advertising—not fine art.

ARTWORK

Graphics, including line drawings, graphs, designs, tables, and decorative rules, can enhance the visual appeal of a piece. Proper use of graphics and photos can increase reader attention, remembrance, and buying behavior. Research reveals that good photography lends credibility to a promotion piece. Do not try to save money with poor/inexpensive photography. Poor photos and poorly edited photos will detract from the pulling power of the piece. The words under a photo are the first words to be read. This space should be used to convey your most motivating sales message, not to explain the obvious ("Here are happy people sitting in the seminar"). While line drawings are usually less costly, reproduce better, and can serve the function of making things look better than they really are, they do not provide the impact and credibility of photos. Graphic representations tend to make a piece easier to read, break up the visual drabness of solid blocks of copy, and often appeal more to audiences raised in the television age, who may have deficient reading skills.

COLOR

By improving the visual attractiveness of a direct mail piece, color can increase readership. In a test that I conducted for a client on the promotion of a seminar on an entrepreneurial topic, four different colors were tested to determine which color had the greatest pulling power. All four brochures were identical. The bulk of the copy was in black on white semigloss paper. The second color, used primarily for headlines, was varied. The results are interesting. A total of 5,000 copies of each brochure was mailed to a perfectly split mailing list in the District of Columbia, Virginia, and Maryland.

| | *Second Color Ink* | | | |
	Red	*Purple*	*Green*	*Orange*
Noticed	9.3%	11.4%	8.8%	10.9%
Read	5.4	6.3	6.2	6.9
Read and remembered	1.4	1.7	2.2	2.1
Number of registrations received	11	14	18	17

I am hopeful that the publication of these results will not create a rash of orange and green seminar brochures. The pulling power of a color tends to change when prospective respondents see the color frequently in other mailings. If you are receiving a great number of brochures using the color red, the next red brochure will be less likely to stand out as much as a green brochure when you haven't seen any green direct mail recently.

FORMAT

A similar phenomenon may be noticed with respect to the general format, appearance, shape, and size of the promotion piece. You have undoubtedly noticed many different formats for promotional brochures. Does one work better than the others? "Yes!" in any given test, but not forever. Here again, readers tend to be attracted to presentations which they are unaccustomed to seeing. Recently, seminar promoters started using a rash of "reader" or "memo" style promotion brochures. Many found them more effective than the standard 11″ × 17″ two-color models they had been putting into the mail prior to this "new" concept. Why? They were new and different. But, as time progressed, they were not as effective; they were no longer new. They really were not new before, either. Style and format and color are like a wheel: choices used in the past get used again after an absence and seem new when they are brought back. Diversity and difference are important here, so pay attention to what the competition, generally and specifically, is making use of.

THE LETTER

After all of these ideas on promotional messages, color, artwork, and format, you might want to consider the advantages of simplicity—a simple letter might get read even where an "attention-getting" brochure would not. A letter, particularly one without a message, indicia, or label on the envelope, does not look like junk mail and will often get the attention needed to secure a registration. (Type your envelopes whenever possible, instead of using labels, and meter your bulk rate mail—it looks like first class.)

AFTER YOU'VE WON THE BATTLE, DON'T LOSE THE WAR

Attracting attention to your seminar or workshop promotional piece is only part of the task of effective program promotion. Once you have captured the reader's attention, you must convince him that registering for your program is a worthy investment of time and money.

Stress Benefits

Once you have attracted the reader's attention, you need to ensure that the whole piece will be read. You can do this by stressing benefits. The new seminar promoter is often surprised to learn that people do not attend seminars to learn technology. They may learn technology as a result of attending, but their motivation to attend a seminar is the fact that they are going to receive some benefit: they will make more money, they will get ahead in their job faster, they will have a richer, more rewarding life, and so on. The brochure should stress benefits and it should be very practical and very specific, to maintain the interest of the reader. One of the advantages that a brochure has over a newspaper or magazine advertisement is space. Because you are paying dearly by the inch in an advertisement, you tend to make your writing concise—the ad is quicker and easier to read than a brochure, but you have only enough space to make your central points. The brochure, however, allows you the luxury of being able to point out benefits in a more leisurely fashion and to pick up "side motivators" to get the reader to attend the program. The principal rationale for a reader's attending your seminar may not be—*will* not be—the only rationale; there may be two or three or four of lesser importance. You may not be able to afford to promote these secondary motivations in the newspaper, but you can raise these issues, promote them, and devote adequate space to them in a direct mail brochure.

What the Participant Will Learn

In addition to stressing benefits, the brochure should contain a specific list of what the participant will learn as a result of attending the seminar. You should find out, either through your own analysis or by talking to potential participants, the most desirable things that an attendee can learn in the program, and these should be listed in the brochure. Make the items specific, tangible, and quantified if possible: "The five ways to do this" or "The seven things you could find out about . . . ." The reader will look at your information and realize that he doesn't know all five ways to do this. If there are seven ways and the reader can think of only three, then he has more motivation to attend the seminar.

Testimonials

When properly presented, testimonials can go a long way toward making a participant out of a potential participant who is unsure about whether to register. Make certain that the testimonials are as strong as possible. Testimonials that are vague or open to other possible interpretations are far worse than none at all. Be sure to include a line that invites people to come to your office and read the original comments for themselves. This not only adds credibility but is a legal requirement in some jurisdictions. If you have no actual testimonials on hand, a listing of the names of individuals or organizations who have taken your seminar can help your credibility. Obviously, the better known and more recognizable these names are, the greater their impact on your credibility. You should obtain written permission from people before using their names in your brochure. Testimonials which list the full name (and company/agency affiliation and title if appropriate) and city/state have greater credibility.

The Seminar Leader

You should also describe the seminar leader, the person who will be conducting the seminar. In describing themselves or those whom they are promoting, people have a tendency to list all of their honors and awards, books they have published, their achievements, recognitions, university degrees, professional designations, and other qualifications. While those data are not unimportant, they are not as crucial as two pieces of information that every seminar attendee looks for. First, does the seminar leader have personal experience doing these things himself in a practical, real-world environment? Second, does this individual have the ability to communicate this information, knowledge, and experience to other people, as evidenced by presentation of this or other seminars in the past? Information that will convince potential participants that the leader does indeed have such experience and abilities should be included in the description of the seminar leader. A high-quality photograph of the leader will also make him more real and credible to the reader.

Seminar Materials

It is also helpful to give the reader as clear a picture as possible of the materials that will be provided to seminar participants. Many potential participants want to feel that they will leave your seminar with some tangible product which will help them make the most of their newly gained information. Generally, the more substantial the materials, the more attractive the seminar will be to the prospective participant. Be as glowing as you can in your description of the "hundreds of pages of material" or the "dozens of useful checklists," or whatever. If your materials are attractively bound, photograph them to give the reader a clearer idea of what he is going to receive. It is generally beneficial to describe and picture the materials in two different situations. If possible, help the prospect to understand and visualize the use of the materials both within the seminar setting and after the seminar as a continuing resource, handbook, or guide. One photograph showing seminar participants using their materials and another showing a participant back home, continuing to use the materials as a deskside reference guide, may be advantageous.

HEAVY COPY VS. LIGHT COPY

"Will my reader actually sit down and read all of this?" is a very hotly contested issue in brochure design. There are those who feel that a brochure needs to be kept as succinct and short as possible because long or complex reading material discourages potential participants. The general consensus, however, holds that before someone is willing to part with valuable time and money for a seminar or workshop, he wants to feel that he has learned everything necessary to make a decision. Research reveals that bounteous copy is more likely to give people this feeling. Certainly, some people will not read the entire brochure and therefore will not attend the seminar, but experience suggests that these individuals would not have attended in any case.

The most important factor in the decision to use light or heavy copy is the audience to whom you are addressing the brochure. If you are offering a $55 seminar on speed reading, then, as suggested earlier, you might want to keep your brochure shorter than if you are offering a $695 seminar on investing. As in all other marketing decisions, consider your target market.

If you are a student of direct mail marketing, you have probably noticed that many large and successful direct mail companies tend to promote with the use of a lot of words—heavy copy. Most of these companies have tested heavy copy versus light copy (few words) and found that the former produces a higher response rate. They have learned that vast numbers of the recipients of direct mail do not read all of those words, but they probably would not make a favorable purchase decision anyway. Those who are truly considering your offer, however, tend to become convinced and make a purchase decision when you have given them sufficient information to encourage them to do so.

One of my clients had a difficult time believing that an abundance of copy was helpful to his promotional efforts. Over a period of almost a year, he tested heavy versus light copy on each of five promotional mailings. In four of the five tests, heavy copy worked better, producing increased revenue of $112 per 1,000 units mailed against an increased cost for paper and printing of $22 per 1,000.

THE COPY

What you say about your program and how you say it are very important. Spending time writing, editing, and further refining the copy is vital if you plan on convincing readers to participate. Just as gaining the reader's attention requires effort, so too does convincing a reader to become a registrant.

When writing your copy, avoid clichés, wordiness, jargon, outdated phrases, and any statements that might cause your reader to toss aside the brochure. The following choices of words and phrases will help to enhance your promotional copy.

Words and Phrases for Sharp, Concise, Readable Copy

Do say:	*Don't say:*
1. then	furthermore
2. however; but	nevertheless
3. so	hence; accordingly; consequently
4. use	utilize
5. learn	ascertain
6. add to	supplement
7. get	acquire
8. look over; review	peruse
9. become known	transpire
10. was enthusiastic about	enthuse
11. over	overly
12. think	deem
13. start; begin	activate; initiate
14. is	comprises; constitutes
15. in conclusion	in the last analysis
16. the future	the foreseeable future
17. to	in order to
18. if	in case of
19. like	along the lines of
20. about; approximately	in the neighborhood of
21. by	on the basis of
22. about	with reference to
23. so that	with the result that
24. for	from the point of view of; on behalf of
25. because; since	for the reason that; inasmuch as; in view of; due to the fact that
26. if	in the event that
27. always	at all times
28. now	at the present time
29. with; by	by means of
30. today; these days	in this day and age
31. mail	send by return mail
32. the reason is	the reason is due to
33. please	will you be good enough to

Rather than merely relying on your own efforts, I would recommend that you provide an edited draft of your promotional copy to a group of individuals similar to those who will likely be prospective participants. Involve them in your own focus group and receive feedback from them about what they like and don't like as well as questions they have after finishing your brochure. You can then fine-tune your copy and your design to make the promotion more effective and productive.

MAKING THE SALE

Now that you have the reader longing to attend your seminar, it's time to get down to business. It's entirely possible to convince a reader to attend your seminar and then lose him because some vital piece of the registration process is either unclear or absent. Keep all aspects of the promotion clear, simple, and straightforward.

Replies

First, you will need to provide one or more kinds of reply mechanism. You are well advised to accept registrations through both telephone and mail response. For many products, including a considerable number of seminars, the toll-free (800) number has largely replaced the postage-paid, preaddressed mailer. Is the added expense of a toll-free number really necessary? The answer to this question depends upon your target audience. If your prospective participants are individuals working for medium and large organizations, typically they will not mind paying for their own phone call and a toll-free number is probably unnecessary. However, if your participants are from very small companies or the general public (consumers), a toll-free number will actually boost sales.

In general, you can apply the same philosophy to postage-paid mail. The real reason you pay the postage is not because the respondents are unable or unwilling to pay the postage, but because they may not have a stamp easily available. In a large organization someone is responsible each day for seeing that outgoing mail is posted and deposited with the Postal Service. However, if your participants are consumers, they may not have a stamp at hand. Rather than have them walk around for a week with your sale (their registration) in their pocket, intending to get to the Post Office, you want them to return the registration immediately.

If you are providing a mail-in registration form, make sure that all of the information on the registration form is duplicated somewhere on the brochure. This serves two functions: first, it gives your first reader, who is by now so bowled over by your presentation that he can hardly wait to go out and tell other people, a means by which others can sign up for your seminar without having to somehow obtain another brochure; second, it provides your participant with all the on-hand information about where he's supposed to be on what date at what time.

Even if you are not planning on accepting registrations by phone, it's a good idea to give readers (potential participants) a phone number they can call for further information. No matter how complete you feel your brochure is, there will be people who have just one more question they need answered before making a decision, and if they can call you and get that settled, it may well garner you additional registrations. Moreover, making yourself available to discuss your seminar with the public makes you appear more accessible, which can be an important factor to some prospective participants.

Figure 3–1 is a sample participant registration card.

Act-Now Kickers and Other Inducements

Readers should feel some motivation to register immediately for your seminar. Once they have put your brochure down, saying that they'll get to it later, your chances of receiving their registrations drop enormously. There are several ways of motivating people to "act now." You can offer a bonus to those whose paid registration is received by a certain date, or to the first x number of people whose paid registration is received. The bonus need not be very substantial. It can be a discount on the cost of the seminar, or, better yet, a small gift such as a book dealing with the subject matter of the seminar. Some providers have had success by offering attendance at a free lunch or dinner combined with an informal discussion with the presenter to the first x number of people. It's usually not a good idea to offer these bonuses to people who register saying they

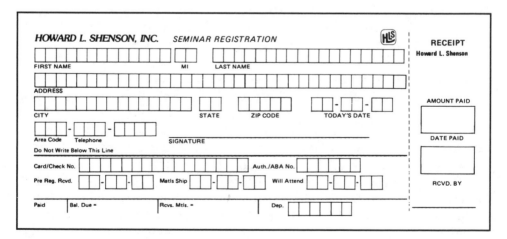

Figure 3–1. Sample participant registration card.

will pay later. Some will sign up on the off-chance that they'll attend, thereby assuring themselves of a bonus if they do decide to attend. The operable language is "receipt of a paid registration by *x* date."

Cancellation Policy

Providing as liberal a cancellation policy as possible helps to ensure that those reading your brochure will sign up immediately. People are much more likely to send in their money immediately if they feel that they can cancel later in the event that something comes up, and the percentage of cancellations on prepaid registrations averages only 2.5 percent. If your cancellation policy is punishing, it will hurt sales.

You may wish to include a cancellation policy for yourself, in case registrations are insufficient to justify the expense of conducting the program. The following standard wording is often used: "If enrollment is insufficient in this program, registered participants will be notified no later than _____," or "All dates and locations subject to cancellation on prior written notice to enrolled participants." When possible, try to avoid having to do this, because prospective participants will feel that the program may be less worthy of their investment.

On the other hand, while a liberal cancellation policy may be advisable, be very cautious about guarantees of satisfaction. Guarantees such as "If you ever, between now and the end of time, have any doubts whatsoever about the value of this seminar, we not only refund your money, but also put your children through college," may act to reassure a prospective participant who is wavering but can make things very difficult for you. More importantly, some promoters have found that the mere mention of a guarantee in promotional literature tends to raise doubts in the minds of prospective participants about the quality of the program and hurts the overall effectiveness of the promotional yield. It may be best not to mention a liberal guarantee policy unless specifically questioned by a prospective or actual participant. This factor should be tested by you for your specific program and target audience. If you feel that a guarantee is an important part of your marketing program, consider giving participants the option of leaving at the first break and receiving a full refund, provided that they have returned their participant materials.

Tax Deductibility

It is almost always in your interest to mention the tax-deductible status of your seminar, assuming that this is applicable. The standard language for this is: "An income tax deduction may be allowed for educational expenses undertaken to maintain or improve professional skills. This includes registration, travel, meals, lodging . . . (see Treasury Regulation 1.162-5) [*Coughlin v. Commissioner,* 203 F.2d 307]."

Education Credit

If your program qualifies for continuing education credit, be sure to include this fact in your brochure. The Council on the Continuing Education Unit, a nonprofit organization, has established a system by which participants of a continuing education program can receive units of credit for their efforts. One Continuing Education Unit (CEU) is given to a participant for every 10 hours spent in a program. CEUs do not *officially* qualify participants in the skills learned but do show that they have completed the program and have the desire to expand their knowledge and skills, which can aid them in their jobs and/or professions. Programs need not be sponsored by the Council, but the seminar provider or sponsoring company must maintain a record of a participant's course completions and be prepared to give the participant a transcript of his record.

However, the Council has an established membership program that sponsors any organization fulfilling its requirements and meeting its approval. Member organizations may use the Council's logo, which can increase a seminar's credibility and show prospective participants that the program has been sponsored by an organized governing body. Member organizations of the Council are benefited in several ways:

1. They are given the opportunity to increase exposure for their name.
2. The use of a common logo links them with other reputable organizations and offers greater credibility.
3. They are kept up-to-date on current advances in the continuing education field through a newsletter and other materials published by the Council.

In general, to be sponsored by the Council, a program must be comprehensive and up-to-date in its field and must expand a participant's skills. Moreover, an organization must have been awarding CEUs in accordance with the official criteria and guidelines for at least one year prior to submitting an application for sponsorship. The Council has two publications which can help you to assess whether your program qualifies to award CEUs: *Principles of Good Practice in Continuing Education* and *The Continuing Education Unit Criteria and Guidelines.* For more information, contact the Council on the Continuing Education Unit, 1101 Connecticut Avenue, Room 700, Washington, DC 20036.

If a professional association is connected with the subject matter of your seminar, its members may be required to involve themselves in a certain number of educational courses relevant to their profession. Be sure to check with the association to find out whether your course meets the requirements; if it does, advertise that fact.

Credit Card

If possible, give registrants the option of paying for the seminar by credit card. Although there is some small expense associated with setting up the account with your bank and a charge on all of the money collected that way, accepting credit cards can increase your registrations from 12 to 28 percent! If you are going to accept credit card payments, make sure that you indicate the cards you will accept and leave sufficient room for the registrants to record the card number, expiration date, and signature. If you are taking telephone registrations, accepting credit cards is really a requirement unless you are willing to invoice participants for the seminar registration fee.

Invoicing

If you expect a substantial portion of your participants to have their fees paid by their employers, you should consider the possibility of invoicing the employers for the seminar fee. Doing so will speed the receipt of registrations and may even permit some participants to attend who otherwise could not. You should require that the invoices be paid prior to or at the time of the seminar; collecting on invoices after the seminar has been given can be difficult. Whatever you decide, include your policy on invoicing in the brochure. If participants tend to come from Fortune 500 corporations, other large private firms, and governmental agencies, you may not feel it necessary to insist on payment prior to or at the time of the program. For smaller private firms, however, you may wish to establish a different policy.

Multiple Registration

Should you offer a discount for multiple registrations? Many seminar and workshop providers feel that such an inducement encourages multiple registrations and improves total program profitability. The evidence is not clear; you should test such an inducement for your program. Offering a discount for multiple registrations can delay receipt of registrations while prospective participants attempt to build a group. And, you run a risk in that if an interested participant is unsuccessful in gathering a group, he may be talked out of a decision to attend your program. In general, if you make such an offer, do not require the prospect to build a group before registering. The following wording has proven effective in several cases:

There is a 20 percent discount when three or more individuals from the same organization register for the same seminar. Take the discount and send in your registration now. Tell the others to mention your name when making their registrations. We will keep track for you!

You have now secured a registration, even if your participant fails to build a team. And, when your participant seeks to build a team it will be from the perspective: "*I am attending* this seminar and I thought it would be useful for you to consider participating too," rather than "Do you think that we should go to this seminar?"

The Obvious

Last but certainly not least, don't forget the obvious. Have you included all of the registration procedure, the price, the location of the seminar, the time, the day, and the date? You would be amazed at how many brochures go out missing one or more of these vital pieces of information.

SELF-CHECK

Once you have finished your first rough draft of the brochure, set it aside for a while and come back to it later. Reread it from the point of view of someone who has just received it in the mail. Using a 10-point scale (1 = low and 10 = high), rate yourself on these factors:

	Rating
I grab the reader's attention immediately and instantly.	
I have avoided being too "tasteful."	____
I have clearly and motivationally described each of the benefits which the participant will obtain by attending my program.	____
I have clearly indicated each item which the participant will learn and, wherever possible, I have quantified.	____
I have included testimonials and they are used in a convincing way.	____
The people who will conduct this program have been described in terms of their practical experience and knowledge and their ability to communicate.	____
I have described the seminar materials in such a way that participants will be able to visualize themselves making use of them in the seminar and afterward.	____

Rating

My offer is plain, simple, easy to understand, and
easy to respond to.

_____

Fee, registration, and payment procedures; sponsor
name, address, and phone; and similar information
have been included on both the brochure and the
reply mechanism.

_____

If you score 80 to 90 on these nine factors, you have done as well as
anyone might expect. A lower score may suggest the need for modifications and improvements. If you are making use of a "focus group" to
evaluate your brochure, as suggested earlier, you may wish to give them
the same factors and rating scale and compare their analysis of your promotional piece to your own.

Make any further revisions indicated as a result of the input of your
"focus group." Once done, you have completed the *rough draft* of your
brochure. Are you ready to take it out and print up 100,000 copies for
deposit in the U.S. mails? No! Give the brochure to a thirteen-year-old
child who is reading at grade level. Have the child mark anything that he
doesn't immediately understand. Take the brochure back to the drawing
board and rework it until you have a piece which a thirteen-year-old can
read and comprehend from cover to cover. You may argue that your potential participants read at a higher level. Many do, but if you cannot
explain why someone should attend your program at a level of communication no more difficult than that of the typical morning newspaper (i.e.,
that of a thirteen-year-old), it will cost you some registrations.

PRODUCTION

The advent of computerized typesetting, desktop publishing, and
computer-aided graphics allows you, at reasonable cost, to produce a
quality piece that is visually appealing and encourages response. You
may buy production services outside or develop, at reasonable cost, an
in-house capability to turn out brochures with a graphic look that com-
plements the quality of the message you have written. Photography,
graphics, design, typesetting, and printing are extremely price-elastic,
so it is well worth your trouble to shop around.

All right, you have finished the brochure copy and you have camera-
ready art. *Now* can you go out and print up 100,000 copies? Maybe.
Remember that only you, your focus group, and a thirteen-year-old
child have seen your brochure, and you have no guarantee of its success.
The only way of knowing whether this brochure is going to work is to test
it. How many should you test? How much risk are you willing to take? If

each brochure deposited in the Post Office costs you 30 cents and you can afford to take a $3,000 risk, you can test-mail 10,000. On the first rendition, I like to test a minimum of 2,500 units. Remember that if a particular version of a brochure doesn't work, it doesn't mean the entire seminar is a failure. Seminars and workshops, when successful, can be incredibly profitable. You cannot always expect to find the pot of gold on your first attempt.

On the following pages, Figures 3–2 through 3–5 give a selection of direct mail seminar brochures. These are typical of promotions used and illustrate many of the principles of brochure design discussed herein.

CONSULTING IN THE '90s

**SURVIVING & PROSPERING
IN AN ENVIRONMENT OF**

TECHNOLOGY LEASING

KNOWLEDGE CONDOMINIUMS

UNEXPECTED COMPETITORS

STRATEGY PACKAGING

INFORMATION MARKETING

BROADCASTED DECISIONS

DATA MANDATED SYSTEMS

TREND MANAGEMENT

ACCELERATING TECHNOLOGY

UNUSUAL CLIENT EXPECTATIONS

*A RESULTS-PRODUCING,
IDEA-GENERATING, 1-DAY SEMINAR
WITH CASE STUDIES
DESIGNED TO REVOLUTIONIZE
THE WAY YOU DO BUSINESS*

DEVELOPED & PERSONALLY CONDUCTED BY
HOWARD L. SHENSON, CMC

Figure 3–2.

WILL YOU BE PREPARED FOR THE CHALLENGES & OPPORTUNITIES OF THE 1990s?
A Personal Message From Howard L. Shenson

The success of your practice during the next decade will depend on your ability to respond to unprecedented — *some say alarming* — trends and conditions. Your ability to interpret and respond appropriately to just-emerging competitive and technological challenges will, quite frankly, determine if you will be among those around to welcome year 2000.

For two decades the vast majority of professionals have prospered (often handsomely) despite a reliance on largely antiquated technology and methods. In the '90s, technological, economic and competitive conditions will be revolutionary in both speed and character. **Those of us unwilling to change dramatically will not survive.**

FIRST SEMINAR IN 15 MONTHS

Consulting In The '90s will be the first program I have presented in 15 months. Time normally spent doing seminars has been devoted to a comprehensive and exhaustive research effort dedicated to defining how you and I must respond to the unprecedented challenges which will characterize the decade of the 1990s.

What I have learned has radically adjusted the way I will do business in the future. I suspect that it will have a similar impact on you.

Survival will be critically dependent upon your ability to embrace a whole new concept of services delivery, a whole new way of looking at what you do, and the strategies which you employ to serve your markets. **Success will require that you respond to opportunity in ways fundamentally different than you have perhaps ever envisioned.**

I look forward to sharing the results of my research and analysis with you and to presenting for your consideration creative new concepts which in my opinion are revolutionary — *some say visionary* — in their own right.

Howard L. Shenson, CMC

SELECT THE MOST CONVENIENT LOCATION

LOS ANGELES
Wednesday, November 1, 1989
9:00 AM until 5:00 PM
Hyatt at Los Angeles Airport
6225 W. Century at Sepulveda

SEATTLE
Tuesday, November 7, 1989
9:00 AM until 5:00 PM
Seattle Sheraton
6th Avenue at Pike

SAN FRANCISCO
Wednesday, November 15, 1989
9:00 AM until 5:00 PM
Hyatt on Union Square
345 Stockton at Post

HOW YOU WILL BENEFIT FROM THIS SEMINAR

Your Seminar is built around thought-provoking and results-oriented case studies designed to reveal what your most visionary and forward-thinking peers are doing (and planning) to ensure prosperity in the '90s. This proven learning method has numerous advantages, including . . .

- You learn, first hand, what the most successful consultants are doing, the results they are getting and the strategic thinking behind their actions.

- *You are introduced to scores of creative, profit-producing ideas and get step-by-step guidance on how to implement similar strategies for your own practice.*

- You enhance your ability to select marketing strategies and services that turn the emerging economic, technological and social/political trends to your advantage.

- *You find out what clients will really require of you in the decade of the '90s, how it will impact the nature of the services you deliver and the ways you will market.*

- You get a guided tour of new technological advances (computer and non-computer) that will dictate unprecedented changes for those who wish to be cutting-edge, state-of-the-art and competitive.

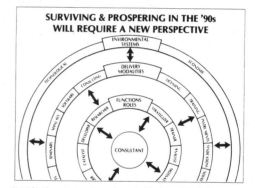

SURVIVING & PROSPERING IN THE '90s WILL REQUIRE A NEW PERSPECTIVE

- *You identify new competitors who seek a big share of the dollars you expected to be spent with you and develop action plans that enhance your ability to out compete.*

- You master innovative ways to contract, set and disclose fees, conduct business which will be essential to survive and profit in a market that can only be described as revolutionary.

- *You explore creative concepts for increasing revenues and profits that produce passive income — reducing/eliminating the strangle hold of the billable hours concept of doing business.*

- You evaluate the wisdom of participating in creative new business development/profit producing mechanisms — including technology licensing and information condominiums.

As with other Shenson programs, your day will be practical and specific. You will open your eyes to new challenges, new opportunities and new perspectives. After this day, you will never again be the same!

The Professional Consultant & Information Marketing Report
20750 Ventura Boulevard, Suite 206 • Woodland Hills, CA 91364
Telephone: 818/703-1415 (Fax: 818/703-6295)

Figure 3–2. *(continued)*

Doing Business, New Client Requirements. ARE YOU READY?

CLINIC INCLUDED:
BRING YOUR QUESTIONS/ PROBLEMS

. For part of the afternoon your Seminar becomes a results-producing, problem-solving, opportunity-generating marketing clinic. Bring your questions and problems. They will be solved on the spot — with particular emphasis on how the decade of the '90s will demand changes. If follow-up information is required, Shenson will call you the very next day with the added information. If you have a question or problem which you believe will require research, please feel free to send it in before the Seminar.

If you have participated in a Shenson-conducted Clinic in the past, you know what benefits you're in for.

SEMINAR FEE & REGISTRATION

The fee for the full Seminar, including all materials and refreshment breaks, is:

$195. if registration is paid by October 15th

$245. if registration is paid after October 15th.

The Program begins promptly at 9:00 AM and concludes at 5:00 PM. Both mid-morning and mid-afternoon breaks are scheduled. The lunch break will be from 12:30 until 1:30. Lunch is not included.

To register please complete the coupon below and mail or telephone your registration to 818/703-1415. If more convenient, please fax your registration. Payment may be made by check or credit card.

A letter of confirmation will be mailed upon receipt of your registration.

If you are one of the first 12 to register at any location, you will receive a valuable gift, a six month subscription (extension) to *The Professional Consultant & Information Marketing Report.*

TAX DEDUCTION

Federal regulations permit a tax deduction for educational expenses (including travel) incurred to improve and maintain skills required for employment or business. Check with your tax advisor.

CONTINUING EDUCATION CREDIT

This program is approved for .7 continuing education units. Such units may have value for professional certification and licensure now or in the future.

©1989, Howard L. Shenson

HOWARD L. SHENSON, CMC

Howard L. Shenson is a Certified Management Consultant. He is the author of more than two dozen books and audio/video learning packages on the marketing and management of professional practices and information business enterprises. More than 100,000 professionals have attended his seminars and workshops. He is a frequent speaker before national professional meetings.

Besides publishing the profession's most widely read/frequently quoted newsletter—*The Professional Consultant & Information Marketing Report*—Shenson authors a monthly column for *Business & Technology Consultant* magazine.

His work has been featured in more than 500 newspaper and magazine articles. His views have been aired on more than 300 radio/TV talk and news shows.

Shenson began consulting part-time in 1968 while involved in teaching and administration at the University of Southern California and The California State University. A full-time consultant since 1971, he will share his vast knowledge, recognized research and authoritative experience generously.

TALK TO THE PROGRAM LEADER BEFORE YOU REGISTER

If you have questions about the suitability of this program for your purposes, don't hesitate to call Howard Shenson directly at 818/703-1415.

3 IMPORTANT REASONS TO REGISTER EARLY . . .

1. You save $50 off the regular fee of $245 if your paid registration is received by October 15th. Benefit from the early registration fee of $195.

2. Seating is strictly limited to ensure individual attention. Early registration ensures that space will be available for you.

3. If you are one of the first 12 to register at any location you receive a valuable gift—a six month subscription to *The Professional Consultant & Information Marketing Report* (Value = $60). Current subscribers receive a six month extension.

REFER A COLLEAGUE & RECEIVE A VALUABLE BENEFIT

If you have friends and associates who would benefit from this program, you could receive a valuable gift. Your choice of any one of these five Shenson-authored best sellers for each participant you refer:

- *The Successful Consultant's Guide To Fee Setting* ($29)
- *How To Strategically Negotiate The Consulting Contract* ($39)
- *How To Create & Market A Successful Seminar Or Workshop* ($29)
- *The Consultant's Guide To Proposal Writing* ($49)
- *The Consulting Handbook* ($59)

Here's how it works. Write your name on the registration coupon below in the space marked "Referred By". Photocopy this complete announcement and send it to interested colleagues. Talk it up if you wish. If you register and attend the Seminar, you will receive a certificate which may be exchanged for any of these books for each person you refer who registers and attends. Those registering by phone will be asked if they were referred to ensure that you receive credit for the registration.

REGISTER TODAY! COMPLETE & MAIL THIS COUPON OR PHONE 818/703-1415 (Fax 818/703-6295)

☐ **YES.** Please reserve _____ seat/s ☐ LOS ANGELES ☐ SEATTLE ☐ SAN FRANCISCO
in the Seminar indicated: November 1 November 7 November 15

I understand the fee is $195. per person ($245 after October 15.)

☐ **Immediately send** _____ copy/ies of How To Build A Profitable Consulting Practice (#676), $175 + $7 shipping and sales tax.

☐ I am attending the Seminar and thus entitled to the special price of $139 + $7 shipping and sales tax.

_____ ☐ Mr. ☐ Ms ☐ Dr.
NAME

FIRM/ORGANIZATION

ADDRESS

CITY   STATE   ZIP

AREA CODE & PHONE

Payment: ☐ VISA ☐ MasterCard
☐ AmEx ☐ Enclosed check

CARD NUMBER

EXPIRES

SIGNATURE

Referred By:

Mail To: *The Professional Consultant & Information Marketing Report,* 20750 Ventura Boulevard, Suite 206, Woodland Hills, CA 91364, Telephone: 818/703-1415

Figure 3–2. *(continued)*

61

A Totally New & Different Seminar Developed & Conducted By HOWARD L. SHENSON, CMC To Prepare You For The Revolutionary Challenges & Unprecedented Opportunities You will Face In the '90s

INCLUDES:
- CASE STUDIES
- MARKETING CLINIC
- NEW RESEARCH DATA

- **LOS ANGELES**
  WEDNESDAY, NOVEMBER 1

- **SEATTLE**
  TUESDAY, NOVEMBER 7

- **SAN FRANCISCO**
  WEDNESDAY, NOVEMBER 15

Once you have experienced this Seminar you will never again be the same. Be prepared to alter the way you do business!

Special Opportunity For Seminar Participants:

HOWARD SHENSON'S DYNAMIC NEW INDEPENDENT-STUDY COURSE

How To Build A Profitable Consulting Practice at a substantial savings . . .

Obtain Shenson's latest, nationally acclaimed, comprehensive guides on building a profitable consulting practice. More than 2½ hours of production grade videos and over 275 pages of detailed, how-to-do-it-with-success information.

Covers every aspect of building and maintaining a successful practice including:

- How to identify the best opportunities/growth arenas;
- Marketing strategies with a proven track record of producing results;
- Fee setting, fee disclosure, invoicing and collections;
- Practice growth & expansion; and
- Maintaining solid client relations (including reporting).

The manual is fully indexed and tab divided to ensure that it serves as a convenient deskside reference source for years to come.

2 Video Tapes + Reference Manual + 101 Proven Marketing Strategies + 73 Proven Referral Business Builders

Order publication number 676, How To Build A Profitable Consulting Practice . . .

Regular price . . . . $175. + $7 priority shipping and sales tax.

Seminar-participant price . . . . $139. + $7 priority shipping and sales tax.

THE PROFESSIONAL CONSULTANT & INFORMATION MARKETING REPORT

20750 Ventura Boulevard • Woodland Hills, CA 91364

BULK RATE
U.S. POSTAGE
PAID
WOODLAND HILLS, CA
PERMIT NO. 89

GET AN EARLY START ON PREPARING FOR THE NEW DIRECTIONS & PROFIT OPPORTUNITIES IN THE DECADE OF THE '90s

Figure 3–2. (*continued*)

SkillPath Seminars invites you to attend a special learning opportunity…

HOW TO MANAGE PROJECTS

The unique, complete-in-one-day project management workshop
guaranteed to show you how to keep your projects
on track, on target, on time

Just $99
Your Satisfaction Guaranteed

We're coming to you in 1990…

Anaheim, CA	January 31
Anaheim, CA	February 28
Bakersfield, CA	February 2
Beverly Hills, CA	March 13
Costa Mesa, CA	January 30
Culver City, CA	February 14
Culver City, CA	March 15
Honolulu, HI	February 9
La Jolla, CA	February 27
Las Vegas, NV	February 8
Long Beach, CA	February 12
Ontario, CA	March 12
Oxnard, CA	February 1
Pasadena, CA	March 14
San Bernardino, CA	February 15
San Diego, CA	January 29
Torrance, CA	February 13
Van Nuys, CA	March 16

INSIDE…

Special Memo from Jerry Brown	Page 3
Your Trainer's Biographical Sketch	Page 4
Workshop Outline	Page 4
Money Back Guarantee	Page 6
Workshop Locations	Page 6
Enrollment Form	Page 7

To enroll, call toll-free 1-800-767-7545
or 1-913-362-3900

SkillPath, Inc. • The Smart Choice™
6900 Squibb Road • P.O. Box 2768 • Mission, Kansas 66201-2768

© 1989, SkillPath, Inc

Figure 3–3.

THE ONE-DAY WAY TO
SUCCESSFUL PROJECT MANAGEMENT

We consulted with the nation's leading project management experts and top project managers in the field to bring you the most comprehensive project management workshop available. You'll find it rich in detail on how to set realistic goals and objectives, plan and track progress, and use real-world techniques for keeping projects on course.

That's the focus of this intensive one-day workshop:

> To provide you with a practical, easy-to-use system for planning and managing projects effectively.

You'll learn how to use scheduling tools like Gantt, CPM and PERT and how to evaluate the relative pros and cons of each for your particular project needs. Plus, you'll learn how to recognize and avoid some of the common pitfalls and mistakes that can sabotage even the most well-conceived projects. And, because "gremlins" always show up, we'll show you how to provide for contingencies and how to creatively solve problems and handle conflicts.

What's more, we bring this unique workshop right to your area at a price that's a fraction of what others charge for similar programs.

YOU'LL GAIN SIX VALUABLE SKILLS THAT WILL SERVE YOU FOREVER

1. **How to Plan Projects**
   What the plan should include, what it shouldn't ... How much time to allow for planning ... Taking into account the "triple constraint" all projects encounter ... How to use powerful tools that can make planning easier.

2. **How to Establish Time Lines**
   How to select and use the appropriate tools for scheduling: PERT, Gantt, CPM ... Step-by-step guidelines for establishing milestones.

3. **How to Keep Things Moving**
   How to select your team, get their support and the support of other key players ... How to motivate and communicate ... How to secure top management agreement and backing.

4. **How to Monitor and Control**
   Reports and reviews -- when to use both ... How to keep tabs on costs, schedules and objectives ... How to monitor checkpoints to measure progress.

5. **How to Solve Problems**
   Creative approaches to solving problems ... Getting the most from available resources ... Specific actions that can save projects in trouble ... How to overcome resistance to adjustments and change.

6. **How to Manage Multiple Projects**
   A systematic approach to staying on top of several projects at once ... How to select team leaders/project managers ... How to set priorities and resolve the conflict between competing priorities.

Like to know more? Turn to page 4 for complete details about this informative day.

TO ENROLL: Call toll-free 1-800-767-7545,
Mail in the enrollment form on page 7 or
FAX your enrollment 1-913-362-4241

Figure 3–3. (*continued*)

SPECIAL MEMORANDUM

TO: Project managers and team leaders
     Managers and supervisors with project management responsibilities

FROM: Jerry Brown

Good things happen to those who know how to manage projects. The ability to make
things happen ... to meet deadlines ... to build and supervise a team ... to get
results. That's what makes people take notice. That's what makes careers soar!

It's a fact. Managers who know how to complete projects on time, on budget, and
with the desired result are in high demand and -- as top management everywhere
agrees -- in short supply.

     That's why we set out to consult with the nation's top project
     managers. We wanted to find out what techniques are working for
     them, gain the benefit of their experience and practical insights,
     and bring the information straight to you.

So, what are the secrets of these project management "superstars?" No secrets,
really. Just a thorough understanding of what it takes to guide a project from
bright idea to bottom-line result. The know-how to create a plan, implement it,
monitor progress, correct as necessary, and deliver as promised. The skills to
make their projects an orderly progression of completed objectives, instead of the
all-too-common helter-skelter race with disaster.

That's our crystal-clear goal in this unique seminar. To equip you with the tools,
knowledge, insights and skills to make you an outstanding project manager. We'll
focus on practical applications and techniques that you can take back to work and
use the very next day. Step-by-step guidelines that you can apply to your current
or next project.

You'll learn how to get projects started in the right direction, set goals and
develop your plan, build your project team, allocate your resources, monitor
progress, adjust and correct as necessary, avoid common project pitfalls, handle
the inevitable problems, and complete the project on schedule.

Whether your project is simple and straightforward or complex and detailed, the
same rules apply. You'll leave this seminar equipped to be more effective than
ever before in leading projects to successful completion.

Managing projects successfully is a challenge. Yet there are great rewards for
those who master the necessary skills.

Let us show you how.

Jerry

Jerry E. Brown
President
SkillPath, Inc.

*P.S.— Whether you manage projects
full-time or as additional duty,
the skills you'll gain in this workshop
can save your organization hundreds of
hours and thousands of dollars.*

Figure 3–3. (*continued*)

One day and $99 — that's all it takes to

THE BEST REASON OF ALL TO ATTEND

Your trainer, Reich Gardner, M.B.A.

A veteran project manager turned full-time project management trainer/consultant, Reich Gardner is one of the nation's most sought-after trainers in this important area.

Reich is "a true professional in every sense of the word" (from a recent program evaluation). From the technical aspect to the human side of project management, Reich has "been there." Now, he's back with the answers to the questions project managers most often ask.

Reich has consulted with such prestigious clients as Bell and Howell, AT&T and United Telecommunications.

From project concept to completion, Reich will detail a systematic step-by-step approach to successful project management. You'll leave Reich's workshop equipped with the tools to manage <u>any</u> project.

Praise from participants of Reich Gardner's Workshop ...

"**The seminar itself was like a well-managed project. Start to finish, I was delighted. Thank you!**"
– Holly Hayes, Marketing Representative, IBM

"**This seminar leader was well-prepared, presented the material in understandable language, and did an excellent job. A great learning experience.**"
– Cary Flynn, Auditor, Centel Corp

" ... he was able to convey some very complex material to me in a way that I could easily understand. I appreciated the humor and personality, but especially the professionalism."
– Marie Brumer, Chief Dietician, Del-Mar Systems

"**Reich was great! Very down-to-earth and made us feel comfortable. I learned so much.**"
– Barbara Stempien, Executive Director, W. Willington Game Farm

"**Thanks for this much-needed 'crash course' on project management. Now I can really get down to work!**"
– Lisa Hughes, Project Manager, Central Telecom

" ... very helpful, covered lots of information...and the instructor covered all areas very well."
– John Fanning, Chief, Office Software Applications, NLRB

"**Reich made it very interesting. He explained the material in a way that made it easily understood.**"
– Jim Decker, Wildlife Biologist, State of California

"**This is one seminar that delivered what it promised. And Mr. Gardner, needless to say, knows his project management.**"
– Lee Anne Hopkins, Software Applications Consultant, MegaThought Systems, Inc. of Kansas City

"... took the time to answer questions. He made what could have been a boring subject into an enlightening learning experience."
– Keith Eyman, Vice President, Ambassador Homes

"**Reich was very good in helping, answering, and explaining. Any questions we had, he took the time for.**"
– Mary Kay Ingenthron, President, MK Communications

"**Mr. Gardner is well-organized, to-the-point, and a quality instructor.**"
– John Paquette, President, Paquette Landscape Design

WORKSHOP OUTLINE:

1. Key Considerations for Project Managers

- The six unique characteristics that distinguish project management from other responsibilities
- Mastering the 5-stage project management process
- Recognizing the "triple threat" constraints you face with every project you start
- Why deadlines are missed — how to avoid, up-front, the single biggest obstacle to meeting the schedule
- Avoiding the four most common problems that plague projects
- How to identify and avoid the three biggest pitfalls that can keep a project's outcome from living up to expectations
- The 10 commandments for successful project management
- The SMART approach to setting clear goals

2. The Fundamentals of Project Planning

- The basic purpose of planning
- How to recognize and overcome the barriers to good planning
- When planning really is a waste of time
- The rule of thumb for determining how much time to allow for planning
- How to use a simple planning "safety net" to make sure nothing falls through a crack
- Planning the time dimension — how to use PERT, Gantt, CPM — choosing the technique best suited to your needs
- How to estimate a project's cost — four straightforward methods
- How to efficiently integrate and allocate the resources at your disposal (and how to make a powerful case for **more** resources when you need them)
- There are three commonly accepted ways to provide for contingencies in project plans — we'll show you which one top project managers prefer

Figure 3–3. (*continued*)

gain the latest Project Management insights

3. Getting Down to Work

- Individuals receive trophies; teams win championships — how to recruit and select the winning project team
- The four staffing rules for building an effective team
- How to instill a high degree of motivation and commitment in team members
- How to get the cooperation and involvement of the critically important "support" team
- Why team member task assignments must include some "give and take"
- How to conduct project meetings that get results
- How to use the WBS system to tie work units to the time dimension
- Choosing the right management tools: internal integration vs. external integration
- Four vital "people factors" you must take into account when setting objectives

4. Monitoring and Controlling

- How to structure reports for maximum value
- How to determine the kinds of reports you'll want
- What written reports can and cannot tell you
- How to determine how much detail reports should include and what the distribution should be
- Recognizing the built-in bias of the report writer
- Using periodic and topical reviews as your "off-course alarm system"
- Communicating and coordinating — how to let everyone on the project know what's expected of them and how they're doing
- How to establish checkpoints and milestones that tell you whether or not your project is on track

5. Problem-solving and Trouble-shooting

- The seven-step problem-solving formula
- How using a decision tree can often make the solution obvious
- Dealing with the special problems of smaller projects
- How to use the principle of "organized disagreement" to ferret out creative alternatives and solutions
- How to handle the seven most common sources of conflict in project management situations
- How to get team members to accept changes when necessary
- How to prepare for the changing nature and intensity of conflict as the project progresses
- Nine specific actions you can take immediately to save bogged-down, derailed projects
- How to recognize and deal with the "dirty dozen" project productivity killers

6. Managing Multiple Projects

- The one management secret that will always serve you no matter how many "top priorities" you're juggling
- Recognizing which projects must take precedence
- Multi-project reporting systems

7. Computers and Project Management

- Recognizing what personal computer software project management programs can do for you — and what they can't
- Seven evaluation criteria to help you select the best software package for your needs
- How to "test the water" before you jump in

8. Putting It All Together

- How to organize what you've learned into your own Project Action Plan.

∞∞∞∞∞∞∞∞∞∞∞∞∞∞∞∞∞∞∞∞∞∞∞∞∞∞∞∞∞∞∞∞∞∞∞∞∞

Seminar Materials

And you won't go home empty-handed. You'll leave this workshop with a Certificate of Completion signifying that you've earned .6 units of Continuing Education credit, a soundly-researched, unabridged workbook, your personal Project Action Plan for implementing what you've learned and step-by-step guidelines for sharing the new ideas with your associates back at work. Plus, we bet you'll also leave with the business cards of at least two other seminar participants for future networking.

About SkillPath Seminars

We train thousands of career-directed, achievement-oriented professionals like you each month. Our participants are from organizations of all sizes and all types — government, business, health-care, education and the military. Our team of managers, trainers and staff is the most experienced group of training professionals providing public seminars and workshops today. It's no wonder that when smart managers are looking for quality training at a fair price they choose SkillPath.

SkillPath *is* **The Smart Choice**™.

MONEY BACK GUARANTEE
If for **any** reason, you're not completely satisfied and absolutely delighted with the seminar, simply call or write us. We'll issue you a refund or arrange for you to attend another SkillPath seminar without paying a penny. Whichever you choose, no questions asked, at any time. Not just within 10 days, not just within one year, **any time.** *That's our guarantee!*

ENROLL BY PHONE: 1-800-767-7545, 1-913-362-3900 BY FAX: 1-913-362-4241 • Or MAIL completed enrollment form to:
SkillPath, Inc. P.O. Box 2768, Mission, KS 66201-2768

Figure 3–3. (*continued*)

ON-SITE SEMINARS, CONSULTING AND KEYNOTE SPEAKING

It's simple. Our people can make your people better. After all, we're America's top trainers and management consultants. We can tailor any of our programs and bring our trainer right to your company's door. We also provide a full range of in-house consulting services and our trainers are always delighted to add sparkle to your next corporate or association meeting with a stimulating keynote speech designed to meet your specific needs. (Our most popular trainers need to be booked many months in advance, so please call early.) For more information regarding all our on-site services, call our training specialists at 1-800-767-7545. Whether you have three or 300 people to train, SkillPath is the answer.

SkillPath's continuing support... We don't just stand behind our seminars, we stand behind **you**. If, after attending the seminar, you're faced with a project management problem and don't know where to turn — try us. Just send a brief description of your particular problem or question and one of our project management specialists will promptly respond. Where else can you find that kind of support? **Nowhere, but with SkillPath.**

IMPORTANT INFORMATION

Our registration table opens at 8:00 a.m. When you arrive at the hotel please check the directory for the exact location of the seminar. Our registrars will greet you, assist you with your registration (or collect your Express Admission Ticket), hand you your seminar materials and direct you toward the refreshments. You'll also want to take the opportunity to meet other professionals from your local area. Introduce yourself! You may meet a new friend. Plan to be registered and ready to go by 8:50 a.m.

We begin at 9:00 a.m. on the dot and wrap up at 4:00 p.m. Lunch is on your own from 11:45 a.m. to 1:00 p.m. Why not invite another participant to dine with you? You can share information, review the morning and make your day (and their's) even more enjoyable.

Parking. We do our best to find seminar facilities which have all the pluses we look for: convenient location, great meeting rooms, courteous staff and plenty of free parking. However, some facilities have paid parking only. You may want to check with the hotel to determine parking fees — often they can direct you to free parking just around the corner.

Tape recording. Our programs — both what you see and what you hear — are fully copyrighted by SkillPath, Inc. No audio or video taping, please.

STILL HAVEN'T PICKED UP THE PHONE?

Five More Good Reasons Why You Will Want To Attend This Program...

1. **Our trainers are the best...period.** We choose only the pros who have a proven track record of training effectiveness, professionalism and expertise. And what's more, they're exciting communicators who'll provide you with one of the most interesting days you've ever spent.
2. **We give you only the most important _important_ information.** There's a lot of information out there and it could take you years to gather it on your own. In six short hours we'll give you what we believe is the best, most important information to help you be the best you can be.
3. **Practicality is emphasized.** You will leave this seminar with specifics you can apply immediately. We promise you'll get results on your very next day back at work.
4. **The value is unbeatable.** Not only is our enrollment fee among the lowest you'll find, when four or more enroll from the same organization, you'll enjoy a significant discount.
5. **Our guarantee is unconditional, straightforward and the very best in the industry.** How can we be so confident? Because we work hard **before** the seminar to make sure you're happy **after** the seminar. Pertinent, up-to-date information you can really use, a convenient meeting location, seminar registrars who are courteous and helpful and a trainer who grabs your attention and takes you on an exciting journey full of fun and **facts.** We believe you'll love every minute of it. Thousands of satisfied participants from around the country are sold on SkillPath seminars. Why not join them?

MONEY BACK GUARANTEE

If for **any** reason, you're not completely satisfied and absolutely delighted with the seminar, simply call or write us. We'll issue you a refund or arrange for you to attend another SkillPath seminar without paying a penny. Whichever you choose, no questions asked, at any time. Not just within 10 days, not within one year, **any** time. That's our guarantee!

Figure 3–3. (*continued*)

REGISTRATION INFORMATION

Three easy ways to register: phone, FAX or mail

1. For the fastest service, phone 1-800-767-7545 or 1-913-362-3900. Our customer service representatives will be happy to reserve a space for you. The easiest way to guarantee your space in the seminar is to pay with a credit card when making your reservation, but if that's not possible simply mail in your payment before the seminar date.

2. If you prefer to FAX us your registration, the number is 1-913-362-4241. We'll reserve a place for you. Please include credit card information, or mail in your payment before the seminar date.

3. Of course, you can complete the enrollment form below, clip it and mail it with payment to: SkillPath, Inc., P.O. Box 2768, Mission, KS 66201.

Whatever your method of registration, be sure to do it right away since space is limited. Upon receipt of your enrollment, we'll send your Express Admission Ticket. Simply bring it with you to the program and hand it to the registrar. If your ticket doesn't arrive before the seminar be sure to go anyway. Your reservation is guaranteed. Walk-in registrations are welcome on a space-available basis only.

Your tuition is tax-deductible. Even the government smiles on professional education. All expenses of Continuing Education (including registration fees, travel, meals and lodging) taken to maintain and improve professional skills are tax-deductible according to Treasury Regulation 1.162-5 Coughlin vs. Commissioner, 203 F2d 307.

Cancellations. Go ahead and register now. You've got nothing to lose and lots to gain. Cancellations received up to five working days before the seminar are refundable minus a $10 registration service charge. After that, we'll issue you a SkillCheck good for any future SkillPath seminar. And if something comes up at the last minute, feel free to send a substitute without prior notice.

This SkillPath seminar is authorized for 6 contact hours (.6 CEUs) in accordance with guidelines set forth by the National Task Force on the Continuing Education Unit. Many national, state and local licensing boards and professional organizations will grant Continuing Education credit for attendance at our seminars when you submit the course outline (save your brochure) and proof of attendance (your Certificate of Completion). You may want to contact your own board or organization to determine what's required.

SkillPath provides you with a Certificate of Completion which serves as your permanent record of attendance. This attractive, 8 1/2 x 11 certificate indicates that you've earned .6 CEUs. You may want to frame it or put it in your personnel file to show that you're serious about success.

	☎	✉		☎
HOW TO	**BY PHONE**	**BY MAIL**		
ENROLL:	**1-800-767-7545**	Complete and mail enrollment form to:	**BY FAX**	
	or	**SkillPath, Inc.,**	**1-913-362-4241**	
	1-913-362-3900	**P.O. Box 2768**		
		Mission, KS 66201-2768		

Yes, I can't wait to attend How To Manage Projects.

(Enrollment fees: $99.00 per person with four or more, $89.00 each.)

[ ] Anaheim, CA .... January 31	
[ ] Anaheim, CA .... February 28	
[ ] Bakersfield, CA .... February 2	
[ ] Beverly Hills, CA .... March 13	
[ ] Costa Mesa, CA .... January 30	
[ ] Culver City, CA .... February 14	
[ ] Culver City, CA .... March 15	
[ ] Honolulu, HI .... February 9	
[ ] La Jolla, CA .... February 27	
[ ] Las Vegas, NV .... February 8	
[ ] Long Beach, CA .... February 12	
[ ] Ontario, CA .... March 12	
[ ] Oxnard, CA .... February 1	
[ ] Pasadena, CA .... March 14	
[ ] San Bernardino, CA .... February 15	
[ ] San Diego, CA .... January 29	
[ ] Torrance, CA .... February 13	
[ ] Van Nuys, CA .... March 16	

Please print or type:

Mrs.
Miss
Ms.
Mr. _____
    Name   Title

Mrs.
Miss
Ms.
Mr. _____
    Name   Title

Mrs.
Miss
Ms.
Mr. _____
    Name   Title

Check Appropriate Boxes:

[ ] Confirming phone registration

[ ] Check enclosed payable to:
    SkillPath, Inc.
    P.O. Box 2768
    Mission, KS 66201-2768

    Check #_____ Check amt. _____

[ ] Purchase order attached: #_____

[ ] Charge to: [ ] MasterCard [ ] Visa
            [ ] Discover   [ ] AmEx

Card # _____

Exp. Date _____

Signature _____

[ ] Invoice my company

Attn: _____

Mrs.
Miss
Ms.
Mr. _____
    Name   Please list additional registrations on a separate sheet and attach   Title

Mrs.
Miss
Ms.
Mr. _____
    Approving Supervisor   Title

Company _____

Mailing Address _____

City, State, Zip _____

Telephone _____ Ext. _____

Note: If you've registered by phone and paid with a credit card, it's not necessary to return this form.

Your VIP Number: ☐ ☐ ☐ ☐
Please complete your VIP Number by filling in the boxes with the number in the upper right-hand corner of the mailing label.

Figure 3–3. (*continued*)

You're invited to attend...

HOW TO MANAGE PROJECTS

The unique, complete-in-one-day project management workshop
guaranteed to show you how to keep your projects
on track, on target, on time

Just $99
Your Satisfaction Guaranteed

Coming to your city:

Anaheim, CA - January 31 • **Anaheim, CA** - February 28 • **Bakersfield, CA** - February 2 • **Beverly Hills, CA** - March 13
Costa Mesa, CA - January 30 • **Culver City, CA** - February 14 • **Culver City, CA** - March 15 • **Honolulu, HI** - February 9
La Jolla, CA - February 27 • **Las Vegas, NV** - February 8 • **Long Beach, CA** - February 12 • **Ontario, CA** - March 12
Oxnard, CA - February 1 • **Pasadena, CA** - March 14 • **San Bernardino, CA** - February 15
San Diego, CA - January 29 • **Torrance, CA** - February 13 • **Van Nuys, CA** - March 16

Our Trainers Train the Best

PIP Printing	Hyundai Motor America	U.S. Customs Service	Ben Franklin Stores, Inc.	U.S. Rentals
Gulf Oil	Prudential	Motorola	McDonald's	Wells Fargo
Ingersoll-Rand	3M	Frito-Lay	IBM	Mitsubishi Electronics
NCR	American Express	Boeing	U.S. Air Force	Ford Motor Company
Ralston Purina	Apple Computers	Memorex	Coca-Cola	Hewlett-Packard
Monsanto	U.S. Army	Wang Laboratories	Scott Paper	Rubbermaid, Inc.
Diamond Shamrock	Ralph's Grocery	Beatrice	General Motors	Weyerhauser Paper Company
U.S. Postal Service	McDonnell Douglas	Dictaphone	AT&T	U.S. Navy
Texas Instruments	University of Iowa	MCI	Xerox	State Bar of California
Anheuser-Busch	Procter & Gamble	Du Pont	U.S. Dept. of Labor	Hughes Aircraft Company
Honeywell	Marriott Corporation	California Highway Patrol	Mobil Oil	Visiting Nurses Association
PepsiCo	Hallmark	Tektronix, Inc.	Pacific Bell	Intel Corporation
Federal Aviation Admin.	NASA	Digital Equipment	Kaiser Permanente	ARCO Oil and Gas Company
Crestwood Hospitals, Inc.	Beverly Enterprises	Univ. of Calif. Med. Center	IRS	City of Los Angeles
The Toro Company	Pizza Hut	Arby's Roast Beef	Hitachi Instruments	USDA Forest Service

	☎	✉	📠
HOW TO ENROLL:	**BY PHONE** 1-800-767-7545 or 1-913-362-3900	**BY MAIL** Complete and mail enrollment form to: SkillPath, Inc. P.O. Box 2768 Mission, KS 66201-2768	**BY FAX** 1-913-362-4241

SkillPath, Inc.
6900 Squibb Road
P.O. Box 2768
Mission, KS 66201-2768

BULK RATE
U.S. POSTAGE
PAID
SHAWNEE MISSION, KS
PERMIT NO. 481

Time Sensitive Material

Attention Mailroom:
If not deliverable to addressee please send to training director

Please don't remove mailing label

HMP #2901A Ⓐ

Figure 3–3. (*continued*)

Dealing with Vendors & Suppliers

Performance Seminar Group

A One Day Seminar

Here are the key benefits of attending this powerful seminar:

Improve your negotiating skills to get the price, quality and service you want.

■ **Hear vital perspectives** on the purchasing function, and learn the key factors in an effective purchasing system.

■ **Get pointers from professional buyers** guaranteed to improve your own performance and your company's profitability.

■ **Pick up tips on using the telephone most effectively** (including special techniques for negotiating on the telephone).

■ **Learn criteria for finding vendors** who will best serve your needs.

■ **Be alerted to safeguards** you can take to avoid common vendor problems.

■ **Use your computer** to speed-up and improve all your purchasing activities.

■ **Remember** . . . Every dollar you save on purchases has the same effect on your profits as $10 to $20 of newly generated sales.

Seminar Locations and Dates

Pasadena
September 19, 1989

Anaheim
September 20, 1989

Los Angeles
September 28, 1989

San Diego
October 3, 1989

Who should attend:

■ This seminar is for anyone who deals with vendors or plans purchases as a regular part of his or her duties.

■ The seminar is targeted at the needs of the full-time professional buyer, but is strongly recommended for secretaries, office managers, administrators and others who deal with suppliers on a full or part-time basis.

How to sound like a pro—no matter what you are buying:

If you are responsible for making purchases, the biggest challenge you face is establishing and maintaining your reputation as a strong experienced buyer. It's the first step in gaining vendor respect and the single most important element in building an effective purchasing style.

By attending this intensive seminar, you'll discover the masterful negotiating and purchasing techniques used by the most sophisticated — and effective — buyers in business. You can learn these techniques in **one day**. And start enjoying a quantum improvement in your dealings with vendors and suppliers.

You'll discover skillful ways to make vendors appreciate your business more and work hard to find ways to express their appreciation. You'll hear easy ways to dramatically reduce the burden of administrative paperwork. And, most important, you'll come to understand purchasing as a **process**, and you'll know the specific steps to take at each stage to ensure the maximum benefit for your organization.

Take a minute to read the agenda inside. Vital information that took years to uncover and polish is now reduced to its essence in a fast paced, one day seminar. It's an opportunity you simply cannot afford to miss.

Figure 3–4.

Dealing with Vendors & Suppli

Seminar Exit Interviews

Comments from attenders immediately upon leaving a recent session of this one day seminar:

"I picked up five techniques I know will cut down time consuming administrative paperwork."

Eva Koenig
Northwest Supply

"The next time I need to respond to a price estimate, I've got a checklist of specific questions to ask that will convince suppliers I'm an experienced buyer."

Paul Walpole
Hightower Electronics Co.

"Now I know the 7 easy steps it takes to become a superior negotiator."

Connie Elich
Wellington, Ltd.

"I learned what information to always hold back from a vendor to make sure I get the best combination of quality, service and price."

Erica Askendahl
Fjord Financial Group

"Not only did I get a list of vendor sources, I also picked up the neatest procedure I ever heard of for quickly finding and sizing up a potential supplier."

Michael Farrucci
M&B Wood Products

"Best of all, I discovered an easy-to-set-up purchasing and inventory control system that will automatically eliminate most of my headaches."

Blanche Treadwell
Detweller Marine

Learn strategies and tactics for skillful negotiating

Know what to tell—and what never to tell—any supplier in order to ensure the best service and price.

Be a good negotiator and bargain with salespeople from a position of strength.

Discover the most powerful negotiating tool a buyer can use.

Learn special strategies for negotiating on the phone.

Become a skillful negotiator by knowing how to combine active and passive bargaining tactics.

Basic techniques to make negotiating comfortable for you and more profitable for your company.

Save time and money with a more effective purchasing system

How to set up a purchasing and inventory control system that can "run itself," involving you only for periodic checks and to handle potential inventory problems.

Learn the 9 key elements of an effective purchasing system.

Know how to apply the principles of the purchasing profession properly: multiple source purchasing, value analysis, contracts and lead time planning.

Get tips on materials management concepts that will help optimize your purchasing activities.

Save administrative time through more efficient practices.

Make use of 20 proven purchasing techniques that will improve your company's profitability.

Get a checklist of successful methods for planning and organizing your work.

Seminar Agenda

Use your "customer power" to negotiate optimum quality, service and price

Learn 4 simple negotiating techniques to assure that you get the quality you are paying for.

Discover how to increase your buying power by making your account more valuable to your vendors.

Exploit the strategic advantage of being the person "who can say no at anytime."

Find out how to use your position as a customer to your advantage in re-negotiating price and delivery terms.

Techniques that earn price reductions and vendor respect

Six questions to ask when you are handed a price quote, in order to let the supplier know you are a knowledgeable buyer.

What to look for in every price quote, purchase agreement, contract and other important supplier forms.

10 ways to make the entire purchasing and inventory control cycle less time consuming and more cost efficient.

Know how to evaluate and choose vendors who can best meet your needs

Get an extensive listing of vendor sources and learn effective procedures for locating and evaluating new vendors.

Learn to use proven price and cost analysis methods to determine your best deal.

Find out about easy actions and remedies to take when vendors don't perform.

Figure 3–4. (*continued*)

72

Performance Seminar Group

Hear about special procedures for handling the unexpected

Find out how to deal with problems such as late or unscheduled delivery, poor workmanship, cost surprises and other risks.

Learn a fast way to inspect shipments for proper quality/quantity and how to resolve deviations to your satisfaction.

Discover ways to turn a vendor problem —half shipment, wrong product, failure to meet specs—into a financial advantage for your company.

Find out how to avoid being intimidated by technical salespeople. Get them to speak in plain English.

How PC's can cut purchasing worktime in half

Understand how to set up the easiest-to-use computer purchasing and inventory control system.

Turn your personal computer into an "assistant" who keeps you ahead of every potential problem, so it can be easily avoided.

Learn how the computer can help you control orders and evaluate vendors.

Get powerful insights that help you work smart

Be able to get the lowest prices by knowing the "art" of telling vendors what price you want.

Learn to avoid the 8 problems areas that can raise the true cost of your inventory 30% to 40%.

Discover how "Win-Win" negotiating can not only get you the best possible deal, but make your suppliers work harder for your business.

Materials For Seminar Attenders

We've worked hard to make sure you will be able to apply the concepts presented in this seminar with confidence. These four manuals will serve as valuable references for years to come.

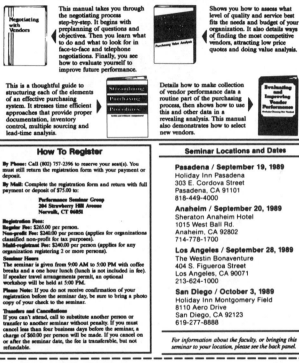

This manual takes you through the negotiating process step-by-step. It begins with preplanning of questions and objectives. Then you learn what to do and what to look for in face-to-face and telephone negotiations. Finally, you see how to evaluate yourself to improve future performance.

Shows you how to assess what level of quality and service best fits the needs and budget of your organization. It also details ways of finding the most competitive vendors, attracting low price quotes and doing value analysis.

This is a thoughtful guide to structuring each of the elements of an effective purchasing system. It stresses time efficient approaches that provide proper documentation, inventory control, multiple sourcing and lead-time analysis.

Details how to make collection of vendor performance data a routine part of the purchasing process, then shows how to use this and other data in a revealing analysis. This manual also demonstrates how to select new vendors.

How To Register

By Phone: Call (802) 757-2396 to reserve your seat(s). You must still return the registration form with your payment or deposit.

By Mail: Complete the registration form and return with full payment or deposit of $75.00 to:

> Performance Seminar Group
> 204 Strawberry Hill Avenue
> Norwalk, CT 06851

Registration Fees:
Regular Fee: $265.00 per person.
Non-profit Fee: $240.00 per person (applies for organizations classified non-profit for tax purposes).
Multi-registrant Fee: $240.00 per person (applies for any organization registering 2 or more persons).

Seminar Hours
The seminar is given from 9:00 AM to 5:00 PM with coffee breaks and a one hour lunch (lunch is not included in fee). If speaker travel arrangements permit, an optional workshop will be held at 5:00 PM.

Please Note: If you do not receive confirmation of your registration before the seminar day, be sure to bring a photo copy of your check to the seminar.

Transfers and Cancellations
If you can't attend, call to substitute another person or transfer to another seminar without penalty. If you must cancel less than four business days before the seminar, a charge of $60.00 per person will be made. If you cancel on or after the seminar date, the fee is transferable, but not refundable.

Seminar Locations and Dates

Pasadena / September 19, 1989
Holiday Inn Pasadena
303 E. Cordova Street
Pasadena, CA 91101
818-449-4000

Anaheim / September 20, 1989
Sheraton Anaheim Hotel
1015 West Ball Rd.
Anaheim, CA 92802
714-778-1700

Los Angeles / September 28, 1989
The Westin Bonaventure
404 S. Figueroa Street
Los Angeles, CA 90071
213-624-1000

San Diego / October 3, 1989
Holiday Inn Montgomery Field
8110 Aero Drive
San Diego, CA 92123
619-277-8888

For information about the faculty, or bringing this seminar to your location, please see the back panel.

Registration Form
MVTG9- -A

Dealing with Vendors and Suppliers

Organization Name: _____

Address: _____ P.O. Box: _____

City: _____ State: _____

Zip Code: _____ Telephone Number: _____
                                      (area code)

Please check the appropriate city and date:

☐ Pasadena / September 19, 1989 (L1)
☐ Anaheim / September 20, 1989 (L3)
☐ Los Angeles / September 28, 1989 (L8)
☐ San Diego / October 3, 1989 (SD)

☐ Full payment of $_____ is enclosed.
☐ Deposit of $_____ is enclosed.
   Balance of $_____ will be paid on course day.

Name _____ Job Title or Position (Please!) _____

Name _____ Job Title or Position _____

Name _____ Job Title or Position _____

Mail with check to:
Performance Seminar Group
204 Strawberry Hill Avenue, Norwalk, CT 06851

Figure 3–4. (*continued*)

Dealing with Vendors & Suppliers

Performance Seminar Group

A One Day Seminar

Pasadena
September 19, 1989

Los Angeles
September 28, 1989

Anaheim
September 20, 1989

San Diego
October 3, 1989

Bring this seminar—and these benefits—to your location:

Cost savings For groups of 10 or more, you can expect a savings over regular registration fees — the larger the group, the greater the savings. In addition, an on-site seminar can save your company the cost of travel, hotels, meals, etc.

Emphasis on topics vital to your organization The same expert instructor who leads our regular seminars can devote more time to those agenda topics you want emphasized and remove any topics you do not need addressed.

Convenience We can accommodate your company's schedule by holding a seminar whenever and wherever you wish.

Company-wide consensus Because everyone learns the same concepts at the same time, the consensus you need to implement new ideas can often be accomplished in one day.

Call Jacqueline Nerette at (203) 331-9888 to find out more about the benefits of on-site training for your organization.

Faculty

Most sessions of our seminars are given by a single speaker. The curriculum is carefully determined in advance and is strongly influenced by the ratings from participants in previous sessions. In the event of a scheduling problem, we reserve the right to substitute a fully qualified faculty member who is not listed below to conduct a particular session.

J. NICHOLAS DeBONIS, Ph.D. has been giving courses on vendor relations for a number of years. He has an extensive consulting clientele and places special emphasis on problems of negotiation and communication. Attenders give him highest ratings for dynamic presentations.

ROBERT BEVARD has spent most of his professional career in the area of financial and administrative management. He is an outstanding seminar speaker, interested in improving management of vendor relations and motivating vendors to high performance.

Performance Seminar Group
204 Strawberry Hill Avenue
Norwalk, CT 06851

Bulk Rate
U.S. Postage
PAID
Performance
Seminar Group

Please: do not alter name or address even if incorrect!

Please forward to person who deals with suppliers

MVTG9- -A

Figure 3–4. (*continued*)

How to Write & Design
Sales
Literature
A One Day Seminar

Anaheim
July 20, 1989

Los Angeles
July 24, 1989

Boston
July 28, 1989

Chicago
August 16, 1989

Use the latest copy and design
techniques to spark the
reaction you want.

Performance Seminar Group

Figure 3–5.

Here are the key benefits of attending this powerful seminar:

■ **Generate more sales** results from your promotional materials.

■ **Discover many ways** to increase your own creative output.

■ **Profit from up-to-date research showing** techniques in copy and design that have proven to be effective.

■ **Be confident** that your sales literature presents your company's image exactly the way you want.

■ **Make all your headlines** and visuals as powerful as they can be.

■ **Know how to create** promotional materials that will be noticed and get read.

■ **Learn how to analyze** your printed materials and strengthen their appeal by eliminating weak or counterproductive copy and design.

■ **Get more value** from your sales literature by improving distribution and introducing new uses.

Who should attend

This seminar will be of interest to all those who write and design or work with those who write and design sales literature.

• Copywriters and artists who work directly on sales literature.

• People who want to enhance their ability to assess and improve work done by others. This includes all managers and administrators responsible for reaching potential customers.

• Personnel from agencies, graphic studios and printers will also find the course relevant.

How to Write &
Sales Liter

A One Day Seminar

Seminar Agenda

Write copy that persuades readers and motivates action

Know how to translate product and service features into benefits that are important to your customers.

Write your copy for maximum impact by knowing people's reading habits.

Learn 9 different copywriting styles and get guidelines on when to use each.

Be able to create a strong and appealing description of any product or service.

Discover the secret of how to make customer testimonials really work.

Be alerted to the 6 most common copywriting errors to avoid.

Get an 11 point checklist to assure your copy is communicating effectively.

Create powerful sales letters that get read and produce results.

Choose your literature format to best achieve the desired result

Know which formats are most involving and which ones will be kept for future reference.

Improve results by knowing when and how to use catalogs, booklets, posters, inserts, rack brochures, unusual folding techniques and other specialized approaches.

Hear which sales literature formats people spend the most time reading.

Learn how to generate more inquiries and convert more of them to customers

Find out about a system for handling inquiries that can dramatically increase your conversion rate.

Discover specific copy and design ingredients that can really help convert readers to customers.

Design your layouts for impact and readability

Be alerted to 13 design errors that can reduce effectiveness of your copy.

Learn how to construct a visual eyepath that directs the reader through your layout to pick up the most important information.

Compel readers to get involved in your layouts with new and powerful ways to use charts, tables, diagrams, cutaways and other graphic elements.

Find out what research has revealed about the relative appeal of various colors in advertising and sales literature.

How to use photos and illustrations to attract readers and help sell your product or service

Profit from research revealing the visual concepts and subject matter that will best attract and involve your audience.

Increase copy readership with 10 proven techniques that maximize the effect of photos and illustrations.

Improve reader reaction to visuals by knowing how to write captions and callouts that drive home the message.

Grab attention and involvement with your headlines

Know the most effective writing approaches and get advice on when and how each should be used.

Get a list of 24 "power" words to make your headlines work better.

Learn techniques to help stimulate ideas for writing powerful headlines that work.

Understand the 4 vital functions that your headlines perform and be sure they do the job in the best way possible.

Figure 3–5. (*continued*)

Design ature

Performance Seminar Group

Be confident you are maximizing the potential uses of your literature

Learn about economical ways to customize your sales literature for sales reps, distributors and others.

Discover additional channels to expose your material to more potential customers.

Know how to design your layouts and literature for several uses.

Hear proven techniques that will get your reps and distributors to use your literature to its fullest advantage.

Know how to position your image in your sales literature

Know how to achieve a strong "personality" when first reaching new prospects.

Learn to "position" your organization properly in relation to your customer's perceived needs and the capabilities of competitors.

Pick up tips on how to enhance the image effects of your copywriting style.

Find out the three basic positioning strategies that will help you generate a productive image in the minds of your target audience and keep it there.

Stimulate new creative approaches for your copy and design

Get 16 tips to help you unlock your creativity and come up with new powerful ideas.

Discover an easy 6-step procedure guaranteed to get your design ideas flowing.

Learn how to get the background information you should have to be able to write effective copy.

Faculty

Most sessions of our seminars are given by a single speaker. The curriculum is carefully determined in advance and is strongly influenced by the ratings from participants in previous sessions. In the event of a scheduling problem, we reserve the right to invite a fully qualified faculty member not listed below to conduct a particular session.

J. NICHOLAS DeBONIS, Ph.D. is a media and marketing consultant specializing in layout design, typography, copywriting and editing.

He has been teaching communications at a major university for a number of years. His dynamic seminar presentations have consistently earned him the respect of our attenders.

KIRK MILLER is president of his own consulting firm concentrating on planning, writing and design of printed materials.

As a seminar speaker he presents vital information in an interesting style emphasizing practical know-how and concrete advice.

Seminar Manual

Attenders take home a manual which details copywriting techniques for sales literature, choosing a successful format, using color, selecting paper, etc. Special chapters cover subjects such as testing readability, handling creative services and multi-purpose uses of sales literature. You'll be able to refer to this thorough reference work as a source of many new ideas.

How to Register

By Phone: Call (802) 757-2391 to reserve your seat(s). You must still return the registration form with your payment or deposit.

By Mail: Complete the registration form and return with full payment or a deposit of $75.00 per person to:

Performance Seminar Group
204 Strawberry Hill Avenue
Norwalk, CT 06851

Registration Fees:
Regular Fee: $265.00 per person.
Non-profit Fee: $240.00 per person (applies for organizations classified as non-profit for tax purposes).
Multi-registrant Fee: $240.00 per person (applies for any organization registering 2 or more persons).

Seminar Hours
This seminar is given from 9:00 AM to 5:00 PM with coffee breaks and a one hour lunch (lunch is not included in fee). If speaker travel arrangements permit, an optional workshop will be held at 5:00 PM.

Please Note: If you do not receive confirmation of your registration before the seminar day, be sure to bring a photo copy of your check to the seminar.

Transfers and Cancellations
If you can't attend, call to substitute another person or transfer to another seminar without penalty. If you must cancel less than four business days before the seminar, a charge of $60.00 per person will be made. If you cancel on or after the seminar date, the fee is transferable.

Seminar Locations and Dates

Anaheim / July 20, 1989
Sheraton - Anaheim Hotel
1015 West Ball Rd.
Anaheim, CA 92802
714-778-1700

Los Angeles / July 24, 1989
The Westin Bonaventure
404 S. Figueroa Street
Los Angeles, CA 90071
213-624-1000

Boston / July 28, 1989
Holiday Inn - Boston Gov't. Center
5 Blossom St.
Boston, MA 02114
617-742-7630

Chicago / August 16, 1989
Howard Johnson's O'Hare Int'l.
10249 Irving Park Rd.
Schiller Park, IL 60176
312-671-6000

Registration Form

SLBC9--P

How to Write and Design Sales Literature

Organization Name: _____

Address: _____ P.O. Box: _____

City: _____ State: _____

Zip Code: _____ Telephone Number: _____
(area code)

Please check the appropriate city and date:

☐ Anaheim / July 20, 1989 (L3)
☐ Los Angeles / July 24, 1989 (L8)
☐ Boston / July 28, 1989 (B8)
☐ Chicago / August 16, 1989 (C6)

☐ Full payment of $_____ is enclosed.
☐ Deposit of $_____ is enclosed.
Balance of $_____ will be paid on course day.

Name _____ Job Title or Position *(Please!)* _____

Name _____ Job Title or Position _____

Name _____ Job Title or Position _____

Mail with check to:
Performance Seminar Group
204 Strawberry Hill Avenue, Norwalk, CT 06851 (802) 757-2391

Figure 3–5. *(continued)*

How to Write & Design
Sales Literature

A One Day Seminar

Anaheim
July 20, 1989

Boston
July 28, 1989

Los Angeles
July 24, 1989

Chicago
August 16, 1989

Use the latest copy and design
techniques to spark the
reaction you want.

Performance Seminar Group

Performance Seminar Group
204 Strawberry Hill Avenue
Norwalk, CT 06851

Bulk Rate
U S Postage
PAID
Performance
Seminar Group

Please do not remove or alter label even if incorrect!

**Please forward to person
concerned with preparing sales literature**

8LBC9- -P

Bring this seminar to your location
Here's how your organization can benefit:

Customization: Let us customize any of our seminars to
meet your organization's specific training needs. We
can even include topics not in the regular course
outline. In most cases, there is no extra cost and you
will be able to spend more time on vital topics and
eliminate the ones that are less important.

Convenience: Your seminar will be held where and
when you wish to accommodate your organization's
busy schedule. That means you save time and eliminate
expenses—no travel, hotels, meals, etc.

Cost: For groups of ten or more there will be a savings
over the regular registration fees. For smaller groups
you'll find that the cost is still very reasonable.

Consensus: Everyone learns the same concepts and
vocabulary at the same time. It's easier to get the group
consensus usually needed to implement new ideas.

Call Jacqueline Nerette at (802) 757-2391 for complete
information about bringing this seminar to your
location.

Figure 3–5. (*continued*)

4

SINGLE PROGRAM
BROCHURES VS.
SEMINAR CATALOGS

A key marketing decision facing the seminar promoter is whether to send to prospects a single brochure for each program or a catalog describing all or several seminar offerings. The promoter may spend endless hours trying to determine which strategy will be more profitable in the long run, using past experience or gut feelings as a guideline.

Arguments can be found to support both choices. Proponents of multiple seminar and workshop listings in a catalog argue that a catalog mailing enjoys a number of economies of scale over the brochure option and results in an overall reduction of promotional costs. The costs of postage, mailing service, list rental, and labor can be amortized over several seminars to yield a profitable ratio over the long run.

Another argument for the catalog approach is that a catalog feels more permanent. Prospects who might readily discard a single brochure would often be less likely to throw away a multipage catalog that looks and feels substantial. (Of course, there is no guarantee that a catalog will be read and acted upon by the prospect, but promoters can reasonably assume a certain level of ongoing interest if their prospects were carefully screened.)

The conventional wisdom in favor of the single brochure holds that despite the loss of economies of scale, the brochure approach will yield a higher return because it focuses specific attention on the program being promoted. Rather than being confronted with multiple long-term decisions, prospects can concentrate on a simple yes/no response for a single program. Single program brochure advocates argue that a favorable decision on a given seminar is more likely with a brochure than a catalog, which is apt to create confusion and delays.

RELEVANT VARIABLES

A philosophical debate on catalogs versus brochures, while interesting to those who seek ready-made solutions, lacks a true appreciation of the complexities involved in this marketing decision. Each seminar promoter is faced with a unique set of problems and opportunities that influence the effectiveness of each approach. The interrelationship of relevant variables—seminar topics, locations, size of mailings, types of prospects, and so on—must be carefully analyzed if an optimal decision is to be reached. Thus, strict adherence to a philosophical school of thought may provide a ready answer for the promoter, but the results may be less than optimal.

A brief examination of a few of the variables that should be considered in the decision of whether to send brochures or a catalog will clarify the need for careful, sophisticated planning and evaluation.

Type of Prospect

The two philosophical schools discussed above attempt to characterize all prospects as either long-range decision makers (catalog) or short-term buyers who cannot deal with multiple decisions (brochures). This rigid typecasting does a disservice to the seminar promoter, whose prospects may fall into either category and sometimes into both. For example, corporations accustomed to long-range planning for seminar attendance by employees might be more responsive to a catalog, which allows them to schedule employee absences and control costs. On the other hand, a single brochure might be more effective for prospects from small companies, where decisions tend to be made individually.

Seminar Topics

The nature and relationship of the seminar topics must be considered in determining which type of promotion will be more effective. Certain topics may lend themselves more favorably to discrete treatment in single brochures; other topics may fare equally well or better as catalog offerings. If a number of seminars on related topics are being offered, perhaps the promoter should consider using a catalog. Prospects interested in one seminar may well find others in the catalog that appeal to them if the topics are related; this "piggyback" effect would be lost if single brochures were used. But again, the relationship of this variable to all the factors that affect the decision must be considered.

Seminar Locations

The number and geographic location of seminar sites may have an impact on the relative effectiveness of a single brochure versus a catalog. If a number of seminars are being offered in multiple locations throughout the country, a catalog might be more cost-effective; if the sites are more localized and fewer in number, this cost differential would be reduced.

Size of Printing and Mailing

As indicated earlier, economies of scale may be achieved by using a catalog rather than brochures. If the print run and the mailing itself are sufficiently large, the per-unit cost may be significantly reduced by using a catalog. For smaller mailings, which would diminish the economies of scale, individual brochures may be more productive in the long run.

Thus far, the discussion of the relative effectiveness of single brochures and catalogs has been largely theoretical. Some empirical studies will provide further insight on this important issue.

STUDY 1. PROMOTION OF SEVEN BUSINESS SEMINARS IN FIVE WESTERN STATES

The relative promotional effectiveness of seven closely related seminar topics was compared using mailings to previous seminar participants and interested prospects in Washington, Oregon, California, Arizona, and Nevada. A mailing list of 13,200 was split on an every-other-name basis, yielding two promotionally identical lists of 6,600 names.

Four of the programs were scheduled in Los Angeles and Seattle, one in Phoenix and San Francisco, and one in Los Angeles and Portland. Five of the seminars were to be conducted twice, and two were to be held four times in Phoenix, Los Angeles, San Francisco, and Seattle.

List A received a two-color, 12-page (8½″ × 11″) catalog featuring the seven different seminars. List B received seven different brochures, one for each of the programs being offered. Five of the brochures were four-page (8½″ × 11″), two-color pieces, and two were single-color. The brochures were mailed weekly over a seven-week period. The comparative costs are shown below:

	List A: Catalog	List B: Brochures
Printing	$2,813	$ 5,105
Preparation of camera-ready art	792	1,156
Mailing list preparation	51	264
Postage	726	5,082
Mailing service	179	463
Totals	$4,561	$12,070

The cost of seven brochure mailings is substantially higher than the cost of one catalog mailing. However, before the relative effectiveness of the two approaches can be determined, a comparison of total revenues is needed. With a fee of $150 for each seminar, the final results were as follows:

	Group A	Group B
Registrations (at $150)	77	219
Total revenue	$11,550	$32,850
Promotion cost per registrant	$59.23	$55.12

The cost of promotion per registrant for Group A and Group B was roughly equivalent (around 40 percent of revenue per participant). While no clear trend is discernible at this point, some additional data indicate that the single brochure mailing was more effective. During the seven-week brochure mailing period, a relatively steady increase in yield was noted; the last mailing was 62.3 percent more effective than the first. The repeated mailings appeared to result in an increased name identification, resulting in higher yields over time.

While the risk was greater for the brochure mailing, so were the potential total profits. Had the brochure treatment been used for the entire list, a projected total of 438 registrations would have been received, for a gross of $65,700 and an average of 24.33 participants at each of the 18 seminars. Had the catalog promotion been used for the entire list, a projected total of 154 registrations and $23,100 gross would have been received. With an average of 8.56 participants per program, the promoter may have found it necessary to cancel some of the sessions. Thus, the use of single brochures rather than a catalog would have been more promotionally effective for this group of seminars offered under these conditions.

STUDY 2. ENTREPRENEURIAL SEMINARS IN NEW YORK CITY

This study compared the relative effectiveness of brochures and a catalog for three workshops on closely related entrepreneurial topics, conducted on successive days in New York City. The promoter rented a combination of compiled and subscriber lists for the New York City tri-state area (New York, New Jersey, and Connecticut). The list of 14,306 was subjected to merge/purge and split into two equal lists of 7,153.

List A received an eight-page (8 1/2" × 11") catalog listing the three seminars. The fee was $95 per seminar, or $250 if all three programs were taken. List B received three separate mailings of a two-page (8 1/2" × 11") flyer, with no provision for a discount for attending all three programs. The costs of the two promotions were as follows:

	List A: *Catalog*	List B: *Brochures*
Preparation of camera-ready art	$ 644	$ 534
Printing	1,729	1,610
List rental	502	1,011
Postage	787	2,352
Mailing service	399	809
Totals	$4,061	$6,316

List A produced 102 registrations at an average fee of $89.10; List B produced 105 registrations at $95.

The List A mailing yielded gross revenue of $9,088 (102 × $89.10). The List B mailing produced a gross of $9,975 (105 × $95) but its profit was lower than that for the List A mailing because the number of registrants from each list was nearly equal:

| List A profit: | $9,088 − $4,061 = $5,027 |
| List B profit: | $9,975 − $6,316 = $3,659 |

In light of the results in Study 1, which indicated that single brochures are apt to be more profitable than a catalog mailing, what factors account for the greater profitability in this catalog mailing? One possibility is that the close relationship of the seminar topics may have yielded a higher gross revenue in Study 1 than otherwise should have been expected. The fee reduction offered in the catalog mailing in Study 2 may have enhanced the promotional effectiveness by encouraging more prospects to register for all three programs.

STUDY 3. SEMINARS FOR BANK EXECUTIVES

Another interesting perspective on the catalog-versus-brochures issue was provided by a publisher who was promoting four repeats of five seminars held for bank executives in New York, Chicago, Dallas, and San Francisco. The publisher's mailing list of 47,377 was split on an every-other-name basis. List A received a catalog promoting both seminars and publications; three pages were given to each seminar. List B received a four-page, two-color, self-mail brochure for each seminar plus a separate publications catalog. The fee for attending any of the two-day seminars was $395 per participant, with a reduction to $345 for groups of three or more. The figures shown at the top of page 84 exclude the costs of publications promotion.

	List A: *Catalog*	List B: *Brochures*
Preparation of camera-ready art	$ 1,567	$ 1,864
Printing	9,862	13,233
Mailing list preparation	122	341
Postage	2,606	13,032
Mailing service	455	1,231
Totals	$14,612	$29,701

The catalog mailing yielded a total of 218 registrations at an average fee of $377; the brochure mailings produced 323 registrations at an average fee of $369. The cost of promotion per participant was $67.03 for List A and $91.95 for List B. The total profits for the two promotions were:

| List A profit: | $ 82,186 − $14,612 = $67,574 |
| List B profit: | $119,187 − $29,701 = $89,486 |

The total profit derived from the brochure mailings would appear to justify the expenditure, which was over twice that of the catalog mailing. But other factors involved are worth considering. The sale of publications from the catalog list came to $23,243 within 90 days of the mailing. Publications sales from List B, which received a separate publications catalog, came to $16,985 during the same 90-day period. Thus, the sale of publications was much more productive for the single catalog promotion.

CONCLUSIONS

In these studies, the per-seminar promotion results did not uniformly favor a brochure promotion over a catalog promotion. In Study 2, the higher-cost brochures promotion produced only three more registrations than the catalog mailings. Thus, what might have appeared to be a definitive conclusion from Study 1, that brochure mailings are more profitable than a catalog mailing, was only a tentative finding, subject to other factors. When a seminar promoter is also marketing publications, a decision to include these publications in a catalog mailing might be made, to enhance overall promotional profits. One such promoter contends that the inclusion of seminars in a catalog of publications and seminar tapes creates a "seminar environment" that encourages publication sales.

As the studies suggest, the decision of whether to promote seminars using individual brochures or a single catalog is a complex one involving a number of interrelated variables. Generally speaking, a more favorable promotion profit results from the brochure promotion despite its higher cost. But this guiding principle is subject to change for a given promotional campaign, depending on the factors involved and the promoter's overall objectives. Promoters who adopt a philosophical position on this issue and adhere to it regardless of changing circumstances have removed some of the uncertainty and complexity from their promotional decision making. But they may also be enjoying a less favorable return than the promoter who risks the uncertainty and carefully evaluates every alternative.

Many seminar promoters use a combination of catalog and single program brochure mailings. One provider first mails a catalog and determines from early returns which of the programs being marketed sells best. The best sellers are enhanced by follow-up mailings of program brochures. Another provider mails catalogs three times each year to all on the house mailing list and sends brochures to only the "best" names— those who have registered for a seminar within the past year.

5

HOW TO SELECT AND
RENT MAILING LISTS

Knowledge of how to select and order mailing lists is vital for the promotion of your seminars and workshops. This chapter deals first with how to find, select, and order lists. It then tells you how to reduce your list rental cost by 20 percent by setting up your own mailing list brokerage and taking advantage of the commission paid to brokers on mailing lists.

FINDING MAILING LISTS

There are numerous ways to obtain information about mailing lists, but the best place to start is with a copy of Standard Rate and Data Service's (SRDS) most valuable publication, *Direct Mail List Rates and Data (DMLR&D)*. Published every two months, *DMLR&D* is a unique source of information on mailing lists. You can subscribe for $240 a year (contact: SRDS, 3004 Glenview Road, Wilmette, IL 60091; phone: 312/256-6067), or you can find the publication in the collection of any quality business library, particularly at major university schools of business and at main offices and major branches of public library systems.

DMLR&D lists in excess of 55,000 direct mail lists that can be rented (almost always for one-time use) or purchased (rarely). (Annual unlimited-use rentals are available from many list owners.) Each issue runs over 1,600 pages and is divided into classifications that enable you to locate the types of prospects you are interested in reaching. (See Figure 5–1.)

As good as *DMLR&D* is for identifying mailing lists, it is not complete. List authorities estimate that another 75,000 mailing lists available for rental have not been listed in the directory. How do you find them? First, talk to list brokers; they often know of available lists that have not been listed in *DMLR&D*. Recognized mailing list brokers are listed in *DMLR&D*.

But even talking to brokers is not sufficient. The little known lists are usually only identifiable by effort—your effort, in carefully analyzing the market to determine which individuals are most likely to be prospective attendees of the seminars and workshops you are promoting. While this is time-consuming, the effort will contribute meaningfully to your profitability.

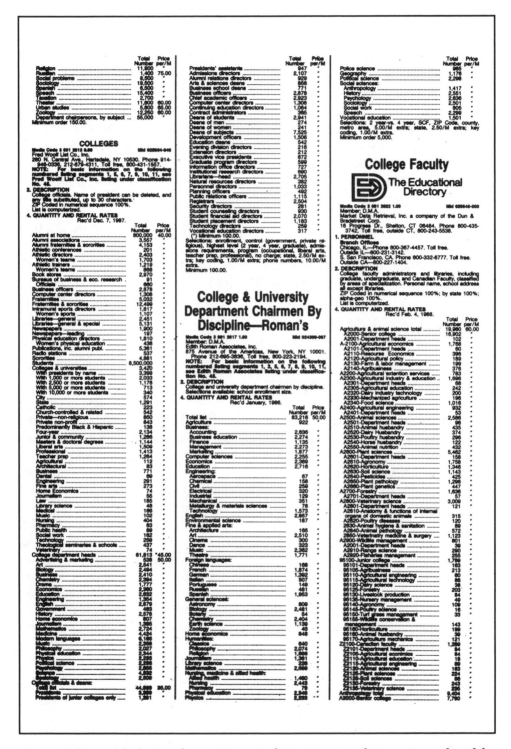

Figure 5–1. Sample listing from *Direct Mail List Rates and Data.* Reproduced by permission of Standard Rate and Data Service, 3004 Glenview Road, Wilmette, IL 60091.

The best way to get responsive lists is to analyze the market by asking yourself: What would my potential participants be doing, reading, joining, participating in, listening to or watching? Or: What would be their identifiable characteristics in terms of income, education, location, lifestyle, career needs? The more precisely you can identify the characteristics of your prospects, the better your chances of finding a mailing list that is just right for your purposes and the more easily you will reach your prospects. By asking yourself these questions, for example, you might determine that the best prospects for your programs are members of some obscure professional or trade association which is not sufficiently market-aggressive to have gone to the trouble of actively marketing its mailing list in any way or having it listed in *DMLR&D*. If, however, you contact that organization, it may well be interested in providing you with its mailing list. Perhaps the list is available immediately, but obscure lists often require additional effort on your part to obtain mailing labels. Is it worth the effort of typing from index cards or a membership roster? Often it is, if the list is particularly strong. Use the form on pages 89–90 to assist you in your search.

SELECTING THE BEST LISTS FROM ALL CANDIDATES AVAILABLE

Your review of *DMLR&D* and other search efforts will likely produce a number of promising candidate lists. You must review the options and select those that have the greatest potential and are in harmony with your budget limitations. I strongly advise that you do not turn over the responsibility for either list identification or final selection to brokers, advertising agencies, or others. They may be extremely helpful to you in the identification and selection process, but no one understands your market and marketing objective as well as you. And, frankly, no one cares as much about your success as you. Get all the help you can but do not abdicate responsibility. Many direct marketing experts firmly believe that mailing list selection is the *most important factor* in the success of any direct mail marketing campaign.

Once you have satisfied yourself about the nature of your prospects and which lists they are likely to be included on, you must again answer questions relative to the specific candidate lists you have identified. You will probably identify more lists than you can afford to rent. Some of the lists may be considerably similar, if not identical, and you probably do not wish to mail to the same people twice. Which lists should you select?

Going with gut feeling or intuition is not at all a bad idea; certain lists just seem to speak to you. Beyond this, however, consider price. Lists that are quite similar or even seemingly identical often rent for very

Think about all the types of people who might attend your seminar. Complete one of these worksheets for each target audience, assigning a number to each group. Your worksheets will help you to identify mailing lists you might use to promote your seminar. Be creative! Don't economize now. You can always reduce your targets or the size of your mailing later.

Target Market # _____

Name/Description _____

Possible Factors to Profile a Target Market	Possible Sources	Mailing List Available (Yes/No)	Source of List (Name/ Address/Phone)
General publications read	1. 2. 3.		
Trade magazines read			
Journals read			
Newsletters read			
Professional association memberships			
Trade association memberships			

Possible Factors to Profile a Target Market	Possible Sources	Mailing List Available (Yes/No)	Source of List (Name/ Address/Phone)
Civic association memberships			
Academic degrees held			
Licenses held/regulated by			
Seminars previously attended			
Books purchased			
Audio/video tapes purchased			
Software purchased			
Products/other services purchased (Whom do they do business with?)			
Other Criteria			

different prices. Among the many possible reasons for the price disparity may be the profit margin of the list owner. Generally, it has been my experience that more expensive lists cost more for a good reason—they are better. List maintenance is not inexpensive. If I clean my list often and/or engage in the necessary research to update and add fresh names, I feel entitled to charge more for my list than a competitor whose list is old and probably outdated.

Price alone is not a sufficient criterion for your decision making. Talk to people who have used the list before and get the opinion of the broker. Here is where brokers can be most useful: They can tell you about the experience of their clients who have rented the list (and the competing lists) in the past.

As a further consideration, look for guarantees. Many list owners guarantee the deliverability of their list. They may say that a particular list is 95 percent deliverable and agree to pay you for any "nixes" returned to them in excess of the guarantee. A higher guarantee often, but not always, denotes a better maintained and probably more productive list.

Evaluate the type of list! There are all kinds of lists. Among the more common are membership lists, buyer lists, subscriber lists, requests for information lists, and compiled lists. A compiled list has been compiled by the owner from directories, address lists, and similar sources. The nature of the list may greatly affect its quality. If, for example, you are selecting between a list of *Fortune* magazine subscribers and a list of people who requested information from in-flight magazines on a commercial airliner, you will likely discover that the lists show quite different responsiveness. Many direct mail authorities believe that the thin air associated with higher elevations, combined with the free flow of alcohol, almost mesmerizes otherwise serious people who then "circle to death" all of those little numbers on the "bingo" cards in the back of the in-flight magazines. These leads have proved to be of such small value that some marketers refuse to use even the "bingo" numbers, contending that anyone who is not serious enough to fill out a coupon or call for information does not qualify as a serious lead.

When you assess these factors, other criteria which you might use, and your own intuition, you will likely have an easier time reducing the number of options to a manageable size.

HOW MANY NAMES TO RENT

When many lists seem promising but your budget is limited, I recommend (initially) renting as many lists as you can afford. Particularly on a new marketing campaign or a market test, rent different lists to determine which ones are most productive for your purpose. Most list providers require that you rent a minimum of 5,000 or 3,000 names. When you want to rent only 1,000 names and request justification for their arbitrary policy, they tend to give long-winded answers about their social responsibility in not allowing you to rent fewer names than are necessary to conduct a statistically valid test of the list. The real reason, of course, is that it is not economical for them to sell fewer than the arbitrary minimum. Some list providers have gone to $100 or $250 minimums rather than minimum numbers of names. Such externally imposed minimums should not be allowed to alter good decision making on your part.

A direct mail promotion, using bulk mailing rates, will cost you around $350 per 1,000 units (35 cents a unit). You can spend less and you can certainly spend more, but $350 is a good average figure to keep in mind. If the cost of a mailing list is $66 per 1,000 units (the current average) or 6.6 cents per unit, it may be in your interest to rent the 5,000 minimum required and mail only the 500 or 1,000 you want to mail. What can you do with the rest? Save them for a later mailing if the list produces results, or throw them away. The printing, postage, mailing service, and time will cost you far more than the mailing list. The less costly the list rental rate—some lists are available for $30 and $40 per 1,000 names—the more relevant is this line of thinking.

In almost all cases, I would prefer to rent several lists and mail to portions of those lists rather than pin my hopes on just one or two lists. Understanding why is very important to your success in direct mail marketing. Numerous variables can affect the response to a mailing: the headline, the copy, the market interest in the product or service being sold, the price, the terms and conditions of selling, the quality of the mailing list selected, and so on. By testing multiple mailing lists you can eliminate one of these variables—the mailing list itself.

Suppose you receive an inadequate response to your mailing. What is the cause? It could be any of the variables mentioned above, or others. But, if you are mailing to several lists and one or two lists produce a high response, while others do not, you have learned something of great value which may well have a significant impact on your future decision making. And, since lists are perhaps the most important factor in the success of a direct mail marketing campaign, your initial test may have taught you the most important lesson you could have learned.

Consider the other possibility: You are a great list selector; you selected a list that exceeded your highest expectations. On the basis of that result you nominate yourself for the position of direct mail authority of the year and roll out a 100,000 mailing to quickly capitalize on the potential. Suppose that test mailing was a fluke and the other lists are only marginally responsive. How are you going to pay the $35,000 promotion bill?

Testing is the key in direct mail marketing.

Saving for future use or even throwing away a few thousand names may be a small price to pay for the value of the information you gain by mailing to multiple lists.

Another important issue in deciding how many names to mail to is the impact your decision will have on profitability. If you approach direct marketing with the idea of making a specific dollar profit, your profit objective can be increased or decreased on the basis of the size of your mailing. The "catch-22," obviously, is that the decision can also impact your loss.

A question almost always asked of me by my clients is: How many pieces should we mail? This is the answer I usually give. Suppose you get zero response: No one registers for your seminar or contracts with you to pay for an in-house training program. How much can you afford to risk? Make your decision on the number of units to mail in terms of how much of a loss you are willing to sustain. This is really the only way to approach a test campaign. After some experience in the market, you will be able to determine a minimum response probability and thus make a more educated determination of the probable risk.

DUPLICATE NAMES

If you are renting several different mailing lists, it is quite probable that a name will appear on more than one list. People who subscribe to *The Wall Street Journal* are also quite likely to subscribe to *Business Week, Fortune, Inc., Forbes,* and related publications. Thus, a person may receive two, three, four, or even more copies of your promotional piece. Those who understand direct mail marketing will know why. Others may feel that the multiple mailing is your error and conclude that your organization is not cost-efficient or well-organized. Depending on what you are marketing, the consequences could be negative. To avoid such an image and to save dollars, many direct marketers do not order mailing labels, but order lists on magnetic tape. They then send the magnetic tapes to their mailing house (letter shop) for a merge/purge—all of the lists are compared, obvious duplicates are removed, and a new combined list is printed. A merged list prints out in zip code order, which may reduce mailing costs because less hand sorting for bulk mail will be required. It is important to remember that a merge/purge is very unlikely to remove all duplicates. Only the obvious duplicates will be recognized. If someone is listed as "John Brown" on one mailing list and "J. W. Brown" on another, some merge/purge programs will not pick up this "human distinction." The cost of a merge/purge is relatively high and unless you are doing mailings of at least 20,000 it will probably not be cost-effective to use this technique.

GEOGRAPHY AND THE SIZE OF YOUR MAILING

One way to control the size and cost of a mailing is to place a limit on its geographic scope. Most mailing lists are available for selection on the basis of zip code and/or state. Your decision to limit the geography of the list you are renting should be at least partially based on the nature of the seminar which you are promoting. Those closest to the site of the seminar are most likely to attend.

You can limit the costs of a test with a geographically limited mailing. Keep this important principle in mind for roll-outs too. You will usually achieve greater impact by promoting closer to the seminar site (vacation and travel seminars excepted). Don't waste valuable promotional dollars promoting those far away when you have not promoted those close at hand. Market in concentric circles. For example, if you are planning on conducting a seminar in Kansas City, approach your marketing as shown in Figure 5–2.

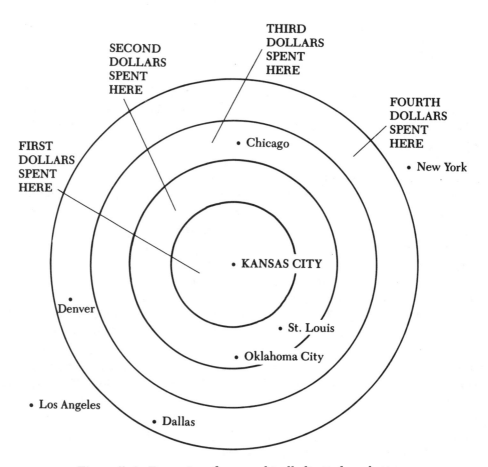

Figure 5–2. Expansion of geographically limited marketing.

ORDERING LISTS AND SETTING UP YOUR OWN DIRECT MAIL BROKERAGE

Identifying and selecting mailing lists (and dealing with the risk involved in the direct mail business) is the hard part. Ordering the list through the broker or directly from the owner/list manager is actually rather simple. Figures 5–3 and 5–4 show two sample forms you can use for ordering lists; you may wish to reproduce them on your letterhead.

Mailing list brokers earn a 20 percent commission on the rental fee (and sometimes some service charges such as selection fees) when they procure mailing lists for clients. If you plan to rent a great number of mailing lists over time, it may well be in your interest to establish your own list brokerage operation to reduce the cost of commissions.

If you were to rent 300,000 names over the next 12 months at an average charge of $66 per 1,000 names, your total bill would be $19,800. The commission on your payments would equal $3,960. If you are a broker, you keep that money—and well you should; you have done the work of the broker, which is not easy work.

Setting up your own brokerage is not too difficult. Declare that you are a broker by selecting a name for your brokerage and handling the usual business start-up activities. Print the list order form on the stationery of your brokerage and begin to insist that list owners and managers recognize you as a broker. Some of the larger list companies will ask you to prove that you are a broker, but most will not. There is nothing illegal in being an in-house brokerage. Once a few list owners/managers have paid you your commission, you have almost totally adequate evidence for others who may ask you to prove that you are entitled to commissions. Brokers provide a valuable service. They do important, time-consuming work. Don't establish an in-house brokerage just to save commissions, but if you are doing the work of the broker anyway, there is no reason you shouldn't earn the commission.

CODING MAILING LISTS

Testing of mailing lists is only productive if you keep accurate records that enable you to track registrations and associate them with the mailing list rented. Do all you can to determine the source of the registrant. Consider having each list "key coded" with a distinctive alphanumeric sequence that identifies the list that produced the response. Instruct those registering to enter the key code on their registration form. Better yet, position the mailing label so that it is returned with the registration. When phone registrations are accepted, ask for the key code. If you are unwilling or unable to key code, consider using a different color of brochure for each list or some other means to ensure that you have the best chance possible of tracking registrants to the mail source. Develop a form to record registration data by mailing list (Figure 5–5).

[Letterhead]

To: _____   Date:_____/_____/_____

_____   Number: _____

_____   Ship via: _____

_____   _____

Date when list must be received: _____/_____/_____

Ship to address above: Yes _____   No _____

Ship to: _____   ____ Prepay charges and invoice

_____   ____ Ship freight collect

_____   ____ Estimated freight charges
                                              enclosed
_____   ____ Invoice for balance

Provide on: _____ Cheshire labels   ____ Mag tape
            _____ Pressure-sensitive labels ____ Other: _____

Additional services:

____ Carbon copy of list   ____ Merge/purge   ____ Key line (____)

Quantity   *List Name/Description*   *$/M*   *Extension*

_____   _____ $_____ $_____

_____   _____   _____   _____

_____   _____   _____   _____

_____   _____   _____   _____

            Estimated freight charges total $_____

Method of payment: _____ Check enclosed _____ Please invoice

Authorized signature: _____

Special instructions: _____

Figure 5–3. Purchase order for mailing list rental.

Date: _____

Account Number: _____

Ship to:

Name   _____

Company   _____

Address   _____

_____

_____

List number: _____

List name: _____

Special Instructions:

List must be received by: _____/_____/_____

Anticipated Charges:

    List rental $ _____

    Pressure-sensitive labels   _____

    Magnetic tape use   _____

    Selection fee   _____

    Merge/purge   _____

    Special shipping   _____

      Total Amount Due $ _____

Terms of Payment: _____

In the event of questions regarding this order, please call:

_____ at _____.

Authorized Signature: _____

Figure 5–4. Mailing list order form.

List # _____

List Supplier: Name _____
Address _____
City/State/Zip _____
Phone _____ / _____ - _____

Key Code _____
No. of Names Rented _____
Date Mailed _____
Expected Date of Delivery _____
First Known Delivery _____

Date	Registrant Name	Participant #	$ Rec'd	Date Rec'd	How Paid*	Undeliverable Mail Returns Rec'd
11-10-89	SMITH, Edward	1	$495	11-10-89	V	2
11-11-89						3
11-12-89	WILSON, Martha	2, 3	$990	11-12-89	C	0
11-13-89	ANDERSON, Eric	4	$495	11-13-89	A	4

Total:

Mailing Cost per Thousand _____
Revenue per Thousand _____

* V = VISA, M = MSTR, A = AMEX, C = CHECK

Figure 5-5. Marketing source/registration tracking form.

6

WHEN TO MAIL
SEMINAR AND WORKSHOP
PROMOTIONS

Seminar promoters are frequently asked: How far in advance of a seminar should the brochure be mailed? The question might be more accurately phrased: How far in advance of a seminar should the promotional piece be received by the prospect, to maximize revenues or profits?

There are two main schools of thought on this crucial question regarding seminar promotion. Proponents of what might be termed the "early" school advocate mailing promotional pieces so that they are received six to 10 weeks in advance of the seminar. This school characterizes seminar participants as long-range planners and slow decision makers—busy people whose crowded, complex schedules require at least six weeks' advance notice.

Proponents of the "late" school take a quite different view of seminar participants, arguing that too much advance notice will lead to procrastination and failure to decide. They believe that most decisions to participate in a seminar are acts of impulse buying. The underlying assumption is that most people have sufficient control over their schedules to accommodate this type of impulsive, last-minute decision making. The optimal timing for receipt of promotional mailings, according to the "late" school, is two to five weeks before the seminar.

RELEVANT VARIABLES

As is often the case, the truth lies somewhere in between these two extremes. A rational, incremental approach will take into account the large number of complex, simultaneously interacting variables that affect the mailing decision. This decision should be based on a careful evaluation of all of the factors that will influence the outcome, not on a prior acceptance of some philosophical school. Of course, for a given seminar, an early or late mailing may be appropriate, but in general the optimal timing falls somewhere between the two extremes.

A few of the significant variables that should be taken into account are discussed here. To help shed further light on this crucial question, several empirical studies are presented in detail.

Nature and Occupation of Prospects

The decision of how far in advance to mail promotion of a seminar will be influenced in part by the prospects' occupations and overall traits. For some practitioners, an earlier mailing may be appropriate; doctors, for example, may require advance notice of eight to ten weeks in order to adjust their schedules. The same may be true for accountants and other professionals who are generally regarded as methodical, long-term decision makers. Conversely, people who have more of an entrepreneurial, risk-taking nature may respond more favorably to a late mailing.

Distance of Prospects from Seminar Site

Another variable to consider is how far the prospects must travel to reach the seminar. Obviously, a mailing must be done earlier if the participants will be traveling cross-country than if the attendees are from a local area. Other things being equal, promotions for a local seminar could be mailed to reach the prospects as late as three weeks prior to the program date and still be effective. At least two weeks should be added to this three-week base time if participants are traveling cross-country.

Type of Mail Service

Promotional mailings frequently are sent out via bulk mail, which offers the least expensive rates. Third-class mail is given low priority by the Postal Service, however, and delivery time is often difficult to estimate. Most direct mail houses (letter shops) are able to make "guestimates" based on the time of year, volume of mail, distance to be sent, performance record of the originating post office, and so on. While first-class mail is generally delivered in one to four working days, and bulk mail in one to three weeks, bulk mail can take as long as six weeks cross-country during peak mail periods.

Time of Year of Seminar

The length of time that it takes for a promotional piece to reach a prospect is affected by the time of year. During the Christmas holiday season, when the mail volume overall is heavier, it will usually take longer for a piece to be received. Also, the prospects themselves may require more time for decision making at certain times of year, depending on their occupations. Accountants were described above as long-term decision makers who should receive their mailings earlier than some other professionals. However, if sending the pieces out early means that they will arrive at the peak of tax season, when most accountants are too busy even to eat and sleep, perhaps the mailing should be delayed (or the seminar postponed, to allow for a sufficient promotional period).

Prospects' Frequency Tolerance

Prospects who have attended seminars in the past tend to have a higher frequency tolerance for promotional mailings for seminars than those who have never attended a seminar. For a low-frequency group that has been recently saturated with seminar announcements, perhaps the seminar promoter should delay mailing so that the response will be more favorable. On the other hand, if the prospects are former seminar attendees, this lag time may not be required to ensure a favorable response.

Length and Time of Day of Program

A program extending over several days, or one that takes place during the workweek, may require more advance notice than a one-day or an evening program, which allows participants more flexibility in scheduling.

Number of Seminars/Seminar Sites

The mailing decision may be affected if more than one seminar session is being held or if the seminar is being offered in a number of cities. Generally speaking, it is not advisable to promote two dates more than a week apart for the same seminar being held in the same city or market area. A seminar being held in both June and September, for example, may be better served by a second mailing prior to the fall program rather than a single mailing prior to the June program. If the program is being held in several cities, the mailing schedule may have to be adjusted so that participants in each city receive sufficient advance notice.

To lend a greater degree of precision to this issue of the optimal time to mail, six empirical studies are presented in the sections that follow. While their findings suggest some general trends that may be useful in your promotional planning, they by no means should be considered definitive. Instead, they should be treated as advisory, with due consideration given to that familiar cautionary statement, "all other things being equal."

STUDY 1. MANAGEMENT SKILLS SEMINAR

Target Market:	Managers and executives with line authority in industrial and commercial firms with sales of $7.5 million to $50 million located in the tri-state (NY, NJ, CT) metropolitan area of New York City
Program:	Two-day management skills/leadership seminar for middle managers
Fee:	$495 per participant; $445 per participant for groups of three or more registering at one time
Promotion:	Two-color, four-page, $8\frac{1}{2}'' \times 11''$ brochure on high-gloss stock; mailed as self-mailer without envelope

This carefully planned study was designed to test the question of when to mail to achieve maximum results. As indicated earlier, a number of factors are influential in this decision. However, this study will help you to establish general parameters that can be used as guidelines in your promotional planning.

In this test, several rented mailing lists were subjected to a computerized merge/purge that yielded 39,000 names. The list was split on an nth name basis to create four promotionally identical lists of 9,750 names. Separate mailings for the four matched lists were sent out at the following intervals prior to the seminar: 10 weeks, 8 weeks, 6 weeks, and 4 weeks. Fifteen pieces were seeded for each list so that delivery times could be determined. The results were as follows:

Weeks Prior to Seminar	Registrations Received	Delivery Time (Days)
10	22	6– 9
8	29	5–11
6	35	7–10
4	19	4–10
	105	

The general conclusion to be drawn from these findings is that mailing too early *or* too late is not advisable. The best results are achieved by mailing somewhere in the middle of the continuum.

Analysis by Size of Employer

The study permitted a breakdown of the results according to the size of the firm employing each participant. The responses yielded some interesting variations.

	Size of Firm (Annual Sales)		
Weeks Prior to Seminar	**Less than $9.99M**	**$10M to $24.99M**	**More than $25M**
10	3	8	9
8	5	7	16
6	16	11	8
4	10	7	4

These data suggest that more time for a buying decision is required by employees of larger firms; for personnel of smaller firms, promotions that are too early may be a deterrent to sales. Perhaps these results can be attributed to the fact that the absence of personnel is usually less disruptive in larger firms, which allows more advance planning than in smaller firms.

Another explanation is more provocative. Perhaps the findings are a function of risk-taking behavior combined with prospect schedule and promotional cycle. Entrepreneurial risk-taking behavior is generally associated with smaller firms, which, therefore, may be more favorably influenced by a later mailing. The following study was designed to test this hypothesis.

STUDY 2. BUSINESS START-UP AND EXPANSION/FINANCIAL SEMINAR

Target Market:	Texas entrepreneurs
Program:	Three-day conference on raising capital for start-up and expansion of entrepreneurial business ventures
Fee:	$595 per participant
Promotion:	Four-color, eight-page direct mail brochure to 15,211 Texas subscribers of entrepreneurial publications; mailed in envelope

There were two separate mailings to the target audience, but they were unequal in size and unmatched for control purposes because the second mailing was unplanned. The promoter rented 7,523 names and mailed the brochure 11 weeks prior to the seminar. Five weeks later, only ten registrations had been received. A second mailing to 7,688 names was sent first class four weeks prior to the seminar. The first mailing resulted in 14 registrations and the second in 24, for a total of 38:

	Registrations Received	
Weeks Prior to Seminar	*1st Mailing*	*2nd Mailing*
9	1	0
8	2	0
7	4	0
6	2	0
5	1	0
4	2	4
3	2	9
2	0	8
1	0	3
	14	24

These results would appear to validate the hypotheses that entrepreneurs are not long-range planners and that an early mailing to this type of prospect may be counterproductive. It could be argued that the difference is due to the fact that the second mailing was sent via first class rather than bulk mail. However, other research suggests that this is not a critical factor in the buying decision.

Because the two mailings were not controlled, it is possible that some prospects received two notices of the seminar. In response to a market research question, only two participants reported receiving two brochures.

In a follow-up study, it was determined that the average number of employees in the firms that responded to the first mailing was 24.3 and in the firms that responded to the second, 11.9. Only one firm in the first group and four in the second reported having no employees.

STUDY 3. DENTAL SEMINAR

Target Market:	Northern California dental practitioners
Program:	One-day practice management and marketing seminar for dentists and staff
Fee:	$175 per dentist; $75 for each additional staff member from the same practice
Promotion:	Two-color, four-page 8½″ × 11″ brochure on semigloss stock; self-mailer without envelope

It was suggested earlier that prospects' occupations should be considered in the mailing decision. This factor was evaluated in this unplanned test. The promoter rented 7,000 names of professional dental practitioners in the urbanized areas of northern California. The lists were split on an every-other-name basis, to create two promotionally identical lists. The promoter intended to send two different sets of brochures, to test promotional appeal, but only one set of 7,000 was actually printed. Nine weeks prior to the seminar, one set of 3,500 pieces was sent; the remaining 3,500 were mailed five weeks prior to the seminar. Both sets were mailed via bulk mail. The results were as follows:

Weeks Prior to Seminar	Registrations Received	No. of Participants	Delivery Time	Average Fee
9	20	31	2 weeks	$134
5	14	26	1 week	$142

For this seminar, an early mailing produced a better result. This finding confirms the hypothesis that for professions such as dentistry, where advance planning is required, an earlier mailing may yield a more favorable response.

Another question to explore further is the degree to which a fee reduction will affect registrations as they relate to the time of the promotion. The following two studies examined this important issue.

STUDY 4. INTERPERSONAL COMMUNICATIONS SKILLS WORKSHOP

Target Market:	General public in greater Boston area
Program:	One-day weekend workshop on interpersonal communications skills development
Fee:	Test #1: $125 per participant; $95 if registration received one week prior to workshop Test #2: $125 per participant; no fee reduction for early registration
Promotion:	Weekly newspaper ads in metropolitan dailies, beginning five weeks and ending one week prior to seminar

In the first test, in which an early registration fee was advertised, 66 registrations were received, including four walk-ins on the day of the seminar. In the second test, conducted 90 days after the first and not offering a fee reduction, 47 registrations were received, including 12 walk-ins.

Weeks Prior	*Registrations Received*	
to Seminar	Test #1	Test #2
5	10	4
4	9	2
3	11	10
2	23	9
1	9	10
0	4	12
	66	47

The results suggest that a fee reduction for early registration does influence the buying decision, even beyond the time when the discount is applicable. However, because these tests were not controlled, there is no way of stating with certainty that the response was caused by the fee reduction.

To help clarify this issue, a second set of tests was run in the Washington, DC area three weeks later, using a four-week promotional period. The discount was provided for the second test rather than the first. Registrations were received as follows:

Weeks Prior to Seminar	Registrations Received	
	1st Replication	*2nd Replication*
4	5	8
3	7	8
2	11	13
1	9	9
0	12	4
	44	42

While the comparisons between these results and those from the Boston tests are not definitive, there is enough of an observable pattern to suggest that a fee reduction for early registration does influence the buying decision. Another trend indicated by these data is that a "creaming" of the market reduces the promotional effectiveness of subsequent replications of a campaign in a given market.

STUDY 5. SEMINAR ON FINANCIAL MANAGEMENT FOR NONFINANCIAL MANAGERS

Target Market:	Business managers and executives in Colorado, Texas, and Florida
Program:	Two-day seminar held midweek
Fee (base):	$295 per participant
Fee Reduction:	If registration received two weeks prior to program: Colorado, $275; Texas, $235; Florida, $195
Promotion:	Direct mail to selected zip codes of same business lists eight weeks prior to seminars

To what extent does the size of the discount influence the buyer's decision? The results in this study were as follows:

Seminar Location	Total Registrations	Number Paying Reduced Fee	Number Paying Regular Fee
Denver, CO	51	15	36
Dallas, TX	62	31	31
Miami, FL	49	37	12

While these findings may be attributable in part to geographical differences, they appear to support the notion that the greater the savings, the more likely a prospect will be an early registrant.

In this study, the overall effectiveness of the promotion (measured by the number of registrations per 1,000 units mailed) was greatest in Colorado, where 51 registrants were received from a mailing of 7,231, and poorest in Florida, where 49 registrants resulted from a mailing of 8,497. The pattern of registration receipts also varied for each test location:

Weeks Prior to Seminar	Registrations Received		
	Denver, CO	Dallas, TX	Miami, FL
6	1	0	2
5	1	1	2
4	2	8	10
3	9	12	20
2	12	22	11
1	19	15	2
0	7	4	2
	51	62	49

These results would seem to suggest that a time-value discount of significant savings encourages early registration, and that it may dry up promotional effectiveness early in the promotional cycle. A small savings does not seem to have much impact on early registrations. In the Colorado test, where early registrants received only a $20 discount, the savings may have been worth less to participants than the value of the time gained by postponing the decision. It is possible that the drastic fee reduction offered to Florida prospects may have discredited the true value of the seminar, causing some participants who missed the discount deadline to decide not to attend. Seven Florida prospects indicated that they would not register if they were too late to obtain the discount; only one such case was noted for Texas and for Colorado, where the discounts were less drastic.

STUDY 6. SALES IMPROVEMENT SEMINAR

Target Market:	Professional sales personnel selling to the business market in California
Program:	One-day seminar on motivational selling
Fee:	$175 per participant; gift of audiocassette tapes (retail value $79) if registration received three weeks prior to program
Promotion:	One-page 8½ × 14 self-mailer brochure to subscribers of sales publications

Many seminar promoters believe that a generous cancellation policy will encourage early registration because participants perceive that they have the freedom to change their minds without suffering economic consequence. In this test, two seminars were scheduled, one in Los Angeles and one in San Francisco. Mailing lists were rented from several sources and a merge/purge produced a total mailing of 33,564 names. The list was split on an every-other-name basis. Both test groups received exactly the same promotional treatment except for the cancellation option:

Group A: "You may cancel your registration at any time prior to the day of the seminar and receive a full refund—no questions asked!"

Group B: "You may cancel your registration at any time up to two weeks prior to the seminar, and you will receive a refund of monies paid minus a $25 processing fee. Cancellations received after this time will receive a $150 credit, which may be used for any future seminar."

The following results were obtained:

Weeks Prior to Seminar	Registrations Received	
	Group A	Group B
5 or more	11	2
4	10	3
3	19	8
2	10	10
1	6	9
0	2	8
	58	40

A significant difference is apparent both in total registrations and in when they were received. Group A, which had the more favorable cancellation policy, registered earlier and in greater numbers than did Group B. Thus, it is fairly safe to conclude that at least for this seminar a generous cancellation policy influenced the buying decision.

CONCLUSIONS

Clearly the timing of promotional mailings to achieve optimal results involves a number of complex variables. The six studies in this chapter should offer some guidelines for your promotional decision making, but it is important that you consider their results in the context of your own target market and seminar program. There are no hard-and-fast rules for making the optimal decision (despite what proponents of the "early" and "late" schools would have you believe). To reach the best determination, sophisticated planning based on empirical evidence and careful evaluation of all the relevant variables is required.

The author's survey of 212 large and small seminar providers (commercial and academically based) found the following averages for the planned number of weeks for mailing in advance of a seminar:

Program Description	Weeks Prior to Seminar— Varied Distances from Site	
	Local	Travel Required
Multiple-day weekday programs	7.5	9.2
Multiple-day weekend programs	7.1	8.4
Single-day weekday programs	6.2	7.3
Single-day weekend programs	5.4	6.8
Partial day or evening programs	4.5	Insufficient data

Remember, time must be added here for delivery of the mail.

The optimal mailing date will differ for each program. Successful providers take great pains to track response data. The typical curve of registration receipts may look like Figure 6–1.

You should track the results of each mailing, for maximum benefit. Comparison of your charts will help you to recognize important changes over time. Figure 6–2 shows the accessibility of data, using this method. Line A reflects the history for the promotion of a particular seminar. Let's assume that line B reflects the response of a partial new mailing list you are testing for the current promotion. By tracking response rate and extrapolating to the future, you discover that the new list is generating a

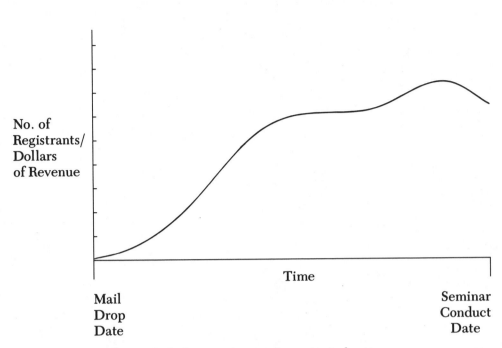

No. of
Registrants/
Dollars
of Revenue

Time

Mail
Drop
Date

Seminar
Conduct
Date

Figure 6–1. Registration receipts—typical pattern.

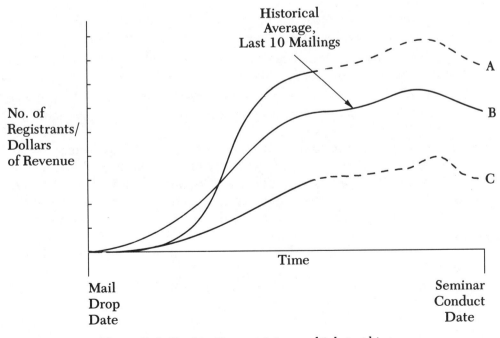

Historical
Average,
Last 10 Mailings

No. of
Registrants/
Dollars
of Revenue

A

B

C

Time

Mail
Drop
Date

Seminar
Conduct
Date

Figure 6–2. Registration receipts—multiple tracking.

111

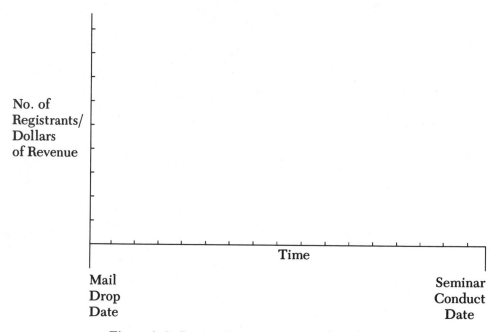

Figure 6–3. Registration receipts—tracking form.

response that is 50 percent greater than you normally receive. Here are just three of the many ways in which this necessary information could be of immediate value:

1. You could rent the balance of the tested list now and mail brochures first class, to increase total registrations for this seminar.
2. You could arrange for a larger room at the hotel you have selected for the seminar, while you still have time to do so.
3. You could increase the press run on participant materials, to avoid having to photocopy more sets on the night before the program.

Now look at line C: for your most recent promotion of this veteran seminar, response is 1/3 less than you normally receive. Now would be a good time to know that you are headed for disaster. You might want to cut facility size, or do more promotion, or duplicate your original promotion with a proven-response brochure you scrapped in favor of your latest creation.

Reproduce the form in Figure 6–3 and be sure to track response data for every promotion (direct mail or other) of every seminar you conduct. It may seem like a lot of work but you will assemble valuable data that will have long-term worth.

7

THE CAPTURE RATIO: CALCULATING EXPECTED DIRECT MAIL RESPONSE

One of the most frequent questions asked by seminar promoters is: What percentage of response on direct mail campaigns can be considered good? They are looking for a definitive figure that will clearly indicate whether the fee charged for their program is sufficient to produce a profit. The conventional wisdom among promoters has been that a capture ratio (response rate) of 1 to 1 ½ percent (.01–.015) or higher is good, and that anything below that modest range is considered unacceptable for most programs.

This quest for a magic formula, while understandable, indicates a misconception regarding the relationship between response rates and promotional decision making. Response rate, or capture ratio, is not a meaningful measure on which to base promotional decision making. In fact, an overemphasis on this measure can be detrimental to the decision-making process.

Consider the following example. A seminar promoter was shocked to discover that his mailings produced a response of only 1/10 of 1 percent (.001). In his prior business, the direct marketing of hardware, he had never experienced such a low capture ratio. After spending a great deal of time trying to increase his capture ratio, he compared his numbers with those of another seminar promoter who had a return of ½ of 1 percent (.005). To his surprise, he found that despite his lower capture ratio, he was actually doing far better than his colleague.

A comparison of the actual figures for the two promoters will illustrate how this revelation came about. The promoter whose capture ratio was .001 mailed 21,300 direct mail pieces at a cost of $0.44 per prospect; his cost of promotion per 1,000 prospects was $440. With a response ratio of .001, he could expect 21.3 participants at his seminar.

When considering these figures in isolation, the promoter might have had good reason to be discouraged. A mere 21 participants from a mailing of over 20,000 seems to be a poor response indeed. Yet all this response rate told the promoter was how large a room to request for the seminar. It did not tell him whether his seminar promotion would be profitable. The relevant measure of success is the promotion cost per 1,000 compared with the revenue per 1,000.

In this example, the fee charged by the promoter to participants was $875. Thus, his revenues were:

$$21 \times \$875 = \$18,375.00$$

and his promotion costs were:

$$21,300 \times \$0.44 = \$9,372.00.$$

The profitability of the promotion was determined by subtracting promotion costs from revenues:

$$\$18,375.00 - \$9,372.00 = \$9,003.00$$

So, even with a capture ratio of only .001, the seminar promotion was profitable. With a total presentation and program delivery cost of $1,844, the promoter's net profit was $7,159.00. Given that his program was three days in length, his per-day profit came to $2,386.33.

Compare his profit with that of the promoter whose capture ratio was .005. With a response rate five times as high as the first promoter's, it might be expected that he would experience five times the profit. In fact, it was substantially less. This promoter sent out direct mail pieces to 102,322 prospects at a cost of $0.29 per prospect. Thus his promotion cost was a modest $290 per 1,000 or a total of $29,623. With a capture ratio of .005, his total response was 511.61 (102,322 × .005). This promoter's seminar fee was $85, yielding revenues of:

$$511 \times \$85 = \$43,435.$$

The net revenue was equal to the difference between revenues and promotion costs:

$$\$43,435 - \$29,623 = \$13,812.$$

Five different seminars were conducted to accommodate the 511 participants. Presentation cost was $1,105 per seminar. Thus, this promoter's per-day profit was:

$$\$13,812 - \$5,525 = \$8,287 \div 5 = \$1,657.40.$$

Despite his higher response ratio, he experienced a lower profit margin than that earned by the first promoter. Thus, capture ratios, considered in isolation, are not an accurate measure of the profitability of seminar promotion. By relying solely on the capture ratio, a promoter may be misled into believing that his seminar is earning an optimum return when in fact it is not.

CAPTURE RATIOS AND FEES

The above example suggests that there may be a correlation between the price charged for the seminar and the capture ratio. This hypothesis is supported by the basic economic law of demand, which states that the higher the price for a product, the lower the quantity demanded. In other words, the higher the seminar fee, the lower the capture ratio, all other things equal. Of course, all other things are never equal, and there may actually be cases where a higher fee yields a higher capture ratio, at least over the relevant range. In markets where people have high discretionary incomes and regard a higher price as an indication of worth and prestige, the response rate may go up with small fee increases.

The basic principle of demand became the basis for a test developed for a promoter who wanted to know exactly how much he should charge for his computer applications seminar in order to earn the maximum profit. First, the names of 45,765 prospects in the Chicago marketing area were obtained from various mailing lists and subjected to merge/purge to eliminate obvious duplications. The list derived from the merge/purge was divided on an *n*th name basis to obtain five lists of 9,153 that would be identical for purposes of the promotional test. An identical direct mail piece consisting of an 8½″ × 11″ sheet printed on both sides was sent via bulk mail to each prospect on each of the five lists. The cost was $0.26 per prospect or $260 per 1,000.

Every variable in the test was held constant except one—the seminar price. Five prices were tested, with the following results:

Fee Charged	Capture Ratio/1,000	Revenue/ 1,000	Promotion Cost/1,000	Net Revenue/ 1,000
$ 65	8.9	$578.50	$260.00	$318.50
95	8.4	798.00	260.00	538.00
125	6.9	862.50	260.00	602.50
165	4.9	808.50	260.00	548.50
225	3.2	720.00	260.00	460.00

Based on these results, the promoter might have been tempted to charge a fee of $65 to ensure the maximum capture ratio of 8.9. But by setting his fee at that level, he would have earned a lower profit, as shown in the column on the right, than if he charged one of the other fees, all of which resulted in lower capture ratios. The optimum fee, based on this test, was $125, which yielded net revenue of $602.50 for each 1,000 pieces mailed.

This was what can be termed a gross test, in that the spread between the high and low prices was quite large. The results, while a useful indicator of the relationship between price and capture ratio, lacked the degree of exactitude needed by the promoter. For example, would a price between $125 and, say, $165 yield an even higher profit?

In order to gain more meaningful results regarding the fee to be charged, a second test was conducted, in the New York metropolitan area. A merged/purged list of 74,707 names, obtained from the same direct mail sources as in the Chicago area test, was divided into eight matched lists of 9,338 or 9,339 names. The promoter and the researcher agreed that prices of $165 and $225 might have been viewed by prospects as being too high for a one-day seminar. Therefore, another variable was added: length of seminar in days, providing results for both one- and two-day programs. Each prospect on the eight lists received the same one-page brochure for the one-day seminar and two-page mailing for the two-day program. The results of this test were:

Fee Charged	Capture Ratio/1,000	Revenue/ 1,000	Promotion Cost/1,000	Net Revenue/ 1,000
		One-Day Seminar		
$115	7.37	$ 847.55	$287	$560.55
125	7.28	910.00	287	623.00
135	7.19	970.65	287	683.65
145	6.70	971.50	287	684.50
155	6.09	943.95	287	656.95
		Two-Day Seminar		
$175	5.76	$1008.00	$369	$639.00
225	5.42	1219.50	369	850.50
265	4.74	1256.10	369	887.10

The results from this more precise test indicated that $125 was not the optimal fee to charge for a one-day seminar. The highest profit was achieved from a price of $145. In comparing the results for the one- and two-day seminars, a fee of $265 for the two-day program appeared to be optimal, given that it yielded the highest revenue–cost ratio. This option was rejected by the promoter because the two-day program would have been more labor-intensive and thus would have yielded a lower return per day than could be achieved by the one-day program at $145.

PROMOTIONAL DECISION MAKING AND PROFITS

The total profit earned by a seminar is a function of both promotion and presentation/delivery costs. Successful seminar promoters focus on increasing the efficiency of their promotion while holding down the costs of presentation and delivery. Given that the latter costs are more subject to the promoter's control, initial emphasis should be on the ratio of promotional yields to promotion costs. The relevant measure, and the one you should pay close attention to, is the relationship between gross registration receipts per 1,000 pieces mailed and promotion cost per 1,000 pieces mailed.

Usually a ratio of 3:1 means that the seminar will be profitable; a 4:1 or higher ratio indicates an extremely profitable program. At a ratio of 2:1, the promoter is making a living but no more. Anything below that figure strongly suggests that significant modifications are required. Hence, a promoter charging $600 for a seminar requires a much lower capture ratio than one charging $150. This is why concentration on capture ratios as a decision-making tool is inadequate. Capture ratio is a useful rule-of-thumb, historically, for determining expected numbers, but little more.

You may not have the resources to subject your seminar to the type of costly research described above. But a clearer understanding of the relationship among price, capture ratios, and profitability should aid you in your promotional decision making and you can certainly afford to do some limited or gross testing. There are several basic concepts to keep in mind as you address this issue:

1. Promotional decision making based on capture ratios is fraught with danger and should be avoided.
2. There is nothing intrinsically wrong with a low capture ratio.
3. The relevant measure of profitable promotion is the cost per thousand compared with the revenue per thousand.
4. All other things equal, the higher the seminar price, the lower the capture ratio.
5. The optimum fee to be charged for a seminar is derived by comparing the promotion cost–revenue ratio for different prices.
6. A ratio of 3 to 1 or higher between registration receipts and promotional costs should result in a profitable seminar, provided the costs of presentation and delivery are kept under control.

A final cautionary note: Be aware that every seminar is different, and that every target market has its own distinctive characteristics. Your promotional and pricing decisions should reflect an appreciation for the type of market you are aiming for and the unique or special features of your seminar.

Measuring promotional yield on the basis of yield per 1,000 permits you to more meaningfully compare the profitability of direct mail to other promotional options. For example, if you find that you have a direct mail cost of $350 per 1,000 names mailed and revenue of $1,100 per 1,000 pieces mailed, you know that your revenue is equal to 3.143 times your promotional cost. Suppose you decide to try magazine advertising. If your ad costs $1,500 and does not produce total revenue of $4,714.50 or more, it is less productive than promoting through direct mail.

8

PROMOTING SEMINARS
WITH ADVERTISEMENTS

Research has demonstrated that more than 63 percent of the newspaper advertisements for seminars fail to produce the minimum result desired by their promoters, and that 47 percent result in lower enrollment than is necessary to cover the expenses incurred in conducting the seminar. In spite of these grim statistics, ads for seminars and workshops can be found in nearly every edition of a newspaper. The difference between disaster and success with a newspaper ad lies in knowing how to use the medium effectively.

As with direct mail marketing, before you make any decisions concerning advertising for your seminar, you must decide: Who is my market for this seminar? Who would be interested in what I have to teach? Unfortunately, many people in the seminar business spend their time developing elegant seminars without giving much thought to the prospective market. They would probably be better off establishing the market and *then* designing the seminar for it. For example, one could research the profile of *Psychology Today* readers, design a seminar that would be optimally appropriate for a typical reader, and then utilize the magazine to advertise the seminar.

WHEN TO ADVERTISE IN THE PRINT MEDIA

Two types of print media are generally available to advertisers: newspapers and magazines. The circumstances under which you should choose one or the other or both are very different and should be given a great deal of thought.

There are two primary situations in which you should consider using a newspaper advertisement: when the seminar appeals to the general public and when your target market is specialized and mailing lists for it are not available. Real estate, investments, career opportunities, and self-improvement are typical subjects for general-public seminars. Remember that only about 63 percent of American households receive a daily newspaper while over 99 percent have a television. There is a considerable difference between the mass market you would be contacting through a television ad and the newspaper-reader market, which is often more literate and more affluent. This is especially important when you are preparing a newspaper ad for a specialized market for which direct mail lists are not available or are not as effective as desired. Suppose you decide to promote a seminar to teach people how to become successful consultants. When you try to find a good mailing list, you discover that there are only limited mailing lists available, and people who are not yet consultants probably aren't on such lists anyway. Good trade publications for consultants are few and do not offer an optimal number of contacts. So you are forced to ask: Are they likely to be reading the daily newspaper? The assumption that consultants do read a daily newspaper is probably accurate.

The reasons for choosing to advertise in magazines are slightly different. Magazines have several advantages over newspapers, but they have disadvantages as well. One advantage is that they are much more tightly targeted, so you can advertise to a specific group. Magazines like *The Saturday Evening Post, Look,* and *Life,* which were once at the top of mass circulation lists, are now dinosaurs. The trend today is for people to read specialized magazines—skiers read skiing magazines and computer buffs read computer magazines. But even that level of specialization isn't sufficient because if you're an IBM PC owner there are specific magazines for you, if you're a Macintosh owner there are different magazines for you, and so on. This increasing specialization also applies to the professions. Every profession, in fact practically every job, has its own magazine or journal—and maybe more than one. This specialization allows you to target your seminar market very tightly.

Another advantage of magazines is that they have a greater shelf life and pass-along readership than do newspapers. Magazines are often passed along to several people and generally stay in the home or office for days, weeks, perhaps even months at a time; newspapers tend to be discarded every day. The longer life of magazines can be a particular benefit if you are advertising a seminar series that will extend over a long period of time or if you are scheduled far in advance.

A disadvantage of magazines is actually the reverse of one of their advantages: because they are tightly segmented, you may miss a significant portion of the potential market for your seminar or even a market that had not occurred to you. Also, some magazines become almost like collectors' items because people don't throw them away. With magazines such as *Gourmet, Architectural Digest,* and *National Geographic,* people are less likely to clip coupons, bend them back to photocopy ads, or loan them to others.

Generally, in all advertising, you have to ask: Who is my market and what is the best, most efficient medium to reach that market? The more tightly defined the group you are marketing to, the more likely that a magazine will be an effective choice for you. There are, however, other considerations.

REGIONAL VS. LOCAL MEDIA

The geographic scope of the publication is another factor when you are deciding where to spend your advertising dollars. Most magazines are national. Therefore, to make the best use of a magazine's circulation, you should plan to conduct several seminars in different geographic locations, unless your seminar is so highly specialized, unique, and valuable that people would be willing to travel great distances.

A newspaper is generally more local in circulation, but even the regionalism of the newspaper market can become an issue if you plan to advertise in a national newspaper such as *The Wall Street Journal* or *USA Today*. If you were to advertise in the Western edition of *The Journal*, for example, it would probably be in your interest to schedule seminars in Los Angeles and San Francisco, at the very least, and perhaps Seattle and Denver as well, in order to get the full pulling power of the circulation of that newspaper.

Publishers seeking your advertising dollars are doing all they can to be more attractive. *The Wall Street Journal*, for example, now has regional and subregional editions. On certain days of the week, you can advertise in the Southern California, Northern California, or Pacific Northwest editions of *The Journal*.

If you think that you should be advertising in a national paper but you are not ready to give seminars in multiple locations, you should consider making available some alternative way for people to get the seminar content, such as via an audio cassette or videotape.

How do you decide whether to use national media, and if so, what editions? We will consider newspapers first. If you are going to be holding seminars in only the southwestern part of the country, then it might make sense simply to buy space in the Southwestern edition of *The Wall Street Journal* and schedule a seminar in Dallas or Houston or New Orleans or all three of those cities. Paying for wasted circulation elsewhere would make no sense. That strategy can also be a good test for *The Wall Street Journal*. Most promoters who test their advertising do it in the Southwestern edition. It's the least expensive regional edition and generally the least effective in most advertisers' minds, so if you do well in the Southwestern edition, you will probably do far better in the other editions.

The same considerations apply to magazines. The most regionalized major magazine is probably *Time*. You can advertise to a very tiny segment of the market—the residents of one state, the residents of a certain part of one city, medical doctors, teachers. *Time* may be more expensive in terms of what you are paying per person reached, but by going to these narrow segments of the market the total dollar outlay is a great deal less and you are assured that your message is being read by people who are likely to be interested in your program. This method also allows you to test the publication at less total dollar outlay. You should be aware, however, that most magazines are not as regionalized as *Time*, although they may have a Western edition and an Eastern edition or even up to eight or 10 different editions. A seminar for the general public, offered in a number of cities within a single region, is probably the principal reason for making use of regionalized editions, because most magazines break out their readers by geography rather than type.

If you are planning to give a seminar in a single city, it may still be in your best interests to consider the regional edition of a national paper such as *The Wall Street Journal.* Your decision depends on your audience. If your target market tends to match the characteristics of readers of *The Wall Street Journal*, then you would probably do well to use *The Journal.* It is also important to analyze the media. For example, the *Los Angeles Times* has such a fine daily business section that many readers don't feel it necessary to read *The Journal* as well. A similar situation exists in New York. Many who read *The New York Times* feel they have no need to read the *Journal*, because the business coverage in the *Times* is so good. The situation in San Francisco is quite different. *The San Francisco Chronicle* and *The San Francisco Examiner* are not regarded as having particularly good business sections; more people there are likely to read *The Wall Street Journal* and an ad in *The Journal* will pull better in the San Francisco Bay area than in Los Angeles or New York. If your dollars are not severely limited, you may do well if you advertise in the *Journal* as well as the local newspapers.

When considering *The Wall Street Journal*, keep in mind that it has both a primary advantage and disadvantage. There is indeed a certain prestige associated with advertising in *The Journal* as opposed to other papers; however, there are also many people who don't read it. They may not be your primary market, but they may be an important secondary market, and you will not reach them by advertising only in *The Journal.* The mass circulation of a daily metropolitan newspaper and the fact that it is widely read by a very diverse audience can be an advantage or a disadvantage, depending on the program you are offering.

Whenever you advertise in a major metropolitan newspaper or in *The Wall Street Journal* you are bound to get telephone calls from what we might call "the fringe competition" of those papers. Publishers who put out specialized city business publications or throwaway papers will offer to pick up your ad from the major metropolitan newspaper and rerun it in theirs, with no effort or trouble to you, and no payment required at that moment because they will bill you. It might be worthwhile to test those kinds of publications, but in all likelihood you will do better spending more money in the major publications rather than buying space in the fringe publications. Generally speaking, the larger the circulation of the publication, the less costly the advertising per person reached, and if an ad is working well in a major newspaper there is no reason for an advertiser to go to other media which will probably be less effective. You would probably do better to put more money back into the major newspaper, but the only way to know is to test.

AD DESIGN

The most important consideration in ad design is gaining the attention of the reader. You don't necessarily want all of the readers, just those who are likely to attend your seminar; it is their attention that you have to grab. In most advertising, this is usually accomplished by a compelling headline that causes the reader who is poring through the magazine or newspaper to wake up and become interested in what the ad is saying.

Graphics also grab the reader's attention. Photographs are a particularly effective way of attracting interest, if they are high-quality, tasteful, and well-reproduced by the publication. At one time the quality of newspaper reproduction was a problem, but photos and other graphics tend to be better reproduced today because of improved newspaper printing technology. Magazines, of course, have always reproduced artwork of all kinds very well. Simple diagrams—graphs, charts, and similar visuals—will also direct the reader's eye into the ad and maintain interest by helping to break up the copy.

Once the ad has attracted the reader's attention, it must sustain it, and the principles for achieving sustained attention in an advertisement are the same as for a direct mail brochure:

1. Stress the benefits of the program.
2. List very specifically what a participant will learn from the seminar or workshop.
3. Describe the seminar leader.

Beyond the basic facts on the seminar, the following information should always be included in your ad:

1. *Cost and Payment Procedure.* Include the credit cards you will accept and your policy on checks and purchase orders.
2. *Your Address and Phone Number.* These basics are often forgotten.
3. *What to Do if Readers Cannot Attend.* Can they attend a later program or buy seminar materials? Should they phone or write, to be put on the mailing list for the next seminar? Provide some options.

4. *Registration Procedures and an "Act-Now" Kicker.* If you are going to require preregistration or award a bonus for early registration, make sure that information on how to do this is included. Newspaper advertising works best when the seminar does not require preregistration because, in order to give people enough time to see the ad one or two times, decide to attend, contact you, mail in their registration, and wait for confirmation, you would need to begin your advertising much earlier and prospective participants would then have enough time to say, "I have plenty of time to register for that, I'll get to it later," and probably forget to do so.

5. *Contact for Further Information.* Provide your name, phone number, and/or address to encourage people to contact you with any questions or for further information.

Once you have finished designing your ad, leave it for a while. When you come back to it, ask yourself the same questions you would ask about your brochure:

1. Is my offer plain, simple, easy to understand, and easy to respond to?
2. Do I grab the reader's attention immediately?
3. Have I clearly and motivationally described the benefits which the participants will obtain by attending my program?
4. Have I clearly indicated each item that the participant will learn and, wherever possible, quantified it?
5. Have I described the people who will conduct this program in terms of their practical experience and knowledge?

Read your ad from the perspective of someone who knows nothing about your program. Make sure that all of your questions are answered and that you know what you are supposed to do when you have finished reading the ad. Obviously, an ad cannot contain as much description as a brochure because space is much more limited—and you are paying dearly for that space—but your advertisement should have as much information as you consider necessary to persuade a potential participant to register for your program or at least to contact you for further information. Figure 8–1 is a checklist to help you evaluate your seminar advertisement.

TICKLER ADS

An interesting variation on the "full information" ad is what is called the "tickler ad," which can consist of only a headline, or a headline and a very short description, and then a referral to a phone number for further

Evaluate the ad for your seminar by giving each criterion listed below a ranking of 1 (lowest) to 5 (highest).

Ranking

1. Cost and payment procedures are clearly stated. _____

2. Name, address, and phone number are included. _____

3. Options are included for those interested but unable to attend. _____

4. Registration procedures are clear and complete, and an "act-now" kicker as a bonus/motivation for early registration is provided. _____

5. The prospect is encouraged to seek further information, and instructions for how to obtain information and whom to contact are clear and easily followed. _____

6. The advertisement is plain, simple, easy to understand and easy to respond to. _____

7. Headlines and graphics attract the reader's attention immediately and sustain it. _____

8. The benefits of attending the seminar are clearly described and are motivating to the reader. _____

9. The ad describes and, whenever possible, quantifies the information, knowledge, skills, and strategies the participant will learn from the program. _____

10. The seminar leader's knowledge and practical experience are described in terms that are meaningful to prospective participants. _____

TOTAL [   ]

If your score is: 42–50   Your ad is probably quite good.
34–41   It needs work.
0–33   Give it a drastic reword or redo it.

Figure 8–1. Checklist for evaluating a seminar ad.

information. Tickler ads are useful when you have a subject for which you know there is some interest but probably not among a widespread market. Rather than put a lot of money into newspapers and magazines to describe the seminar, it may be much more profitable to run a very small ad that piques the curiosity of those interested in the topic and causes them to write or call for additional information. You can then mail out a brochure with complete details of the program to the select few who have inquired, knowing that you are mailing to individuals who are truly interested and therefore very good candidates for your seminar. This strategy allows you to use the newspaper or magazine as a screening device.

SIZE VS. COST

The advertising industry tends to be built on the principle that more is better than less, more frequent is better than less frequent, and larger is better than smaller. The principle undoubtedly has some truth but there is no linear relationship between the size and frequency of an ad and the results from the ad. An advertisement that is twice as big as another is unlikely to pull twice as many participants, and an ad run four times is not likely to produce four times the response of an ad run once. Obviously, the ad needs to be large enough to command attention and not be overlooked amid the other advertising, but beyond those general guidelines you must test each ad individually to determine the right size and frequency for your promotions.

TESTING

Because advertising is a very inexact science, the only way of finding out whether a given ad will produce results is to try it in the market. This doesn't mean that you must commit yourself to a complete advertising campaign without having any indication whether it will be successful. You can get a good idea of what will work for you by testing in relatively inexpensive publications. Some promoters test their seminars in high-visibility but expensive newspapers such as the *New York Times* or the *Los Angeles Times* and because they do not have extensive resources they run a rather small ad. The ad may not work for them, possibly because of its size, and they become discouraged about the advantages of advertising. They have not adequately tested the pulling power of the medium.

   A far more useful approach is to find a market that has demographics similar to the one you intend to penetrate but is smaller and has lower advertising rates. If you are thinking of advertising in the New York area, for example, you may want to pick a market that is less expensive but sufficiently convenient to New York to give you a good test of the New York market. Advertise in a paper like the *Bergen County Record* in New Jersey. Since you will pay a fraction of what it would cost you to advertise in the *New York Times*, you will be able to run a bigger ad and find out if it works. If it works there, it will probably work as well, if not better, in the *Times*.

In designing a test of your advertising, it is important to resist greed and not believe your own hype. In testing a seminar, many promoters want to jump in immediately and spend $5,000 to $10,000. They want to start in Los Angeles or San Francisco or some other very expensive market. They are afraid to start off in a small market because there is less potential profit. They forget that there is also less potential loss. These people believe their own hype so much that they are convinced they will make a profit and they are dying to get into the big market. If they are right, of course, it would be smart to go into the big market, but if they are wrong it is a very costly mistake. They may have spent several thousand dollars when they needed to spend several hundred. If they have the several thousand dollars to spend, it would be much safer and more prudent to do their testing in several-hundred-dollar increments to determine what works, and then roll out to the larger, more expensive, and more profitable markets.

HOW TO CHOOSE A NEWSPAPER

In some markets, it will be very clear and obvious which newspapers you ought to buy. For example, if you are doing a professional or business seminar in New York City, you will not need a significant amount of analysis to realize that your potential participants are much more likely to read the *New York Times* and not the *Post* or *Daily News*. In other markets your newspaper choice may not be as clear and you will need to do some reasonably sophisticated media research. One of the most useful tools for newspaper research is Standard Rates and Data Service's (SRDS) *Newspaper Circulation Analysis,* which contains demographic information about the readership of most newspapers in the United States. It is published once a year and is made available to subscribers of SRDS's *Newspaper Rate and Data.* SRDS also publishes *Consumer Magazine and Farm Publication Rates and Data* and *Business Publications Rates and Data.* These publications together provide a complete market picture of the print media and can be found in most public and/or business libraries. For each type of publication indexed they give the following information:

1. Editorial profile
2. Representatives and branch offices
3. Commission paid to advertising agencies
4. Advertising rates and charges
5. Deadline for submitting copy
6. Circulation
7. Ad sizes and (for newspapers) number and width of columns

Figures 8–2 and 8–3 show sample listings from *Newspaper Rates and Data* and *Newspaper Circulation Analysis* respectively.

You can obtain information about their readership directly from newspapers, but look at it very carefully because it is primarily marketing information and so may be a bit slanted. You should obtain copies of all the newspapers published in a target-market city. The major newspapers maintain advertising representatives in many large cities nationwide. If you call the paper you are considering, the representative will be happy to supply you with a media kit and copies of the newspaper so that you can make a complete evaluation.

When you are evaluating a newspaper, magazine, or other publication, take a look at who is advertising in it. If you are doing an upscale professional business seminar, it will probably be useful for you to see where the upscale retailers are advertising and where most of the financial and business advertising is placed. Then you can draw some conclusions.

An important factor to be aware of in choosing a newspaper is that only a handful of markets in the country now have competitive daily newspapers. More often, an area has only one newspaper or two newspapers that are owned by the same company or are under a joint marketing agreement. In such cases, usually no significant dollars are saved in advertising in just one. You should probably buy both papers and pick up the added circulation, since the additional cost tends to be negligible.

In many areas the real competition for the metropolitan daily newspapers is not other major daily papers. Particularly in the larger markets of the country, the primary competition comes from a very healthy suburban press. In Los Angeles, for example, the *Los Angeles Times* is the dominant metropolitan daily newspaper and a very successful one, yet it pulls a rather small percentage of the total market. About 27 percent of the households in the total market area receive it on weekdays and about 31 percent receive it on Sundays. What is everyone else reading? The suburban press. There are about eight to 10 very well-read suburban newspapers in the Los Angeles area, no one of which has a significant share of the market. However, when you add them all together, they become important.

Generally, for higher-level business and professional seminars, it is in your interest to advertise in the major metropolitan daily newspaper. For some seminars—particularly those relating to avocational interests, lifestyles, and self-improvement—the local suburban press may be better. Again, look at the papers, then test and find out what works best for you.

PLACEMENT

Proper placement of your advertisement is absolutely vital. Research reveals that people tend to throw away entire sections of the newspaper

Modesto

Stanislaus County—Map Location B-5
See SRDS Consumer market map and data at beginning of the state.

BEE

Box 3926, 14th & "H" Sts., Modesto, CA 95352.
Phone 209-578-2064.

The Bee's INLAND VALLEY GROUP BUY

Media Code 1 105 4890 1.00 **Mid 016177-000**
MORNING AND SUNDAY.
Member: INAME, ACB, Inc.

1. **PERSONNEL**
General Manager—John Ward.
Advertising Director—Alan Truax.
Display Adv. Mgr.—Don Wallace.
Nat'l Adv. Sales Mgr.—Denise Nordell.
2. **REPRESENTATIVES and/or BRANCH OFFICES**
Creamer, Woodward, O'Mara & Ormsbee, Inc.
3. **COMMISSION AND CASH DISCOUNT**
15% to agencies; no cash discount.
4. **POLICY-ALL CLASSIFICATIONS**
30-day notice given of any rate revision.
Alcoholic beverage advertising accepted.

ADVERTISING RATES
Effective January 1, 1988.
Received November 5, 1987.

5. **BLACK/WHITE RATES**

	Morn.	Sun.
SAU open, per inch	31.78	34.32

Inches charged full depth: col. 21.25; pg. 127.5; dbl truck 265.5.

BULK CONTRACT RATES

Within 1 year:	Per inch Morn.	Per inch Sun.
50"	29.95	32.32
100"	29.82	32.19
150"	29.69	32.06
250"	29.47	31.83
500"	29.21	31.52
1,000"	28.95	31.26
1,500"	28.60	30.86
2,000"	28.25	30.50
2,500"	27.90	30.10
3,500"	27.51	29.70
5,000"	27.03	29.17
6,000"	26.33	28.42
7,000"	25.51	27.53
10,000"	22.89	24.73

NEWSPLAN—SAU

Pages	% Disc.	Morn.	Sun.	Inches
6	8	29.21	31.52	765
13	10	28.60	30.86	1,657
26	12	27.90	30.10	3,315
39	15	27.03	29.17	4,972
52	17	26.33	28.42	6,630

See Newsplan Contract and Copy Regulations—items 5, 6, 8, 9, 10, 11, 13, 14, 16, 17.

6. **GROUP COMBINATION RATES-B/W & COLOR**
Bees' Inland Valley Group—see listing at beginning of State.
7. **COLOR RATES AND DATA**
B/w 1 c, 2 c or 3 c available daily (leeway required on b/w 2 c & 3 c); and Sunday.
Use b/w rate plus the following applicable costs:

	b/w 1 c	b/w 2 c	b/w 3 c
Extra	395.00	450.00	495.00

Color premium increase pro rate if space is more than full page.
Closing dates: Reservations as early as possible; order and material daily, noon, 4 days before publication; Sunday, 2.00 p.m. Wednesday before publication. Special colored inks must be ordered by number or sample 10 days before publication.
9. **SPLIT RUN**
Geographical split available by special arrangement.
Replate charges: b/w 30.00, 30.00 each additional plate, plus 3.00 per inch for body changes other than dealer signs.
11. **SPECIAL DAYS/PAGES/FEATURES**
Best Food Day: Wednesday.
Agri/Business, Sunday; Page for Children, Religion: Saturday; Art, Theatre, Music; Travel: Sunday; On the Go, Thursday; Home and Garden, Friday.
12. **R.O.P. DEPTH REQUIREMENTS**
Ads over 18 inches deep charged full col.
13. **CONTRACT AND COPY REGULATIONS**
See Contents page for location of regulations—items 1, 3, 5, 6, 7, 13, 15, 16, 18, 25, 29.
14. **CLOSING TIMES**
Orders and materials: 3 days in advance for Thursday and Friday; Noon Wednesday for Saturday; 4:30 p.m. Wednesday for Sunday; 4:30 p.m. Thursday for Monday; noon Friday for Tuesday, Wednesday deadline: 4:30 p.m. Friday.
15. **MECHANICAL MEASUREMENTS**
For complete, detailed production information, see SRDS Print Media Production Data.
PRINTING PROCESS: Photo Composition Direct Letterpress. (NAPP.)
6 col; ea 2-1/16"; 1/8" betw col.
Inches charged full depth: col. 21.25; pg. 127.5; dbl truck 265.5.
17. **CLASSIFIED RATES**
For complete data refer to classified rate section.
18. **COMICS**
POLICY—ALL CLASSIFICATIONS
Alcoholic beverage advertising not accepted.
Place all orders through Metro Sunday Comics Network—see that listing.
Sold in combination with Sacramento Bee.
Effective January 1, 1988.
Received February 17, 1988.

COLOR RATES AND DATA
Four colors:
(insertion in Modesto Bee and Sacramento Bee)

1 page	12,129.40
2/3 pages	8,611.86
1/2 page	6,657.18
1/3 page	5,111.22
1/6 page	3,161.61

DISCOUNTS

Within 1 year:		Within 1 year:	
3- 5 times	2%	26-38 times	12%
6-12 times	4%	39-51 times	15%
13-25 times	8%	52 or more times	20%

MECHANICAL MEASUREMENTS
Standard page size 13" wide x 19-3/4" deep.

19. **MAGAZINES**

TV Today

SUNDAY.
Effective January 1, 1988.
Received November 5, 1987.

BLACK/WHITE RATES
Open, per inch 34.32
Bulk R.O.P. or frequency discounts apply.
COLOR RATES AND DATA
Minimum 1/2 page:
Full color, per page 300.00
Spot color, per page 150.00
Available on 8 alternate pages in addition to 8 process color positions. Same color used on first alternate color page must be same on all other alternate color positions.
CLOSING TIMES
B/W: 3 Fridays prior to publication. Reservation and copy for one proof, 4:30 p.m. Friday. Proofs must be cleared and returned prior to 4:00 p.m. Wednesday.
Color: 1 week prior to black/white.
Holidays: Deadlines advance 24 hours.
MECHANICAL MEASUREMENTS
PRINTING PROCESS: Offset.
Page size 7-1/8" wide x 10" deep. 5 cols. to page.

20. **CIRCULATION**
Established 1884, per copy daily .25; Sunday 1.00.
Net Paid—A.B.C. 9-30-87 (Newspaper Form)

NEWSPAPER DESIGNATED MARKET

	Total	NDM	Outside
Morn	76,275	61,954	14,321
Sun	81,835	65,228	16,607

Total City Zone: Morn 37,940; Sun 38,546.
Max-Min CPM rate: Morn Max 13.12; Min 9.45.
For county-by-county and/or metropolitan area breakdowns, see SRDS Newspaper Circulation Analysis.

Monterey

Monterey County—Map Location C-6
See SRDS Consumer market map and data at beginning of the state.

HERALD

P. O. Box 271, Monterey, CA 93942.
Phone 408-372-3311.

Media Code 1 105 4950 4.00 **Mid 016179-000**
MORNING AND SUNDAY.
Member: INAME, NAB, Inc; ABC Coupon Distribution Verification Service; ACB, Inc.

1. **PERSONNEL**
General Manager—Paul Ayars.
Advertising Manager—James Rutledge.
Retail Adv. Mgr.—Jerry Meltzer.
Advertising Services Mgr.—Nanette Maysonave.
Nat'l Adv. Mgr.—James Rutledge.
2. **REPRESENTATIVES and/or BRANCH OFFICES**
Branham/Newspaper Sales.
3. **COMMISSION AND CASH DISCOUNT**
15% to agencies; 2% 15th following month.
4. **POLICY-ALL CLASSIFICATIONS**
30-day notice given of any rate revision.
Alcoholic beverage and cigarette ads accepted.

ADVERTISING RATES
Effective January 1, 1988.
Received November 3, 1987.

5. **BLACK/WHITE RATES**
SAU open, per inch (daily or Sun.) 16.94
Inches charged full depth: col. 21; pg. 126; dbl truck 273.
NEWSPLAN—SAU

Pages	% Disc.	MorS	Inches
6	5	16.09	756
13	7.5	15.67	1,638
26	10	15.25	3,276
52	15	14.40	6,552

See Newsplan Contract and Copy Regulations—items 2, 3, 4, 5, 6, 7, 9, 11, 13, 15, 17.

6. **GROUP COMBINATION RATES-B/W & COLOR**
Monterey-Santa Cruz Unit—see listing at beginning of State.
7. **COLOR RATES AND DATA**
Available daily and Sunday. Leeway not required. Minimum 30".
Use b/w rate plus the following applicable costs:

	b/w 1 c	b/w 2 c	b/w 3 c
Extra	180.00	280.00	315.00

Closing dates: Noon, 3 publishing days before publication; Saturday & Sunday Morning, Tuesday; printing material & cancellation, 3 days before publication.
9. **SPLIT RUN**
30" minimum. Service charge 40% extra. Minimum charge 203.28.
11. **SPECIAL DAYS/PAGES/FEATURES**
Best Food Day: Wednesday.
Garden, Saturday; Travel, Sunday.
12. **R.O.P. DEPTH REQUIREMENTS**
As many inches deep as columns wide. Ads 19-1/2 inches in depth or greater billed for at full column rate.
13. **CONTRACT AND COPY REGULATIONS**
See Contents page for location of regulations—items 1, 3, 6, 7, 8, 9, 10, 11, 12, 13, 14, 15, 16, 18, 19, 20, 23, 25, 26, 27, 28, 29.
14. **CLOSING TIMES**
Noon 3 publishing days before publication.
Saturday and Sunday morning—Tuesday deadline.
15. **MECHANICAL MEASUREMENTS**
For complete, detailed production information, see SRDS Print Media Production Data.
PRINTING PROCESS: Photo Composition Direct Letterpress (NAPP).
6 col; ea 2-1/16"; 1/8" betw col.
Inches charged full depth: col. 21; pg. 126; dbl truck 273.
16. **SPECIAL CLASSIFICATIONS/RATES**
Political (cash with order)—general rates apply.
POSITION CHARGES
Alongside reading 15%; full position (min. 3 inches) 25%; specified page (when available) 25%.
17. **CLASSIFIED RATES**
For complete data refer to classified rate section.
18. **COMICS**
POLICY-ALL CLASSIFICATIONS.
When orders are placed through Puck The Comic Weekly—see that listing.
Effective January 1, 1986.
Received November 1, 1985.

COLOR RATES AND DATA

1 page	800.00	1/3 page	280.00
2/3 page	552.00	1/6 page	192.00
1/2 page	416.00		

MECHANICAL MEASUREMENTS
Page size 7 cols. wide x 280 lines deep.
Material and copy of insertion to Western Colorprint, 1540 South Coast Highway, Laguna Beach, CA 92651.

19. **MAGAZINES**

Weekend Magazine

SUNDAY.
Effective January 1, 1988.
Received November 3, 1987.

BLACK/WHITE RATES
Flat, per inch 16.94
COLOR RATES AND DATA
Minimum size 2 columns x 13 inches.
Use b/w rate plus the following applicable costs:

	b/w 1 c	b/w 2 c	b/w 3 c
Extra	180.00	280.00	315.00

CLOSING TIMES
Reservations and copy 3 weeks before publication.
MECHANICAL MEASUREMENTS
Page size: 10" wide x 13" deep, 5 cols to page.

20. **CIRCULATION**
Established 1876. Per copy .25, Sunday .75.
Net Paid—A.B.C. 9-30-87 (Newspaper Form)

NEWSPAPER DESIGNATED MARKET

	Total	NDM	Outside
Morn	33,167	30,363	2,804
Sun	34,675	31,241	3,434

Total City Zone: Morn 24,197; Sun 24,759.
Max-Min CPM rate: Morn Max 15.82; Min 13.44.
For county-by-county and/or metropolitan area breakdowns, see SRDS Newspaper Circulation Analysis.

Napa

Napa County—Map Location B-4
See SRDS Consumer market map and data at beginning of the state.

REGISTER

A Scripps League Newspaper, Inc. Newspaper
P. O. Box 150, 1615 2nd St., Napa, CA 94558.
Phone 707-226-3711.

Media Code 1 105 4725 4.00 **Mid 017682-000**
EVENING (except Sunday).
Member: ACB, Inc.

1. **PERSONNEL**
Publisher—Bill G. Daniel.
General Manager—Greg Stevens.
Nat'l Advertising Manager—Jim March.
Nat'l. Adv. Coordinator—Geraldine Nalley.
2. **REPRESENTATIVES and/or BRANCH OFFICES**
The Papert Companies.
3. **COMMISSION AND CASH DISCOUNT**
15% to agencies; 2% 20th following month.
4. **POLICY-ALL CLASSIFICATIONS**
30-day notice given of any rate revision.
Alcoholic beverage advertising accepted.

ADVERTISING RATES
Effective July 1, 1987.
Received February 27, 1987.

5. **BLACK/WHITE RATES**
SAU flat, per inch 12.34
Inches charged full depth: col. 21.5; pg. 129; dbl truck 274.5.
6. **GROUP COMBINATION RATES-B/W & COLOR**
Golden Horseshoe Wine Country Group & Northern California Bay/Valley Group—see listings at beginning of State.
7. **COLOR RATES AND DATA**
Available daily. Minimum 32 inches.
Use b/w rate plus the following applicable costs:

	b/w 1 c	b/w 2 c	b/w 3 c
Extra	120.00	200.00	290.00

Closing date: Reservations 1 week in advance; printing material 3 days in advance. Cancellation date: 4 days in advance.
11. **SPECIAL DAYS/PAGES/FEATURES**
Best Food Days: Tuesday, Wednesday.
Automobile, Friday: Home Economics, Wednesday.
12. **R.O.P. DEPTH REQUIREMENTS**
Ads over 19 inches deep charged full col.
15. **MECHANICAL MEASUREMENTS**
For complete, detailed production information, see SRDS Print Media Production Data.
PRINTING PROCESS: Offset.
6 col; ea 2-1/16"; 1/8" betw col.
Inches charged full depth: col. 21.5; pg. 129; dbl truck 274.5.
16. **SPECIAL CLASSIFICATIONS/RATES**
Amusements, Political (cash with order)—general rate applies.
POSITION CHARGES
Definite page and/or page position, when available, 25% additional.
17. **CLASSIFIED RATES**
For complete data refer to classified rate section.

April 12, 1988 **Newspaper Rates and Data**

Figure 8–2. Sample page from *Newspaper Rates and Data.* Reproduced by permission of Standard Rate and Data Service, 3004 Glenview Road, Wilmette, IL 60091.

COUNTY AREA ANALYSIS

(For city zone and/or NDM data, see SECTION IV entitled CIRCULATION ANALYSIS OF NEWSPAPERS AND NEWSPAPER GROUPS.)

	ADJUSTED CIRCULATION DATA								CONSUMER MARKET DATA 4-1-86						
	MORNING		EVENING		MORN. & EVE. (Combined)		SUNDAY OR WEEKEND								(000 OMITTED)
	CIRC.	%Circ. of HSHLDS	CIRC.	%Circ. of HSHLDS	CIRC.	%Circ. of HSHLDS	CIRC.	%Circ. of HSHLDS	HSHLDS	POP Women 18+	Men 18+	HH EXPEND Teens 12-17	FOOD EXPEND Children 0-11	DRUG EXPEND	GROSS HH INC
CLARK *(Cont'd)*															
BUY ONE IN NWS G					1,720	26	1,710	26							
CLAY (D)									6.09	15.5	5	82,555	18,451	3,006	132,910
DECATUR HER REV =	426	7					404	7		6	5	1	3		
EFFINGHAM NEWS			512	8											
FLORA ADVOCTE-PR +			3,800	62											
STLOUIS POST-DIS							327	5							
CENTRAL ILL GRP					426	7	404	7							
CLINTON (A)									11.46	33.7		174,921	37,881	5,917	317,726
BELLEVILLE N DE =	890	8					1,458	13		12	12	3	7		
CENTRALIA SENTIN			4,488	39			4,759	41							
†STLOUIS GLOBE D ■	1,160	10					1,210	11							
†Seven-month audit.															
STLOUIS POST-DIS	942	8					1,718	15							
STLOUIS USSPI GR + •			WEEKLY CIRCULATION		5,296	46									
STLOUIS-ILL M GR					890	8	1,458	13							
STLOUIS-ILL S GR					890	8	1,458	13							
COLES (C)									19.24	52.3		279,775	61,335	9,745	497,584
CHICAGO TRIBUNE ▲							1,224	6		22	19	4	8		
DECATUR HER REV =	1,021	5					2,791	15							
MID-ILL NEWSPAP	14,156	74													
CENTRAL ILL GRP					1,182	6	3,326	17							
COOK (A)									1,945.94	5,274.0		30,735,800	6,594,220	1,016,340	64,871,700
CHICAGO CALUMET =	10,473	1								2,079	1,836	468	891		
CHICAGO DEFENDER +	32,245	2													
CHICAGO HERALD	62,640	3					59,281	3							
CHICAGO SO ECONM + =			16,048	1			31,111	2							
CHICAGO SUN-TIME	536,130	28					554,919	29							
CHICAGO TRIBUNE ▲					493,945	25	716,636	37							
CHICAGO USSPI GR			WEEKLY CIRCULATION		399,670	21									
CHICAGO USSPI GR +			COMB. DAILY/WEEKLY CIRC.		426,191	22									
CRAWFORD (D)									8.33	20.9		124,659	27,120	4,263	230,119
EVANSVILLE CO PR							532	6		8	7	2	3		
ROBINSON NEWS +			6,710	81											
TERRE HAUTE TR-S =							498	6							
BUY ONE IN NWS G							498	6							
CUMBERLAND (D)									4.10	11.0		56,920	12,636	2,042	93,387
DECATUR HER REV =	267	7					508	12		4	4	1	2		
EFFINGHAM NEWS			530	13											
MID-ILL NEWSPAP	1,819	44													
CENTRAL ILL GRP					267	7	508	12							
DEKALB (C)									24.17	72.2		374,439	80,731	12,531	702,728
CHICAGO SUN-TIME							1,373	6		29	27	6	10		
CHICAGO TRIBUNE ▲					3,409	14	5,891	24							
DEKALB CHRONICLE =			11,060	46			11,615	48							
†GREATER CHICAGON			1,675	7			1,950	8							
†Publishing frequency is evening and Sunday, except Waukegan News-Sun which is evening and weekend.															
ROCKFORD RG STAR	1,761	7					2,246	9							
N IL NEWS NETWOR			DAILY CIRCULATION		11,060	46									
N IL NEWS NETWOR			COMB. DAILY/WEEKLY CIRC.		11,060	46									
ROCK AREA NWS NT			DAILY CIRCULATION		11,060	46									
ROCK AREA NWS NT			COMB. DAILY/WEEKLY CIRC.		11,060	46									
DE WITT (D)									7.02	18.0		109,094	23,499	3,642	205,105
BLOOMINGTON PAN	2,854	41					3,047	43		7	6	2	3		
CHAMPAIGN NE-GAZ =			390	6			472	7							
CLINTON JOURNAL ✶			3,673	52											
DECATUR HER REV =	883	13					1,081	15							
CENTRAL ILL GRP					1,273	18	1,553	22							
DOUGLAS (D)									7.35	19.6		113,271	24,451	3,802	213,328
CHAMPAIGN NE-GAZ =			2,969	40			3,176	43		7	7	2	4		
DECATUR HER REV =	656	9					620	8							
MID-ILL NEWSPAP	810	11													
CENTRAL ILL GRP					3,625	49	3,796	52							
DUPAGE (A)									249.84	717.9		4,495,970	934,891	137,403	11,054,700
CHICAGO SUN-TIME	35,220	14					44,463	18		270	256	67	125		
CHICAGO TRIBUNE ▲					85,012	34	135,564	54							
CHICAGO USSPI GR			WEEKLY CIRCULATION		77,787	31									
CHICAGO USSPI GR +			COMB. DAILY/WEEKLY CIRC.		77,787	31									
EDGAR (D)									8.33	21.1		118,368	26,117	4,186	206,958
DANVILLE COM NEW			389	5			499	6		8	7	2	4		(Continued)

• This group is comprised entirely of weekly newspapers. = Member of Newspaper Group. ▽ Six-month Initial Audit. ✦ Nine-month Audit. ○ Twenty-four-month Audit.

Figure 8–3. Sample page from *Newspaper Circulation Analysis*. Reproduced by permission of Standard Rate and Data Service, 3004 Glenview Road, Wilmette, IL 60091.

without ever reading them. If you advertise in topical suburban sections or special advertising supplements, your intended audience may not read your ad simply because they never see it. Rates often reflect this. If advertising in a particular section is a great deal less expensive, the reason may be that it doesn't pull as well. Rates for prime time television and late night television are based on a similar principle. Many people watch late night television, but the advertising rates are much lower on late night TV because its viewers are a very small percentage of the total market. If someone is going to watch one television show, it will probably be during prime time, which is where prime time got its name.

In choosing which section of the newspaper to use, an advertiser needs to ask: If no other section of the newspaper were read that day, what section would my potential participant be most likely to read? If you are putting on a seminar on sports psychology, it is very likely that your target audience reads the sports section even if they don't read any other part of the paper. If you are giving a seminar on real estate syndication, your target audience is apt to read the business and real estate sections, even if they junk the rest. The rule of thumb here is: Don't be clever, be dumb; go with the section that you suspect your target market is most likely to be reading. Research has correlated, by gender, the likely audiences for some newspaper sections:

	Males	*Females*
General readership	Sports, main news	Main news, life-style
Affluent readership	Business	Business, life-style

The best place to locate your ad in the paper is on the right-hand side, near the top of a right-hand page, next to and under reading matter. Early pages in a section are usually more desirable than later pages, and it may sometimes be worth the additional cost to pay a premium for these positions if they are available.

Classified advertising is generally not effective for seminars. Classified ads are read very intently, but only by approximately 8 to 12 percent of the total readership of the paper. If your seminar is likely to be attended by people who for some reason are reading the classified ads, then you should probably consider the classifieds, but they are not as effective as advertisements in the general paper. If you are running an ad for a seminar on how to buy a business, advertising in the business opportunities section of the classifieds appears to make sense, but experience suggests that those who read the classifieds also read related sections of the paper. So do many others who may bypass the classified business opportunities that day but who are interested in buying a business. You will probably attract more interested readers by being in the display sections of the paper. If you can afford to run a second ad, do consider the classifieds, but test the placement very carefully because it is seldom as effective.

WHEN TO ADVERTISE

Most Sunday newspapers are more carefully and widely read than daily newspapers. Although advertising on Sunday may cost a bit more because of the greater circulation, it is usually a worthwhile investment that will produce a higher response rate. In a survey I conducted nationally of 415 seminar and workshop developers and promoters, the following priority orders were revealed:

Best Days of the Week to Advertise in Newspapers	*Best Days of the Week to Advertise on Radio*	*Best Months of the Year to Advertise in Magazines*
1. Sunday	1. Monday	1. September
2. Tuesday	2. Wednesday	2. January
3. Wednesday	3. Tuesday	3. March
4. Monday	4. Thursday	4. October
5. Thursday	5. Friday	5. April
6. Saturday	6. Sunday	6. February
7. Friday	7. Saturday	7. May
		8. December
		9. June
		10. November
		11. August
		12. July

Pay close attention to when your ad will run. Try to avoid advertising on holidays or at times that conflict with major public events, when the paper is less likely to be read.

REDUCING THE COST OF ADVERTISING

Newspaper advertising can be expensive, but there are a few ways to keep the costs down. Most newspapers offer a dual rate structure based on whether the advertiser is a local or out-of-town business. If you are planning to offer seminars in a particular market on a regular basis, consider setting up a business address in that area to qualify for the local (sometimes lower) rates. Although it is becoming increasingly rare, some newspapers still offer a 2 percent discount for cash payments. Almost all newspapers offer discounts to people who advertise either frequently or copiously; if you spend a lot of money with them, they will usually give you a better rate on your advertisements. Unfortunately, that sort of discount is usually unimportant to seminar marketers, who rarely advertise more than a few times a year in a given market.

SETTING UP YOUR OWN AD AGENCY

Almost all media pay a 15 percent commission to advertising agencies, and about 20 percent of the newspapers and magazines have a 2 percent cash discount accorded only to advertising agencies. By establishing your own agency, which can often be accomplished with little more investment than the cost of having stationery printed, your up-front savings on newspaper advertising alone can result in a reduction of from 15 to 17 percent of the total cost.

The main requirement for setting up an advertising agency is simply to have the nerve and determination to do it. The procedure is quite simple:

1. Select a name that is different from that of your other business.
2. File the name with your state registration agency if required.
3. Open a checking account in this name and always write checks for advertising expenses on this account.

Few will dispute your right to become an ad agency. You can even serve outside clients if you wish.

Once you have created an advertising agency, you can deal with media representatives and media agencies whenever possible, instead of placing your ads directly with a newspaper, magazine, or other publication. About 85 percent of all newspapers, and most magazines, have representatives in major cities. Since they profit from advertising sales, they will be less likely to challenge your right to take an agency commission.

Figure 8–4 is an advertising insertion order form that you can reproduce or adapt as you wish. Figures 8–5 through 8–10 are reproductions of actual advertisements, to give you an idea of the types of newspaper and magazine ads being used to promote seminars and workshops. In any newspaper you will also see a tremendous variety of ad styles, formats, and copy. Review them carefully. Many providers find newspaper and magazine advertising a productive means to promote their seminars and workshops.

[Letterhead]

Advertising Insertion Order

TO: Name
          Publication
          Address
          City/State/Zip

Number: _____

Date: _____

Terms: _____

       _____

       _____

- -

Please run the enclosed camera-ready copy _____ in

_____ in accordance with the following schedule:

_____

_____

_____

Request best position possible: _____

Rate: _____

Total due $_____

Please send tear sheets/checking copies to address above.

Authorized Signature _____

Figure 8–4. Order form for an advertising insertion.

3 New Seminars From *MagazineWeek*

MagazineWeek will offer three specialized 3-day intensive seminars in 1989

#1 Secrets of Profitable Magazine Management

Designed as an advanced refresher course for senior level magazine executives and as a cross training opportunity for department head level personnel on their way to senior management. The course is divided into six half-day sessions on magazine economics, advertising marketing, circulation marketing, magazine production, list rental management and financial planning. The six areas are linked using a case study approach to revising the business plan of a dying magazine. Emphasis is placed on interdepartmental relationships in the strategic positioning of a successful magazine. Seminar leaders include Alex Brown, Stuart Jordan, Donn Rappaport, Don Nicholas and David Orlow. This seminar will be held in June on Cape Cod, in September in New York, and in December in Los Angeles.

#2 Effective Circulation Management

Goes beyond the basics of circulation management to explore how each circulation skill area can be used to enhance overall magazine profitability. This seminar combines the best of three programs we offered last year: Direct Mail Management; Budget Preparation and Strategic Planning and; Effective Renewal Management. The three-day program is divided into six half-day sessions on the following topics: circulation source management and testing, direct mail campaign management, creating winning renewals, wholesale and direct single-copy marketing, fulfillment analysis and reporting, and circulation modeling and budgeting. Seminar leaders include Mike Gumbinger, Stuart Jordan, Pete Savage, Tom Low and Don Nicholas. This seminar will be held in June on Cape Cod, in September in New York, and in December in Los Angeles.

#3 Maximizing Advertising Profits

Designed to provide participants with a complete set of revenue enhancing tools that will allow them to increase the advertising profit contribution of their own publication(s). The three-day course includes six half-day sessions on the following topics: advertising merchandising, creating advertising that sells, advertising positioning and marketing, advertising pricing, management of the sales force and creative selling. The course topics are designed to cover the entire advertising job spectrum — from tips to increase individual ad sales, to the strategic management of the advertising revenue stream. Seminar leaders include Jack Edmonston, Michael Perlis, Bob Ziegel, Marty Walker and David Orlow. This seminar will be held in September in New York, and in December Los Angeles.

For More Information Call:

Hilary Gamache at (508) 650-1001 or return the information request coupon to:

MagazineWeek
Seminar Information
5 Commonwealth Road
Natick, MA 01760

Please Send Me Complete Information:

❏ Secrets of Profitable Magazine Management
❏ Effective Circulation Management
❏ Maximizing Advertising Profits

Name/Title _____

Publication _____

Address _____

City/State/Zip _____

Phone _____

MagazineWeek Educational Conferences
Five Commonwealth Road , Natick, MA 01760   MW9C

Figure 8–5.

135

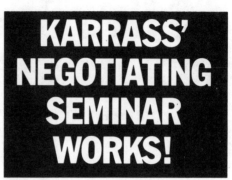

KARRASS' NEGOTIATING SEMINAR WORKS!

Forbes Magazine said it simply: "Sure, there are dozens of guys — too many — running around giving seminars. But Karrass' client list is a breed apart: Mobil, General Motors, Ford, IBM, General Electric, Arco, Shell, ITT, Phillips Petroleum, — 9 out of the nation's 15 largest companies — plus 140 others." Forbes added: "Kaiser Aluminum & Chemical, which spent about $15,000 over several years on Karrass Seminars, asked employees to identify specific savings they had made through better company negotiating. The total ran into millions of dollars. A Boeing sales executive says the same about a single Mideast negotiation. At General Electric, renowned for its own in-house training programs, 90 percent of the employees called the Karrass course their most significant career training ever. The seminars are even regarded as a fringe benefit. 'You wouldn't believe how many of our employees have told me what a good

Dr. Chester L. Karrass

deal they got on a boat or a car because they adopted Karrass' strategies,' says the head of training at a major oil company." (Forbes Feb. 15, 1982) Since that article appeared in Forbes, February 15, 1982, the number of Fortune 500 companies sending executives, managers and other key staff members through the Karrass Seminar has risen to 260. And these companies have been joined by hundreds of smaller business and professional organizations, as well as governmental agencies on the federal and state level.

In all, over a quarter of a million people have attended EFFECTIVE NEGOTIATING®, and gone away armed with all

KARRASS

◀ • • • • • • •
Continued next page

Figure 8–6.

TWO QUICK EASY WAYS TO REGISTER:

1 Simply choose the City and Date of the seminar you wish to attend and

CALL (213) 453-1806

2 Mail the Enrollment Form below to: Karrass, 1633 Stanford Street, Santa Monica, CA 90404

Enrollment is limited to personalize individual coverage, so lose no time in choosing the date and place of the seminar you wish to attend.

FEE INCLUDES: • Tuition • 11 hour Audio Cassette Series • Give and Take (hardcover book) • The Negotiating Game (hardcover book) • Workbook • Luncheons • Certificate of Completion

FEE: $595 individual fee — $550 for individuals from licensed companies (see list at right) — $545 per person for two or more, registering at the same time. (All individuals need not attend the same seminar) — Fee includes $35.00 registration charge (non-refundable). Price may be higher for seminars held outside of the United States. Call for current price.

SEMINAR TIME: First Day 8:30 am registration; Seminar, 8:45 to 5:30 pm. Second Day, 8:15 to 4:30 pm.

TAX DEDUCTION OF EXPENSES: An income tax deduction is allowed for expenses of education (including registration fees, travel, meals and lodging) undertaken to maintain and improve professional skills. (Treas. Reg. 1.162-5 Coughlin v. Commissioner 203 F2d 307.)

These fine reference materials are yours FREE when you attend.

DO YOU QUALIFY FOR A DISCOUNT?

Organizations listed below hold license agreements with Dr. Karrass' in-house EFFECTIVE NEGOTIATING® program; you qualify for a discount if you work for a company or subsidiary of any organization listed.

• AM General • Aerojet General • Air Products • Allen Bradley Co. • Allied-Signal • American Can • American Standard • Armco, Inc. • Army Air Force Exchange Service • Arvin Industries • Associated Spring • AT & T Technologies • Avantek • Avco Aerostructures • Ball Brothers • Bechtel Corp. • Bell Helicopter • Bell Communications • Boeing • Borg-Warner • Catell • Celanese Corp. • Chicago Bridge & Iron • Chrysler Corp. • CIL, Inc. • Cincinnati Milacron • Coca Cola USA • Continental Forest Industries • Control Data Corp. • Convair • Coulter Electronics • Crown Zellerbach • Cummins Engine • Digital Equipment • Dow Corning • Dow Chemical • DuPont • Duquesne Light Co. • Eastman Kodak • T. Eaton • Envirotech Corp. • Exxon • Fairchild • Fannie Mae • Florida Power & Light • FMC Corp. • Ford Motor Co. • General Dynamics • General Electric • General Motors • Georgia Pacific • B.F. Goodrich • Gould, Inc. • Goodyear • GPU Nuclear • Green Giant Co. • Grumman Aerospace • GTE • Harris Corp. • Hamilton Standard • Hanscom AFB • Hewlett Packard • Home Federal Savings • Homequity • Hughes Aircraft • Hughes Helicopters • Hussmann Corp. • IBM • ICI Americas Inc. • Inland Steel • Intel Corp. • International Paper • ITT • Jet Propulsion Lab • J.A. Jones Construction • Kaiser Aluminum • Litton • Lockheed • Lubrizol • R.H. Macy & Co., Inc. • Martin Marietta • McDonnell Douglas • Meijer • Merck & Company • MGIC • Mobil Oil • National Semiconductor • Navistar • Navy Resale • NCR Corp. • New York Telephone • Northrop Corp. • Oscar Mayer • Otis Engineering • Packaging Corp. of America • Paradyne • Phillips Petroleum • Picker International • Pillsbury Co. • Polaroid • Pratt & Whitney Aircraft • Procter & Gamble • Rank Xerox • Raytheon • RCA • Republic Steel • Roadway • Rockwell International • SAMSO • Sandia Nat'l Laboratories • Shell Oil • Sikorsky Aircraft • Siemens Allis • Southern Bell Telephone • Sperry Univac • Standard Oil of Ohio • Storage Technology • Target Stores • Tektronix, Inc. • Texas Instruments • Tinker AFB • Trane Co. • Travenol Labs • TRW • Turner Corporation • University of California • Uniroyal • Unisys • USX • United Technologies • Virginia Chemical • Wang Labs • Washington Metro Transit • Western Electric • Westinghouse • Wright Patterson AFB • Weyerhaeuser Co. • Xerox.

INDICATE DATE AND CITY AND SEND ENTIRE COUPON

This is your FREE copy. Take the magazine with you.

ALBANY
☐ Feb. 5-6 '90—Marriott

ATLANTA
☐ Dec. 14-15 '89—Hyatt Regency
☐ Jan. 11-12 '90—Hyatt Regency
☐ Feb. 15-16 '90—Hyatt Regency
☐ Mar. 12-13 '90—Hyatt Regency

BALTIMORE
☐ Nov. 27-28 '89—Stouffers Harbor Place
☐ Feb. 15-16 '90—Marriott Inner Harbor

BOSTON
☐ Nov. 13-14 '89—The Colonade
☐ Jan. 22-23 '90—The Colonade
☐ Feb. 22-23 '90—The Colonade
☐ Mar. 22-23 '90—The Colonade

BUFFALO
☐ Jan. 11-12 '90—Hyatt Regency
☐ Mar. 29-30 '90—Buffalo Marriott

CHARLOTTE
☐ Jan. 22-23 '90—The Registry
☐ Mar. 19-20 '90—The Registry

CHICAGO/OAKBROOK
☐ Dec. 7-8 '89—Palmer House
☐ Dec. 18-19 '89—Stouffer Oakbrook
☐ Jan. 22-23 '90—Palmer House
☐ Feb. 26-27 '90—Palmer House
☐ Mar. 5-6 '90—Oakbrook Marriott
☐ Mar. 22-23 '90—Palmer House
☐ Apr. 26-27 '90—Palmer House

CINCINNATI
☐ Dec. 12-13 '89—The Westin
☐ Jan. 25-26 '90—Cincinnati Marriott

CLEVELAND
☐ Dec. 7-8 '89—Stouffer Tower
☐ Feb. 12-13 '90—Stouffer Tower

COLUMBUS
☐ Dec. 11-12 '89—Pickett Suites
☐ Feb. 26-27 '90—Marriott North

DALLAS
☐ Dec. 11-12 '89—Fairmont
☐ Feb. 8-9 '90—Fairmont
☐ Mar. 12-13 '90—Fairmont

DENVER
☐ Nov. 30-Dec. 1 '89—Hyatt Tech Ctr.
☐ Jan. 11-12 '90—Marriott Tech Ctr.

DETROIT
☐ Dec. 7-8 '89—Omni International
☐ Feb. 8-9 '90—Omni International
☐ Apr. 2-3 '90—Omni International

HARTFORD
☐ Nov. 9-10 '89—Harley Hotel
☐ Feb. 5-6 '90—Harley Hotel

HONOLULU
☐ Feb. 8-9 '90—Hyatt Regency Waikiki

HOUSTON
☐ Jan. 18-19 '90—Westin Oaks
☐ Mar. 22-23 '90—Westin Oaks

INDIANAPOLIS
☐ Jan. 18-19 '90—Adams Mark
☐ Mar. 26-27 '90—Adams Mark

IRVINE
☐ Dec. 4-5 '89—Balboa Bay Club
☐ Feb. 1-2 '90—Balboa Bay Club

JACKSONVILLE, FL
☐ Mar. 5-6 '90—Sawgrass Marriott

KANSAS CITY
☐ Nov. 9-10 '89—Marriott Plaza
☐ Jan. 25-26 '90—Marriott Plaza

LAS VEGAS
☐ Nov. 14-15 '89—Caesars Palace
☐ Feb. 8-9 '90—Caesars Palace

LOS ANGELES
☐ Nov. 16-17 '89—Beverly Hilton
☐ Dec. 14-15 '89—Beverly Hilton
☐ Jan. 12-13 '90—Marina Beach Hotel
☐ Feb. 12-13 '90—Marina Beach Hotel
☐ Mar. 15-16 '90—Marina Beach Hotel

MEMPHIS
☐ Jan. 22-23 '90—Omni Hotel
☐ Mar. 26-27 '90—Omni Hotel

MIAMI
☐ Dec. 14-15 '89—Hyatt Regency
☐ Jan. 29-30 '90—Hyatt Regency

MILWAUKEE
☐ Nov. 13-14 '89—The Pfister
☐ Feb. 8-9 '90—Marc Plaza

MINNEAPOLIS
☐ Nov. 9-10 '89—Vista Marquette
☐ Jan. 18-19 '90—Vista Marquette

NEW ORLEANS
☐ Dec. 14-15 '89—Hotel Inter-Continental
☐ Feb. 15-16 '90—Hotel Inter-Continental

NEW YORK/NEW JERSEY AREA

NEW YORK CITY
☐ Nov. 16-17 '89—Hotel Westbury
☐ Jan. 29-30 '90—Grand Hyatt
☐ Mar. 29-30 '90—Hotel Westbury

LONG ISLAND
☐ Nov. 30-Dec. 1 '89—Long Island Marriott
☐ Feb. 15-16 '90—Long Island Marriott

WESTCHESTER COUNTY
☐ Jan. 18-19 '90—Tarrytown Hilton
☐ Apr. 26-27 '90—Tarrytown Hilton

ATLANTIC CITY
☐ Nov. 30-Dec. 1 '89—Bally's Park Place
☐ Feb. 22-23 '90—Bally's Park Place

MORRISTOWN
☐ Dec. 11-12 '89—Governor Morris Inn
☐ Feb. 12-13 '90—Governor Morris Inn

OKLAHOMA CITY
☐ Feb. 15-16 '90—Sheraton
☐ June 14-15 '90—Sheraton

PALM SPRINGS
☐ Feb. 1-2 '90—Stouffer Esmeralda

PHILADELPHIA
☐ Dec. 4-5 '89—Adams Mark
☐ Jan. 25-26 '90—Adams Mark
☐ Mar. 22-23 '90—Adams Mark

PHOENIX
☐ Dec. 7-8 '89—Hyatt Regency
☐ Feb. 15-16 '90—Hyatt Regency

PITTSBURGH
☐ Dec. 11-12 '89—Vista International
☐ Feb. 12-13 '90—Vista International
☐ Apr. 9-10 '90—Hyatt Regency

PORTLAND
☐ Dec. 7-8 '89—Marriott Hotel
☐ Feb. 26-27 '90—Westin Benson

SACRAMENTO
☐ Feb. 15-16 '90—Hilton
☐ May 14-15 '90—Hilton

SALT LAKE CITY
☐ Dec. 4-5 '89—Doubletree
☐ Jan. 29-30 '90—Doubletree

SAN ANTONIO
☐ Feb. 26-27 '90—Wyndham San Antonio

SAN DIEGO
☐ Dec. 11-12 '89—Westgate
☐ Feb. 26-27 '90—Westgate
☐ Apr. 26-27 '90—Omni

SAN FRANCISCO
☐ Dec. 7-8 '89—Stanford Court
☐ Jan. 11-12 '90—Park Hyatt
☐ Feb. 12-13 '90—Park Hyatt
☐ Mar. 15-16 '90—Park Hyatt

SAN JOSE
☐ Nov. 9-10 '89—Fairmont Hotel
☐ Jan. 29-30 '90—Fairmont Hotel

SEATTLE
☐ Nov. 16-17 '89—Seattle Hilton
☐ Jan. 22-23 '90—Crown Plaza Hotel
☐ Mar. 29-30 '90—Crown Plaza Hotel

ST. LOUIS
☐ Nov. 13-14 '89—Hyatt
☐ Feb. 1-2 '90—Marriott Pavillion

TAMPA
☐ Nov. 13-14 '89—Hyatt Regency Tampa
☐ Jan. 18-19 '90—Hyatt Regency Tampa

WASHINGTON, DC
☐ Dec. 4-5 '89—Madison Hotel
☐ Jan. 22-23 '90—Madison Hotel
☐ Mar. 12-13 '90—Madison Hotel

MELBOURNE, AUSTRALIA *
☐ March 1-2 '90—Hyatt on Collins

SYDNEY, AUSTRALIA *
☐ March 5-6 '90—Hyatt Kingsgate

CALGARY, CANADA *
☐ Nov. 27-28 '89—Westin Hotel
☐ Mar. 22-23 '90—Westin Hotel

MONTREAL, CANADA *
☐ March 1-2 '90—Le Grand Hotel

TORONTO, CANADA *
☐ Nov. 27-28 '89—Sheraton Centre
☐ Feb. 8-9 '90—Sheraton Centre

VANCOUVER, CANADA *
☐ Jan. 29-30 '90—Hyatt Regency

TOKYO, JAPAN *
☐ Mar. 19-20 '90—Miyako Hotel

GUADALAJARA, MEXICO *
☐ Feb. 1-2 '90—Camino Real

MEXICO CITY, MEXICO *
☐ Nov. 9-10 '89—Westin Camino Real
☐ Jan. 15-16 '90—Westin Camino Real
☐ Mar. 8-9 '90—Westin Camino Real

MONTEREY, MEXICO *
☐ Nov. 7-8 '89—Hotel Ambassador
☐ Feb. 5-6 '90—Hotel Ambassador
☐ Apr. 2-3 '90—Hotel Ambassador

SAN JUAN, PUERTO RICO *
☐ Jan. 25-26 '90—Condado Plaza

* *Call for prices*

Name _____ Title _____
Name _____ Title _____
Name _____ Title _____
Company _____
Street _____ Phone (_____) _____ Ext. _____
City _____ State _____ Zip _____

PRIORITY CODE AW059

☐ CONFIRMATION ONLY – RESERVATION BY PHONE **(213) 453-1806** FAX – **(213) 828-4739**

☐ Enclosed is my check, payable to: Karrass, 1633 Stanford St., Santa Monica, CA 90404

☐ Charge to my credit card as checked: ☐ American Express ☐ Visa ☐ MasterCard

Card # _____ Expires _____

Signature _____

☐ Please send more information about Effective Negotiating® Seminars and speeches, available at my company's facility.

Cancellation of a reservation does not affect registrant's financial liability unless we receive notice seven days before the meeting. SUBSTITUTIONS ANY TIME. Please make your own hotel reservations. A limited number of rooms have been set aside. Please mention that you are with the KARRASS group for special attention. Due to the exclusive confidential and copyrighted material of EFFECTIVE NEGOTIATING®, no tape recording will be permitted under any circumstances.

KARRASS

THE WORLD LEADER IN NEGOTIATING PROGRAMS

Figure 8–6. *(continued)*

Continued from previous page

the strategies, tactics, techniques and skills of negotiation that Dr. Karrass learned and has tested in three decades of practical negotiation, advanced academic study, and pioneering research in the field.

Why are more people attending EFFECTIVE NEGOTIATING® each year? They know that successful negotiators are successful people. And successful negotiators aren't born—they're trained.

They also realize negotiation isn't something reserved for diplomats and labor relations people. We all negotiate, and we all spend a great deal of time at it. We negotiate in business with the people we buy from, and the people we sell to. We negotiate with our own bosses. We negotiate with our own employees. We negotiate in our personal lives, time and time again.

As Newsweek once said: "Negotiation is the game of life."

◀ • • • • • • •

This is YOUR copy
tear out and take with you

NEGOTIATING SKILLS ARE KEYS TO YOUR SUCCESS IN BUSINESS AND LIFE.

Your agreements, understandings and relationships mean the difference between success and failure. Poor agreements with other companies and individuals are always breaking down. They bring nagging dissatisfaction and aggravation into your business and personal life.

But good agreements help you reach and exceed your own objectives; and they leave the other party gaining more satisfaction at the same time.

This is true whether you are:

· Determining the price and terms at which you buy or sell

· Closing with an important customer

· Persuading others to work with and not against you

· Setting or meeting budgets

· Finalizing and administrating simple or complex contracts

· Working on a problem with someone important to you

· Managing and supervising those responsible for doing the work properly in your organization, in other departments and on the outside

· Breaking or avoiding a serious impasse

Dr. Chester L. Karrass

EFFECTIVE
• • • • • • • • •

It is no surprise that the most successful negotiation seminar in the United States would be created and designed by Dr. Karrass. No other negotiator in the country has a similar background. Dr. Karrass has combined over 25 years of on-the-job experience with advanced academic credentials in negotiation techniques.

After earning an Engineering degree from the University of Colorado and a Masters in Business from Columbia University, he became a negotiator for the Hughes organization. There he won the first Howard Hughes Doctoral Fellowship Award and spent three years conducting advanced research and experimentations in negotiation techniques before earning his Doctorate from the University of Southern California. He then returned to Hughes as a negotiation consultant.

In 1969 Dr. Karrass used his research and experience in his pioneering EFFECTIVE NEGOTIATING® seminar, assisting other business people to master the strategies, tactics and psychological insights of negotiating.

When he began holding these seminars, most business executives and professionals did not realize how much they actually negotiated. Now over 250,000 professionals, including salespeople, buyers, corporate leaders, managers, engineers, financial officers, C.E.O.s and international business people have attended Dr. Karrass' EFFECTIVE NEGOTIATING® seminar.

Many of the participants have attended the EFFECTIVE NEGOTIATING® seminar in-house, and more than 170 of the Fortune 500 corporations currently license the Karrass program.

Dr. Karrass is the author of four books on negotiation, including "The Negotiating Game," and "Give and Take." They are all best-sellers in their field.

His EFFECTIVE NEGOTIATING® seminar is packed with the strategies, techniques, tactics, tips and skills Dr. Karrass learned, practiced and tested over the past three decades. He designed the seminar program to be practical, hard-hitting and to pay off – literally. He constantly updates it. Karrass Seminar course leaders are carefully selected for their experience and skill; and specially trained for their seminar roles – leading, teaching, discussing, motivating, and making it all as enjoyable as it is educational.

And at the Karrass Seminar you'll broaden your range of business acquaintances, sharing not only learning sessions but meals and coffee breaks with presidents, vice presidents, sales and purchasing executives, and other business and professional people from a wide spectrum of enterprise.

Gary Karrass, author of Simon & Schuster's "Negotiate to Close," is a recognized national authority on negotiation, especially from the sales and marketing side. As president of KARRASS he spends over 200 days a year conducting speeches for companies, associations and conventions of all sizes and all areas of business.

Mr. Karrass joined KARRASS Seminars in 1974. And under his direction, KARRASS has grown into the worldwide leader of its field. Since he became president, the number of annual public seminars has more than tripled. And through offices in Los Angeles and Great Britain, hundreds of Effective Negotiating Seminars have been held on every continent. ■

• • • • • • • • •
Gary Karrass

Figure 8–6. (*continued*)

NEGOTIATING WORKS!

• • • • • • • • • • •

See back page for two-day seminar schedule and fees

EFFECTIVE NEGOTIATING® TWO-DAY SEMINAR TOPICS:

STICKING TO YOUR OWN GAME PLAN
What People Forget To Do • Pyramid of Planning • First Things First • Product Strategy • Fact Finding • One Useful List, **Plugging The Leaks On Your Side** • Smoking Out Their Concessions

YOU HAVE MORE POWER THAN YOU THINK
Using Hidden Leverage • Power of Legitimacy • Commitment Power • Word Power • Power of Knowledge • Risk-Taking Power • Hard-Work Power • The Limits of a Seller's Sole-Source Power • The Limits of a Buyer's Power to Use Competition • Putting Time on Your Side • Power of Rules and Precedent • Team Power • Power of Status and Appearance, Strengths and Weaknesses • Self-Evaluation, What Your Opponent Really Wants • Stated Motives • "Under the Iceberg" • Using Hidden Needs, Long-Term Relationships Versus One Shot Deals • Who Benefits Most • Making Long Term Relationships Work For You • Turning Things Around

BETTER AGREEMENTS RIGHT NOW!
Both Sides Win • Ten Tips That Always Work • You Can Negotiate Specifications, One Win • Do Well For Yourself • How To Get More Information • Who Talks Too Much? • Better Questions For You • Don't Trust Assumptions • Cost Breakdowns – Yes or No? • How To Make A Concession,

Personal Negotiating • Goodwill and Rapport Mean Business • Negotiating an Organization – Five Modes

YOU CAN'T HIT A TARGET YOU NEVER SET
How To Set And Achieve Your Targets • A Practical Method For Team Target Setting • Gaining Personal Targets • The "Must" and "Give" Issues • Min-Max Positions, When You Expect Less You **Get Less** • How Expectations Affect Outcomes • How Expectations Go Up and Down in the Other Person's Head • Achievers and Non-Achievers • Risk Takers and Avoiders, **What Makes A Good Negotiator** • Change The Negotiator – Keep The Initiative • Tying the Plan Together

USING YOUR STRENGTH IN –
Business • Selling • Purchasing • Manager/Employee Relations • Real Estate Transactions • Contracts, Legal Conflicts, Engineering Specifications, Personal Needs and Transactions

SOME TIPS FROM THE COMPETITION
How Other Cultures Negotiate • Opening Moves • Authority Limits • Measuring Concessions • "Fair and Reasonable"

TRAPS AND TACTICS
Keeping Your Eyes Open • Quick Deals

Deadline! • Telephone Mistakes • Using the Phone To Your Advantage • Summary For Success, **Applying Time Tactics** • Patience – Japanese Power • How To Build Patience Systematically • Buy Now – Negotiate Later • Acceptance Time • Change of Pace – Initiative Tactic **Applying Authority Tactics** • Authority and No-Authority • Escalating Authority – A Movie Industry
Tactic To Watch Out For – Why Authority Mixes You Up • Limited Authority • Full Authority Pitfalls • How The Highest Executives Escape From Authority When They Want To

COUNTERMEASURES
Demand And Offer Tactics • Testing A Firm Price – "Take It or Leave It" • When a Firm Stand is Necessary • How To Reduce Resentment, Learning To Walk Away – And Come Back! • Taking On Higher Authority, Zeroing In • How To Pin Down What The Other Party Will Take • Why And How Every Contract Changes Silently Over Time • Projecting For Real-World Results And Reactions

DEALING WITH DEADLOCKS...YOU WIN
Breaking A Deadlock or Making One • Is The Price Right? Why You Must Negotiate Anyway • 15 Ways To Break Deadlocks and Avoid Impasses • How To Get Someone To

Deal With You Who Won't! – AN ABSOLUTELY UNIQUE EXERCISE TO HELP YOU RIGHT AWAY

GUARDING AGAINST TRICKS
Psychological Ploys Meant To Corner You • Good Guy – Bad Guy • Averages and Statistics • Why All Facts Are Negotiable • Negotiating Tricks From The Movie Industry

MORE SUBTLETIES – MORE SKILLS!
Understanding For Self-Defense • How Funny-Money Can Work For or Against You • Issues Even Experienced Negotiators Miss • Planning Purpose Traps That Salespeople Fall Into • The Reverse Auction, A Very Tough Tactic • Competition Face To Face, **Nibbles That Add Up** • How To Stop Them In Any Agreement • How To Stop a Buyer's or Seller's Hidden Nibbling, Four Tactics Hard To Cope With • Dirty Trick Escalation • The Big Proposal Puzzle • Backing Off A Concession • Mistakes – Real or Otherwise, The Bogey Works Almost Every Time • What It Is and Why It Works • Why Tiger Teams Get Results • Is Any Budget Constraint Real? • Countermeasures, The Krunch • Dangers and Opportunities • How The Seller Should Handle The Krunch and Turn It Around, **What Will Work For You In The Toughest Negotiation?** • Time To Think • Proven Techniques To Give Yourself More Time • Why Teams Make Sense – Pitfalls and Opportunities

YOUR HELPFUL CONCESSIONS; WHY THEY CAN HURT YOU
Opening Offers • How Fast Should You Move? • Should You Split The Difference? • Much More On Doing It Right, How Winners Win – With Real Money • The Critique – What Went Wrong – What Went Right

GAINING SUCCESSFUL AGREEMENTS AND KEEPING THEM
Attendee Discussion • Negotiating Problems • How To Deal With Them, How Hard A Bargain Should You Drive After The Negotiation • How You and Your Company Benefit, Review – Prescription For Continuing Success

Yours Free When You Attend

YOURS FREE WHEN YOU ATTEND THE SEMINAR

No other seminar offers so much.

Everyone who attends receives free to take home the most comprehensive, state-of-the-art package of materials on negotiation available anywhere today.

This multimedia package is not only a constant reminder of everything you learn at the seminar but includes additional material not covered in the two-day program. The package assures you can keep the course working for you in the years ahead.

Your take-home reference materials will include:
- Effective Negotiating® Reference Cassettes, 11 one-hour audio tapes designed for review and reinforcement.
- "The Negotiating Game," Dr. Karrass' definitive best-selling hardcover book, the choice of three book clubs.
- "Give and Take, The Complete Guide To Negotiating Strategies and Tactics," another best-selling book by Dr. Karrass, chosen by four book clubs.
- "Effective Negotiating® Workbook and Action Guide," outlining the Karrass Seminar with provocative questions and exercises.
- Certificate of Completion, suitable for framing.

For Those Who Cannot Attend The Seminar

This multimedia package – the two hardcover books, the workbook, and the 11-hour set of audio tapes – is available by mail order.

The set is $317 including handling, shipping and insurance. There is a money back guarantee, if you are not satisfied and return it within 10 days. Send check (no purchase orders), New York residents add 8% sales tax. To: Negotiating Books, 84 Lone Oak Path, Smithtown, NY 11787.

KARRASS

• • • • • • • • • •

Figure 8–6. (*continued*)

HOW TO GET ON TALK SHOWS WITH ROSS SHAFER'S

TALK SHOW WORKSHOP

CRACKING THE TALK SHOW CIRCUIT

As you may have discovered, getting booked on talk shows can be difficult. Unfortunately, being qualified or writing a book isn't good enough anymore. With more and more shows cutting into the same ratings pie, T.V. and radio producers on major shows usually won't gamble on a new face who doesn't know how the game is played. However, they will always book guests they feel are "broadcast ready." And believe me, a producer can tell within three minutes of your initial inquiry if you are "bookable." Your job is to know how to score in those first three minutes.

WHO SHOULD ATTEND?

Talk shows need experts, speakers, authors, inventors, psychologists, performers, business & professional people. With more than 2,000 talk & issue T.V. and radio shows who use guests regularly, the demand is insatiable.

WHAT YOU WILL LEARN.

• How to get on T.V. & radio shows with or without a book • What turns producers on & off • How to become a "regular" • How to score in the critical phone pre-interview • What to say in your introduction letter • How to reverse a turndown into a booking • When to plug your products or services and when not to • Picking the right shows to do • Fee guidelines • How to become quotable • Scripting vs. planned ad libs vs. winging it • Making your entrance • Advice on hiring agents and P.R. firms and when not to • Developing your T.V. personality • What to wear and not to wear • How to treat other guests • Green room etiquette • What the camera sees that you do not • Broadcast standards and practices • 4 key elements of every great guest • Standing out "on the panel" • How to "connect" with the host • How far in advance to contact shows • Pre-show preparation tips • Talk show storytelling hints • Evaluating your performance • Publicizing your appearances • Avoiding blunders that can blackball you and much, much more.

GUARANTEED EXPOSURE TO PRODUCERS

Not only is this workshop endorsed by major talk show producers, each enrollee is guaranteed a free listing in our monthly TALK SHOW GUEST DIRECTORY which is received by all network and syndicated T.V. talk shows alerting them that you have completed this workshop.

UNABLE TO ATTEND?

You may order the live cassette recording, course study notes, and talk show source list, $129.00 + 4.45 S/H by check, MC/Visa, or Amex.

ROSS SHAFER

Ross Shafer is an emmy-award winning talk show host and producer. You have seen him as the network host of A.B.C.'s Day's End, The Late Show on Fox, Almost Live w/Ross Shafer and his upcoming syndicated talk show Not For Men Only. He has interviewed thousands of guests over the years and can show you how to succeed on the talk show circuit.

REGISTER BY MAIL OR PHONE BEFORE JANUARY 10TH FOR THIS INVALUABLE ONE DAY SEMINAR.

WHEN: Saturday, January 13, 1990

WHERE: Sheraton Universal Hotel/Los Angeles

COST: $195 per person

METHOD OF PAYMENT: CHECK ☐   MC/VISA ☐   AMEX ☐

CARD # _____ EXP. DATE _____

SIGNATURE _____

EXPERTISE _____

NAME _____

ADDRESS _____

CITY _____ STATE _____ ZIP _____

DAYTIME PHONE (   ) _____

DATE _____

ADVANCE REGISTRATION NECESSARY. PRIVATE CONSULTATIONS ALSO AVAILABLE.
CALL FOR MORE INFORMATION AT (818) 348-2702.

Figure 8–7.

SEMINAR: *HOW TO BUILD AND MAINTAIN*
YOUR OWN PART-TIME/FULL-TIME

© HLS
1980

CONSULTING

PRACTICE

You too can earn substantial income as a part-time or full-time consultant to business, government and the professions. Attend this successful seminar and learn how to turn weekends, evenings, and other free time into increased income.

WHO SHOULD ATTEND?

Any man or woman with a marketable skill gained through education or experience. Managers, engineers, professors, psychologists, manufacturer's reps., scientists, executive recruiters. Personnel specialists, military, grad students, editors, authors, real estate professionals, investors, accountants, designers, data processing specialists, architects, lawyers, trainers, etc.

SEMINAR LEADER

Your Seminar conducted by H.L. Shenson, a recognized, successful consultant who began consulting part-time while department chairman at a major university. Now a full-time consultant with significant industrial experience.

Seminar fee of only $195 includes over 300 pages of written material, handbook, strategy guide, cassette recording of Seminar, and follow-up consultation. This is the original Consulting Seminar attended by more than 12,000, featured on ABC TV news, radio/TV talk shows and newspapers.

WHAT WILL YOU LEARN?

How to Price (Value) Your Services · How to Market Your Skills · Strategies to Benefit You in a Recession · **How to Build Client Dependency** · How to Obtain Government Contracts · How to Identify Bad Consulting Jobs · How to Start Your Own Newsletters & Seminars · **How to Avoid Giving Away Free Consulting** · How to Idenfity Consulting Opportunities · How to Create Your Own Demand · **Low Cost/No Cost Ways to Gain Professional Exposure** · How to Get Clients to Seek You Out · How to Turn the First Meeting into a Signed Contract · Contracts · Billings · Collections · **How to Get Retainers** · Performance Contracts · Knowing When & How to Turn Down Consulting Jobs · How to Get and Broker Grants · **Dealing with Conflicts of Interest** · Making the Business Cycle of Consulting Work for You · How to Market a Professional Practice · Consulting Corporations & Partnerships · Practice Management & Expansion · **Dealing with Your Professional Liability** · Effective Silent Marketing · Creating Information Products from Your Know-how · **What to Do When You Meet the Client Face-to-face** · How to Get Follow-on Contracts · How to Write the Consultant's Proposal · **Advertising Your Services — What Not to Do** · Estimating and Pricing Strategies · How to Profit from Regulatory Legislation, · and more.

AN ADDED BENEFIT

Seminar participants may contact Shenson at any time with their questions.

LOS ANGELES
Friday, September 12th
9:30 A.M. to 4:30 P.M.
Los Angeles Marriott
Airport at Century Blvd.

SEATTLE
Wednesday, October 15th
9:30 A.M. to 4:30 P.M.
Red Lion Inn - Airport
18740 Pacific Highway South

DENVER
Thursday, October 16th
9:30 A.M. to 4:30 P.M.
Executive Tower Inn
1405 Curtis Street

UNABLE TO ATTEND? Order complete Seminar Materials — live cassette recording, 300 plus pages of written material, follow-up consultation, $145 plus tax. Check, Mastercharge, VISA, American Express. Attend any future Seminar by paying the difference between Materials Kit and Seminar fee.

Registration, 30 min. prior to seminar. Bankcards, Checks accepted.

(HLS) The Howard L. Shenson Seminar

Figure 8–8.

SEMINAR
HOW TO FIND MONEY

Being able to obtain all of the money you need at the most favorable terms and conditions for business, personal and real estate transactions is vital for your success. Yet, the strategies and techniques for successful money finding — for clout with lenders — is known by a very few. Most are far less successful than they could be. Uncertainty about getting money, not knowing how banks work, or alternatives to banks, even fear of lenders results in missed opportunities. This powerful, insightful Seminar unlocks the little known, proven strategies and techniques of the money game so that you can get all of the money you need.

WHO SHOULD ATTEND?
Every man and woman who now borrows, or expects to borrow in the future, from banks, savings and loans, commercial lenders or who seeks private investment sources for current or future business operations, new business ventures, personal use or investments in real estate, securities, etc. Whether you need funds yourself or serve as advisor to those who need funds, (ie., CPA's, consultants, attorneys, etc.) you will benefit from this eye opening Seminar.

WHAT YOU WILL LEARN
How to prepare presentations/proposals for lenders. . .How to determine the lender's rules. . .What lenders look for. . .How they check you out. . .What information to give them. . .How your financial statements are read, interpreted, and analyzed. . .How to win the ratio game. . .What really happens in loan committee. . .How to select a bank. . .When to change banks. . .When not to change banks. . .When to have more than one bank. . .When to use commercial credit instead of banks. . .The strategic advantage of different kinds of loans. . . What you should know about collateral and collateralizing loans. . .Compensating balances. . .How to restructure financial statements for different uses. . .When not to sign personal guarantees. . .How to create financing in-house with your banker. . .How to make him a part of your team. . .How to borrow on 2nd TD's and mortgages. . .How lenders read appraisals. . .What ratio determines 91% of R.E. loan approvals. . .How to know how much to ask for. . .How to know how much you need. . .How to figure the real cost of interest. . .How a loan committee decides yes or no. . .Real estate loan packaging. . .How to identify lenders interested in making your kind of loan. . .And much, much more.

YOUR SEMINAR LEADER
Thomas J. O'Malia is uniquely qualified to conduct this important Seminar. He has been on both sides of the banking desk. His experience as a seeker of bank credit includes responsible positions in the capacity of corporate treasurer, public accounting and nationally recognized financial consultant. But one side of the coin is insufficient. As a grantor of bank loans he has also served as Senior Commercial Lending Officer of the First Eastern Bank and Corporate Center Vice President, Lloyds Bank of California. O'Malia is author of the best selling Banker's Publishing Company book, "Banker's Guide to Financial Statements" and is a frequent lecturer to major banks on the loan making process.

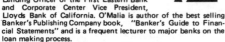

SHOULD YOU ATTEND THIS SEMINAR NOW?
If you know that you (or your clients) could be more successful in banking relationships, in acquiring new sources for funds or in finding private investors, you will have already decided to attend this dynamic, authoritative Seminar. If you think that you may not need this information now, consider this: the need to borrow money arises with little warning. Successful money finding relationships are based upon pre-planning. You should establish a line of credit in advance of the need to borrow; you should establish credit with the lenders when you are financially healthy. Procrastination is unhealthy for financial success and causes you to look unworthy. Don't be sorry later. This vital Seminar will unlock the most important, but least understood, factor in business/financial success. This is the only time that this Seminar will be given in this area this year. DON'T MISS IT!!!

CONTINUING EDUCATION CREDIT:
Approved for AICPA credit. Also, 1.1 CEUs are awarded for successful completion of this program.

TAX DEDUCTION:
An income tax deduction may be allowed for education expenses undertaken to maintain or improve professional skills. This includes registration, travel, meals, lodging . . . (see Treas. Reg. 1.162-5) Coughlin vs. Commissioner 203 F 2d 307).

HLS **HOWARD L. SHENSON, INC.**

WHAT PAST PARTICIPANTS SAY
I got my money's worth in the first hour...I wish every customer of this bank was smart enough to have attended this Seminar before they come to me... Worth the whole day just for the question and answer period...Could have filled two days with the information presented...

The handbook alone was worth the price of admission...I wish I had gone three years ago when I first started...The lender's checklists and interview questions removed all my prior fears about getting money...

Fantastic! I am sending every one of my accounting clients...I am particularly appreciative of the fact that you took time to arrange an introduction at the bank for me...Having every question answered was the greatest benefit...

I am glad that I came now. With today's economy I can use all of the help I can get...With my experience I thought I knew it all, thanks for opening my eyes. I learned more than I can tell you...

BRING YOUR QUESTIONS AND FINANCIAL DATA
Bring your specific questions, they will be answered during and after the Seminar. Bring business cards, etc., you are likely to meet bankers and money brokers at the Seminar.

BRING THIS AD WITH YOU FOR A VALUABLE GIFT
Tear this ad out and bring it with you to the Seminar. Give it to the Registration Secretary when you register and receive without charge "The 7 Keys to a Favorable Real-Estate Loan Decision."

DALLAS
WEDNESDAY, JAN. 21st
9:30 a.m. to 4:30 p.m.
Loews Anatole Plaza
2201 Stemmons Freeway

OR

HOUSTON
FRIDAY, JAN. 23rd
9:30 a.m. to 4:30 p.m.
Houston Oaks Hotel
Houston Galleria

SEMINAR FEE $95
INCLUDES ALL MATERIALS.

REGISTRATION: Registration at the Seminar begins at 9:00 a.m. Fee may be paid by check, VISA, Mastercharge, American Express or cash.

Figure 8–9.

EXCLUSIVE ONE DAY WORKSHOP

CREDIT REPAIR: SECRET OR SCAM?

Millions of Americans are experiencing the anxiety and frustration of having bad credit! However, not every credit problem can be "repaired". Before you rush out and hire a credit consultant to "repair" your credit, attend this EXCLUSIVE ONE DAY WORKSHOP sponsored by the Foundation For Consumer Credit Education, a non-profit organization, and learn from our EXPERT GUEST SPEAKER:

DR. MICHAEL HSU, Attorney-at-law, one of the nation's foremost experts on consumer credit, and author of several books on credit improvement.

* How to detect and avoid credit "repair" scams
* How to consolidate your debts and avoid bad credit
* The exclusive CREDIT REBUILDING PROGRAM—a new and effective 4-step process to rebuilt your credit
* SPECIAL STRATEGIES in improving, removing or neutralizing bad credit from credit reports
* Step-by-step instructions on how to reestablish good credit
* Recent state laws, federal laws, FTC opinions and case laws regarding consumer credit rights

A $595 VALUE WORKSHOP
NOW ONLY $35 ADMISSION FEE
LIMIT TO 200 STUDENTS PER WORKSHOP!
NO CHECKS ACCEPTED ● NO TAPE RECORDING

DON'T MISS THIS DYNAMIC WORKSHOP!
SPONSORED BY: Foundation For Consumer Credit Education (A nonprofit organization)

SATURDAY, NOV. 18	**SUNDAY, NOV. 19**
9 A.M.-5 P.M.	9 A.M.-5 P.M.
IRVINE MARRIOTT HOTEL	WESTIN BONAVENTURE HOTEL
18000 VON KARMAN AVE. OFF I-405	404 SO. FIGUEROA OFF I-110
IRVINE	**LOS ANGELES**

Figure 8–10.

9

WHERE AND WHEN
TO HOLD SEMINARS
AND WORKSHOPS

One of the most important steps in ensuring a successful, profitable seminar is the selection of the city or cities in which the seminar is to be conducted. The effectiveness of your marketing strategy is enhanced by the care you take in selecting an appropriate site. Size, location, accessibility, and media availability are just a few of the factors to be considered in selecting the optimal geographical locations for your program.

You probably have a "hunch" as to which cities are ideally suited to your program and will provide the largest market window. Your own experience with particular cities, the images they convey, and the fit of your topic to a certain region will help you to narrow your list to the right selections. Intuition, shaped by experience and good judgment, may suggest which of the cities on your list would be the best choice.

To eliminate some of the guesswork from selecting a city and to provide a more scientific basis for your selection, a number of selection criteria have been identified through controlled research involving 117 seminars and developed into a highly reliable model. This model (Figure 9–1) is presented at the end of the chapter (pages 154–157), following the discussion of the individual criteria.

POPULATION

The population of your seminar city will strongly influence the ultimate success of your program. Other factors being equal, a city with a population size of 1 million is far more likely to be a profitable site than a city with fewer than 1 million. The population of the metropolitan area in which the city is located (Standard Metropolitan Statistical Area or SMSA) also influences the suitability of a site. An SMSA of 2 million or more should provide a strong drawing card for most seminars.

In considering the size of your prospective cities, be aware of the existence of "sleeper cities"—for example, Albuquerque, New Mexico—which, because of their smaller size, would not seem to be optimal choices for seminars but which have proven to be excellent locations that draw very well.

Growth rate is another factor to be considered. A metropolitan area in decline is not apt to be a desirable location for your seminar whereas one that is experiencing a healthy growth rate (4 percent a year or more) is more likely to generate interest, exposure, and higher attendance. In cities with declining growth rates, seminars may do well if their topic is connected with the decline and oriented toward a concerned audience.

Population demographics should be carefully evaluated when selecting a seminar site. The age, sex, education, income level, and skills of the population all have a bearing on the marketability of your seminar in that area. For example, a city with a high percentage of well-educated, higher-income professionals could be a preferred location for a seminar on a high-tech or sophisticated financial topic.

While not of primary importance, the relation of the city to nearby cities and to others in the state and region affects the suitability of your choice. If the city is the largest in the state, it is likely to be a profitable choice as a seminar site. Conversely, if it lies in close proximity to a larger city, attendance may be negatively affected, especially if residents of the larger city tend to view the smaller one as being of secondary importance. For example, many residents of San Francisco would not be inclined to attend a seminar in Oakland, even though it lies just across the Bay, because they perceive it as a "second city." Oakland residents, accustomed to going into San Francisco to do business, would be favorably disposed toward a seminar held there.

ECONOMIC CONDITIONS

Prevailing economic climate should be considered in choosing a seminar site. During a recession, corporate managers tend to be more cost-conscious and a seminar in a nearby city is more appealing than one in a city that requires more travel. This is especially true if the seminar is being paid for by a corporation or other benefactor rather than by the individual participants.

Your market's perception of the location will also come into play. Exotic resort-type cities may generate high attendance during a growth period, when the prevailing mood is more optimistic, but people may shy away from these locations during a belt-tightening crunch, especially if they have to answer to an employer for the expenditure.

The unemployment rate of a city may affect attendance. People who are out of work are less likely to spend money to attend seminars (unless the topic happens to be "How to Market Your Job Skills" or "How to Cope With the Stress of Unemployment"). Nor will choice of a city in a depressed economic state reflect favorably on the seminar being held there; prospective participants are not as likely to be attracted to a seminar held in a city they perceive as unprosperous, unsuccessful, and undesirable. The national rate of unemployment provides a useful benchmark: a city with a higher-than-average rate usually is less desirable than one with a rate below the average.

A comparison of the median household income in the metropolitan area with that of the nation as a whole will provide you with another economic index with which to rate your selection. An area whose income exceeds the national average by 5 percent or more should be given higher consideration than one with an income equal to or below the national average.

Seminar attendance is affected early in the business cycle. During the first stages of a growth period, seminar promoters have noted an increased interest in seminars; expenditures for training tend to fall off in the early stages of a recession. An awareness of trends in the economic cycle will help you to select the appropriate types and numbers of sites for your seminar or workshop.

ACCESSIBILITY

The ease with which participants can get to your location will affect attendance. Check on the number of daily nonstop flights from major cities into your city; 16 or more is considered optimal. The degree of accessibility also serves as an indication that the city is regarded as being dynamic and sophisticated, making it more appealing as a seminar site.

COMPANIES AND INSTITUTIONS

The presence of Fortune 500 companies indicates a dynamic, vigorous city that serves as a center for business and trade. A city with corporate headquarters of more than a dozen major corporations may provide a ready-made market for your seminar. Similarly, universities or colleges with at least 4,500 students and located within 15 miles of the city limits offer a strong professional orientation and expanded market base for your seminar. Law and medical schools are another indication of a city's prominence and interest in education and professional advancement.

Government agencies—state and federal—broaden your marketing opportunities even further. Their employees are apt to have more time and discretionary income to allocate to seminars, and many of these workers are on the lookout for ways to improve skills and marketability.

PROMOTION

Cities with a broad newspaper readership and the availability of a number of television stations suggest a well-informed, sophisticated populace and a high level of activity and stimulation. A high percentage of newspaper readership, in particular, may be beneficial to your promotional campaign if you are seeking promotional support from newspaper advertising or public relations.

Certain cities may be more amenable to direct mail campaigns than others, which could have important repercussions for your seminar. A well-populated Sun Belt city may appear to be a good choice for your seminar until direct mail possibilities are considered. If a large percentage of the populace is Spanish-speaking and does not have a strong facility in English, a direct mail campaign is not apt to generate the attendance level that might be expected for a city that size, unless your direct mail pieces are geared specifically to that audience. Awareness of the relation between the city selected and promotional opportunities is an important element of a successful marketing strategy.

FACILITIES

Cities with a number of first-class hotels with 100 or more guestrooms indicate a high level of tourism and business activity, which is likely to have a positive effect on seminar attendance. Moreover, you will have more options in choosing a facility that is both convenient for participants and good for your image as a seminar promoter. You can avoid the areas that have high crime rates, and you can choose a site that is easy to get to from the airport (unless the airport is viewed as being inconveniently located, as for example, among residents of Dallas and Houston).

In major markets, multiple facilities might be used and can offer two advantages: if you have a large enough market, you can schedule concurrent or consecutive seminars at different hotels within the metropolitan area; and, you will have the means to work around the travel mentality of the target population. People in some areas simply are not willing to travel to other locations in the area to attend a seminar. Sometimes referred to as the "7-11 phenomenon" after 7-11 Stores ("24 hours a day, close to you"), this mentality is found even in areas such as Los Angeles where people are accustomed to commuting great distances to get to work. Long-distance commuters seem to expect other services to be brought to them. Thus, multiple facilities can be an advantage.

Depending on the type of program you are offering, the availability of a convention center able to accommodate a large audience may be required. Even if you are planning to hold all of your meetings in a hotel, your marketing potential is slightly improved in cities with large-scale convention facilities. If nothing else, such facilities suggest a center for trade and tourism.

ENTERTAINMENT

Cities with a wide offering of entertainment are generally more sophisticated and dynamic, and people are more likely to travel to those sites. A metropolitan area with multiple major league sports franchises is a definite marketing asset as a seminar location. A city with a professional opera company, symphony orchestra, and theater company will also enhance the drawing card for your program. You may even want to include opportunities to attend a sporting, theatrical, or cultural event as part of your seminar promotion.

THE SEMINAR TOPIC

As already indicated, your seminar topic will influence your choice of sites. A topic specific to a particular region or audience may mean eliminating choices that otherwise might be desirable. Boston and New York may be ideal choices for seminars on sophisticated financial topics, for example, but this type of seminar may not play well in Peoria. Topics geared toward a certain age group or educational level should be scheduled where they will have the greatest appeal. If you design your seminar with marketing potential in mind, your topic must appeal to a broad audience base so that you can hold your seminar in a number of locations. Sensitivity to the match between topic and audience is an important factor in site selection.

IMAGE—THE CITY'S AND YOURS

People's perceptions of a city, admittedly a very subjective concept, influence how well the city will draw for a seminar. A city perceived as upscale or exotic will attract more participants than one viewed as depressing or dull. These perceptions may or may not be colored by facts; Detroit and Pittsburgh, for example, have undertaken large-scale civic improvements to recoup their image, yet many people continue to have a negative impression of them as "smokestack cities." This is not to suggest that these cities should not be chosen as seminar sites; for certain topics and at appropriate times of the year they may be ideal. But be aware of how your target market perceives a certain city before selecting it as your seminar location.

The city's image, whether good or bad, will reflect on your image as a presenter. If you choose a city with a positive image, you are more apt to be perceived positively than if you choose a city which, accurately or not, is viewed as undesirable.

A direct correlation exists between the city's image and the fee you can charge for your seminar. People in an upscale, sophisticated market are accustomed to spending more money for products and services and will not be put off by higher fees, provided they perceive that the seminar will benefit them.

FOREIGN COUNTRIES

Your seminar or workshop may also have profit potential outside the country. In many foreign cities, fluency in English is widespread among the business and professional communities. Any English-speaking countries are candidates, as are many cities in western Europe, including Paris and most of the industrial centers of Germany. Japan or Latin America might be viable choices, depending on the nature and appeal of your topic. Many American and Canadian seminar providers who do seminars abroad find it useful to work with a sponsor/promotion agency in the host country. While such firms add to expenses, their knowledge of the market makes use of them advantageous.

REDUCING THE RISK

No decision is completely risk-free, but the more you can reduce the element of uncertainty in your selection of a site, the better your chances for a profitable, successful seminar. One obvious technique for risk reduction is to rate locations based on past experience—your own and that of other seminar presenters. What type of response have you received to sites you have used in the past? To what degree was attendance influenced by the site, in your judgment? What did participants like or dislike about the site? Your hunches about which cities make good seminar locations are no doubt based on past experiences, but it might be valuable to write down your impressions and determine what exactly made those cities desirable (or undesirable) locations.

Do not overlook the experiences of other seminar sponsors in your selection of a site. By talking to other promoters, reading their reports and newsletters, and eliciting comments from their attendees, you can eliminate choices that have not worked well for others and focus on those where seminars in general seem to draw well. Remember: Every seminar is different. A city that was a "dud" for another seminar may be the ideal location for yours. Experience of others is one variable in your decision matrix, not an acid test.

The following list shows in priority order the twelve most profitable cities for programs geared to business managers and professionals, based on the opinions of 212 seminar providers surveyed by the author:

1. Los Angeles—Orange County
2. Washington, DC
3. New York City (metropolitan area)
4. Denver
5. Chicago
6. Dallas
7. San Francisco/San Jose
8. Boston
9. Atlanta
10. Minneapolis
11. Seattle
12. Tampa

TIMING

When to conduct your seminar is as important as where to conduct it. The following data suggest in priority order the best months of the year and days of the week to present seminars, according to the author's survey of 212 seminar providers:

Best Months and Days to Conduct Seminars

Business/Professional Programs (someone else pays the fee)		*Consumer/Personal Programs (fee paid by participant)*	
Months	*Days*	*Months*	*Days*
March	Wednesday	January	Thursday
October	Thursday	September	Saturday
April	Tuesday	October	Wednesday
September	Friday	March	Sunday
November	Saturday	April	Tuesday
January	Monday	June	Friday
February	Sunday	November	Monday
June		February	
May		May	
July		July	
August		December	
December		August	

When you are selecting the month, day, and time for your seminar or workshop, you should consider several important factors.

Vacations

Heavy vacation periods, such as the month of August or the last week in December, mean light seminar attendance. Even if potential participants might be willing to attend your seminar during vacation times, hotels may be booked up with tourists and other vacationers. Plan around popular vacation times so that your seminar does not suffer.

Holidays

National and religious holidays are bad times to run a seminar or workshop, as are dates of major national or local events such as political elections and sports events. Again, even if participants might be willing to attend, hotels may be booked up.

Special Events

Avoid conflicts with events of major significance to your potential participants, such as trade association or professional meetings. The leading trade publications within specific fields will usually list major events; keep informed and prevent scheduling conflicts. However, you may be able to take advantage of a national meeting in the same city by scheduling your seminar either immediately before or after, so attendees of the national meeting can attend your program as well, without additional travel expenses.

Transportation

Schedule your seminar to avoid rush-hour traffic patterns, particularly in highly congested, sprawling cities such as Washington, Houston, or Los Angeles. If your participants will be traveling to the seminar or workshop by plane, bus, or train, avoid peak travel days and times. You might do well to start your program a little later in the day—perhaps 9:30 A.M. instead of 8:00 A.M.—to allow participants to fly in from nearby cities on the day of the seminar instead of the night before.

Potential Labor Strife

As unlikely as it may seem, labor problems—strikes or job actions by airline personnel, taxi drivers, transit workers, or hotel staff—do occur and can wreak havoc with your scheduling. Check out the possibility of any such problems in your seminar site.

Convenience of Time and Day

Some professions have, by tradition or workload, light and heavy schedules on different days of the week or months of the year—you certainly would not want to schedule a program aimed at accountants during tax season. If the profession or trade your seminar is aimed at has a "light" day or month, make use of this advantage and schedule your seminar during that time, allowing sufficient travel time for out-of-town participants.

As a general rule, seminar promoters try to schedule seminars in northeastern cities for the fall and spring, and Sun Belt and West Coast seminars for the winter. This rule can be relaxed for cities where people are accustomed to coping with weather conditions. A seminar held in Minneapolis in February may draw surprisingly well, as people there are not fazed by snow and ice. A seminar held in Los Angeles during the rainy season may run into trouble, however, as people in that area are inclined to stay home when it is raining.

You can repeat your seminar once or twice or even several times in a city in one year, perhaps conducting it once in January and again in June. But some cities cannot sustain repeat seminars within a year, and others can sustain only a limited frequency of repeats. Topic and market size will be the determining factors. Research has revealed the profitability potential of repeat seminars in 27 cities, as follows:

Recommended Seminar/Workshop Repetitions in Major Market Areas for Maximum Annual Profit

Market Area	Times Per Year	Market Area	Times Per Year
Los Angeles	6	Kansas City	2
New York	6	Miami	2
Chicago	5	Milwaukee	2
Washington	4	Minneapolis	2
Boston	3	New Orleans	2
Denver	3	St. Louis	2
Detroit	3	San Diego	2
Houston	3	Cincinnati	1
Philadelphia	3	Phoenix	1
San Francisco	3	Pittsburgh	1
Seattle	3	Portland	1
Atlanta	2	San Antonio	1
Cleveland	2	Tampa	1
Dallas	2		

WEIGHING THE FACTORS

Once you have compiled some preliminary data and reviewed the factors important in site selection, what do you do with this information? How do you validate your hunches?

A model has been developed that assigns weights to the various factors discussed in this chapter (see Figure 9–1). These values are a reliable means of comparing both the relative importance of the different factors for a given city and the suitability of several cities.

The worksheet in Figure 9–1 lists the major factors in site selection and their weights. Four columns are provided for ranking the cities on your preselection list for each category. Simply enter the appropriate value for each criterion for every city, then add up the figures for each one and compare the totals. The city with the highest overall ranking would be your best selection, based on this evaluation.

Compare this finding with your initial hunch. Does the result support your intuitive feeling as to which city would be best? If so, the decision is an easy one. If not, you may want to reexamine your initial premises about which city is best. On the other hand, if your "hunch" city ranks a close second, or your gut feeling that your hunch is correct persists, do not be afraid to override the results obtained in this evaluation and go with your intuitive choice.

Criteria		City	City	City	City
Population of City:					
Under 100,000	1				
100,000–299,999	2				
300,000–599,999	4				
600,000–999,999	7				
1,000,000–1,399,999	11				
1,400,000 or more	16				
Population of SMSA (1)					
Under 450,000	1				
450,000–699,999	3				
700,000–1,299,999	6				
1,300,000–1,899,999	10				
1,900,000–2,799,999	16				
2,800,000 or more	22				
Growth Rate of SMSA Population: **Last 5 Years**					
Declined by more than 3%	0				
No growth to 2.9% decline	1				
Growth under 2.0%	3				
Growth of 2.1 to 4.0%	7				
Growth of 4.0% or more	12				
Unemployment Rate Compared **to National Average**					
Less by 3 %age points or more	15				
Less by 0.1 to 2.9 %age points	11				
Equal to national average	8				
Greater by 0.1 to 1.9 %age points	4				
Greater by 2 %age points or more	0				
Proximity to a City with **Population Equal to 150% or** **More of Candidate City**					
Less than 25 miles	0				
26 to 45 miles	2				
46 to 75 miles	5				
76 to 125 miles	8				
126 to 200 miles	11				
201 to 400 miles	15				
More than 400 miles	23				

Figure 9–1. Site selection worksheet.

Criteria		City	City	City	City
Availability of Daily Scheduled **Non-Stop Airline Service** *(2)*					
To 3 or fewer cities	1				
To 4 to 8 cities	4				
To 9 to 15 cities	9				
To 16 or more cities	17				
Number of Households in SMSA **Receiving a Metropolitan** **Daily Newspaper** *(3)*					
Under 50%	0				
50 to 59.9%	3				
60 to 64.9%	5				
65 to 69.9%	9				
70% or more	15				
Number of First Class Hotels **with 100+ Guest Rooms** *(4)*					
None	0				
1 or 2	1				
3 to 5	3				
6 to 10	7				
11 to 20	12				
21 or more	18				
Number of Major League **Sports Franchises in SMSA**					
None	2				
One	5				
2 or 3	11				
4 or more	17				
City Is Largest City in the State					
Add	8				
City Has Convention Center **Which Seats 1,500 or More** **Theater Style**					
Add	6				

Criteria		City	City	City	City
Number of Colleges and Universities in City and Within 15 Miles of City Limits with 4,500 (FTE) Students or More *(5)*					
None	0				
One	2				
2 to 4	7				
5 to 9	15				
10 or more	22				
Colleges or Universities Within City Limits with 20,000 (FTE) Students or More					
None	0				
One	7				
Two	11				
Three or more	19				
Number of Fortune 500 Companies with Corporate Headquarters Within City Limits					
None	0				
1 to 3	3				
4 to 7	8				
8 to 12	16				
13 or more	29				
Percentage of Work Force Within the SMSA in the Employ of Government Agencies					
Less than 3%	1				
3.0 to 6.5%	3				
6.6 to 15%	6				
15.1 to 22.4%	10				
22.5% or more	15				
Median Household Income in SMSA					
Below national average by 5%+	0				
Below national average by less than 5%	3				
Equal to national average	6				
Above national average by less than 5%	10				
Above national average by 5%+	14				

Criteria		City	City	City	City
City Has the Following:					
Professional opera company, add	9				
Professional symphony company, add	6				
Professional theater company, add	3				
City Has the Following:					
Medical school enrolling 100+	9				
Law school enrolling 125+	6				
City Is Served by 3 or More Interstate Highways					
Add	9				
Number of Television Stations with Broadcasting Studios Within City Limits					
Three or less	1				
4 to 6	5				
7 or more	11				
Percentage of Total National Population Living Within 300 Miles of City Center					
Three percent or less	0				
3.1 to 6.4%	5				
6.5 to 10.4%	9				
10.5 to 18.4%	15				
18.5% or more	22				
Distance from State Capital					
150 miles or more	1				
90 to 149 miles	6				
45 to 89 miles	7				
20 to 44 miles	10				
Less than 20 or capital city	14				
Totals					

Notes:

(1) SMSA (Standard Metropolitan Statistical Area) population figures are available from the United States Census Bureau and a wide variety of other sources.

(2) This information is available from either the pocket or office editions of the *Official Airline Guide*.

(3) Consult *Newspaper Circulation Analysis*, published by Standard Rate and Data Service.

(4) It is suggested that you use one of the standard tour guides' two highest classifications.

(5) FTE: Full Time Equivalent.

10

SELECTING HOTELS AND CONFERENCE FACILITIES

Choosing the right facility to host your seminar or meeting can be a critical factor in its success. Improper selection can leave you with a huge, empty room, or a room which, even if it is filled, is so expensive that making a profit becomes impossible. In this chapter we will discuss what to look for in a facility and how to deal with your chosen facility to ensure that all of your needs are met.

In evaluating a facility, the first question you need to ask is: Where will my participants feel most comfortable? Don't enter your search with the assumption that you absolutely must give your seminar in the Grand Ballroom of the fanciest hotel in town. You may want to use a hotel, or you may find it appropriate to use a church basement or the local high school auditorium. Your site should not be so fancy that your participants feel uncomfortable, nor so downtrodden that they are uneasy or concerned for their safety.

Try to select a place that most of your participants will find accommodating and easy to locate. Most business seminars are conducted in first-class business hotels because business people are accustomed to going there and they feel comfortable there. For the same reason, some seminars are conducted in church basements: people who attend those seminars are comfortable there—and rental is certainly less costly for a church basement than for a first-class hotel. On the other hand, be aware that the location of your site will affect people's perceptions of your seminar. Even if people feel comfortable in a church basement, they may not feel that first-class business seminars would be given there.

In this chapter, we will primarily discuss hotels as sites for seminars and meetings, but keep in mind that few hotels can handle more than 500 participants at a time; if you are expecting more than 500 attendees, you should consider a convention center. Be aware, however, that convention centers usually have very little to recommend them other than size. Compared to business hotels, they tend to be less intimate, they often have fewer services immediately available, specific areas and rooms are usually more difficult for people to find, and their parking facility is generally more complicated and farther away from the meeting rooms.

Once you have decided on the type of site you want, you need to begin considering the area in which you want to hold your seminar. There are a number of factors to consider. The first is traffic and transportation. What are the traffic conditions around the facility? What is the availability of public transportation, if public transportation is important in that market area? For example, in New York City, San Francisco, or many traditionally concentrated smaller cities, you wouldn't want to be located where public transportation almost to the door of the facility is unavailable, because many prospective participants do not have cars or will not drive them into the business district if they do have them.

On the other hand, in some of the newer and more spread-out market areas like Los Angeles or Dallas, public transportation is probably a negligible factor but traffic congestion is a major concern. You don't want to dump people out in downtown Los Angeles at 5:00 P.M., when the area suffers from a severe case of gridlock. Look carefully at where facilities, particularly the more recently built hotels, are located. Airport locations are often very good and quite convenient. Los Angeles International Airport, for example, is one of the most convenient places in the entire metropolitan area. The noise factor at an airport must be evaluated, however, especially if the buildings are not new enough to have proper acoustic insulation.

If you are holding a multiday seminar, does your location offer anything for your participants to do after the seminar is over for the day? One of the problems of dumping people out in downtown Los Angeles at 5 P.M. is that there are few places in the immediate area for them to go. There are very few shops, restaurants, or bars, and they are difficult to get to. People in downtown Los Angeles drive rather than walk from one end of the area to the other, but you have quite the reverse situation in New York or San Francisco, where there are plenty of things to do and people would appreciate having an hour or two in the city to have dinner, go to the theater, or do some shopping or sightseeing. You should probably avoid airport hotels for multiday seminars in cities such as Houston, where it is somewhat difficult (or costly) to get from the airport into the city. There is simply nothing to do at most airport locations after you have walked around and looked at a gift shop. People would usually prefer to be in the city, particularly if it has attractions.

Participant safety is a vital factor, particularly in major industrial cities with high crime rates. You may not want to hold seminars in central city areas because of the crime problem and the risk to your participants. From that perspective, suburban locations might be better, but be aware that some people will not come into the central city and others will not go to the suburbs. For example, it is usually to your advantage to hold two seminars in Chicago—one in the Loop or on North Michigan Avenue and the other in the suburbs, perhaps near O'Hare International Airport. People will contact you and proudly say that they haven't been in downtown Chicago in 27 years and they are never going there again; you are going to lose these people unless you offer your seminar in the suburbs. But other prospective attendees in Chicago don't have cars and can't go to the suburbs, so two programs are in order, to service the market adequately.

Once you have chosen an area, it is time to begin considering specific sites. If possible (and inexpensive), try to visit the sites you are considering. Make sure that they have adequate facilities: good lighting, quality audiovisual equipment, moderately priced restaurants that serve during advantageous hours, reasonable parking, comfortable sleeping rooms, and so on. The conference rooms should allow easy entry and exit for numbers of people, offer accessibility for the handicapped, be well ventilated, have adequate safety features, and be reasonably close to restrooms. Hotel and conference facility sales personnel sometimes leave you with the impression that small, confining rooms will hold "hundreds of people"; make sure that your meeting room will hold as many people as the facility management claims. (Where fire-safety capacities are posted, you can be sure your space has not been undersold.)

Can the room be found? Many hotels have tacked on additional meeting rooms in barn-like structures accessible only through obscure passageways off the main facility. Don't make your participants take elevators, search down narrow corridors, or follow paper arrows taped to walls to find your meeting room.

Another common practice among hotels anxious to capture more of the lucrative conference business is to convert sleeping rooms into meeting rooms. These typically have low ceilings, bathrooms jutting into the middle of the meeting room, and inadequate ventilation, and should be avoided if at all possible.

Be wary of old properties. They tend to suffer from certain realities of age which may make them less-than-ideal places to hold a seminar or a meeting. Old buildings are often plagued by posts that obscure view, inadequate air conditioning, poor traffic movement within the property, room configurations not designed for seminars and workshops, inadequate parking, insufficient lighting, inadequate power supply, and less than state-of-the-art visual support and public address systems.

LEAVING YOUR HOMETOWN

All of this information is relatively easy to obtain about the facilities in your hometown, but seminar presenters rarely enjoy the luxury of offering seminars only in their own backyard. If you are going into a city of which you have no knowledge, how do you select a hotel? The best way to start is to obtain a travel guide published by the American Automobile Association (AAA), Mobil Oil Corporation, or any of several others. Turn to the city you are considering and read about the general layout. Try to determine which part of town is the up-and-coming area, and which section is downtrodden. Get as much information about the city's character as you reasonably can in a short period of time, and then look for any hotels that are well-rated (three or four stars).

Once you have identified all of the three- or four-star hotels, look for the major chains. More specifically, look for chains such as Hyatt, Westin, Marriott, Four Seasons, and other companies who almost always own their own properties, or who have historically demonstrated a concern for the quality of the property that bears their name. Be careful here: some major chains do not own most of their own properties. They will allow any motel willing to accept their reservation service to hang a sign outside with the name of their chain on it and dupe people into thinking that the facility is the equivalent of a property with the same name in another city—which it may well not be.

You don't need to be too concerned about the locations of the major hotels. Most of the leading hotel chains have large market research departments which spend literally millions of dollars a year figuring out where their properties should be and of what quality their properties should be in each locale. There is no sense in reinventing the wheel.

Once you have identified the major chains whose properties in the area are available and of good repute, you need to take a look at the "rack rate," the open general rate which a hotel advertises for a sleeping room. Everything else being equal, you should go with the hotel that has a rate at the higher end of the spectrum. For example, you may find that your candidate city has a Marriott, a Hyatt, and a Westin (all four-star hotels), but the Hyatt can extract an extra $20 a night for its rooms. There must be a reason for this difference, and the reason is often that the more expensive hotel is regarded as a better hotel. It is probably newer and perhaps is enjoying "in" status at this time; if you are picking a place for a business or professional seminar, it would probably be in your best interests to go there rather than to a less expensive hotel.

You might have to reconsider, however, if you are offering a multiday seminar and/or your marketing suggests that participants coming in from out-of-town are going to stay overnight. In such cases a hotel with a lower rack rate would be better, since the cost of staying overnight may well be an important factor in prospects' decision to attend your seminar.

To assist you in your search, the following list of favorite hotel locations for holding seminars and workshops in the major market areas may be helpful. This list was compiled from the preferences stated by 209 seminar and workshop promoters:

Atlanta	Hyatt Regency, Westin, Marriott-City Center, Hilton
Boston	Hyatt Regency, Marriott Long Wharf, Marriott (West suburbs)

Chicago	Westin, Hyatt Regency-Chicago, Hyatt Regency-O'Hare, Marriott-Airport, Chicago Marriott, Palmer House, Holiday Inn-Merchandise Mart, Grand Hyatt (Water Tower)
Dallas	Hyatt Regency, Anatole, Marriott-Market Center
Denver	Fairmont, Marriott, Marriott Tech Center, Brown Palace, Clarion Denver Inn, Stapleton Plaza
Houston	Westin-Galleria, Westin-Oaks, Hyatt Regency, Houston Sheraton
Los Angeles	Marriott-Airport, Hyatt-Airport, Sheraton Universal, Century Plaza, Beverly Hilton, Hyatt Regency, Pasadena Hilton
Miami	Marriott, Hyatt Regency
Minneapolis	Marriott, Hyatt Regency, Radisson South
New Orleans	Marriott, Hilton, Hyatt Regency
New York	Essex House, Warwick, Marriott-LGA, Hilton-JFK, Grand Hyatt, New York Hilton, Saddle Brook Marriott (NJ), Stamford Marriott (CT)
Orange Co., CA	Westin-South Coast Plaza, Newport Beach Marriott, Newporter, Disneyland Hotel, Anaheim Hilton
Phoenix	Hyatt Regency, Biltmore
Portland, OR	Marriott, Westin, Hilton
San Diego	Town & Country, Sheraton Harbor Island, Executive, Little American Westgate, Hilton
San Francisco	Westin St. Francis, Grand Hyatt (Union Square), Hyatt Regency, Airport Hilton, Clift, Mark Hopkins, Fairmont
San Jose	Red Lion Inn, Hyatt, Marriott-Santa Clara
Seattle	Four Seasons Olympic, Red Lion Inn-Airport, Westin, Meany Tower
Washington, DC	Hyatt Regency, Madison, Capital Hilton, Four Seasons, Washington Hilton, Key Bridge Marriott, Twin Bridge Marriott, Hyatt Regency-Crystal City, Marriott-Crystal City, Stouffer's National Center

Remember that there are many other fine hotels for giving seminars in these cities. These are not the only hotels or even the best, merely the preferred choices of the respondents to a survey. Also, there are new hotels opening in these cities on a fairly regular basis. Because newer hotels are less likely to have been used by the survey respondents, they are less likely to show up on such a preference survey.

HOW LARGE A ROOM?

Determining how large a room to rent can be very tricky. If this is not the first time you have given this seminar, then you probably know how many people to expect. The first time out, however, you don't know and you have to take a risk. You will need to choose between spending less money and having a room that may be inadequate for the number of people who show up, or spending more money and having a big room that may be sparsely populated. You must decide which risk you prefer to take the first time out.

How you set up the room will affect the size of the room you choose. Allowing for numerous variations, there are four basic ways in which the chairs and tables in a room are set up for almost all programs. The first is called *conference style:* one large table with chairs set around it. This style is best suited for small conferences, particularly when a great deal of participant interaction is encouraged. The second style is *U-shaped:* tables arranged in a U with chairs on the outside facing in. This style is recommended for slightly larger groups where ongoing group interaction is anticipated. The third style is *classroom:* several rows of tables, usually with an aisle down the middle, with chairs all facing toward the front of the room. This is best suited for lecture-type seminars where a great deal of note taking is expected. The fourth style is *theatre style:* rows of chairs, all facing the front of the room. This is suitable for large groups where the participants are not expected to do much writing. Obviously, any one of many variations to these basic arrangements might be preferable for your seminar. For example, one variation is workshop style: round tables with chairs, allowing participants to interact in smaller groups as well as to view front-of-the-room activities.

Using these differing styles of room setup can allow you flexibility in the numbers of participants you can accommodate. For instance, you might order a room set up classroom style and find that you have far too many participants, in which case you can switch to theatre-style seating. This will typically allow you to seat 50 to 60 percent more people, which means that you will not have to turn away paying participants. Last-minute cancellations are not uncommon for hotels. You may find that the hotel can move you to larger or smaller quarters, as need dictates, as you near the seminar date. Figure 10–1 may serve as a useful checklist for evaluating candidate properties. Even after selecting your facility, keep

FACILITIES SELECTION CHECKLIST

City _____ Seminar _____ Date(s) _____

Anticipated Registration _____

Set-up Required _____

Property Name	Used Before: Rated Low (1) to High (5)	Guide/ Tour Book Rating	Charge for Rental	Capacity This Type Set-Up	Guest Room Charge	Food & Bev Charge	Notes

Figure 10–1. Checklist/record for selecting seminar facilities.

completed forms in a file; you may save time when you next have to book a facility in that city.

You have chosen your hotel. It is in the right area, it is part of a reputable chain, and its rack rate is high enough to convince you of its quality. Before you call the hotel to make the arrangements, there are some things of which you should be aware. First, you have to understand that there are really no fixed prices in the hotel business. Everything is based on what the traffic will bear. This is true of guest rooms, meeting rooms, meal prices, and extras. The entire conference business is predicted on how much hotels can extract from *this* customer and how many times a day they can rent *this* room and *this* projector, or resell *this* coffee. Once you realize this, you know that you are in a position to dicker.

The first trick to getting a good price for a room is knowing whom to talk to. Most major hotel chains have national sales offices, with branches in many cities. Booking through them will save the cost of a few toll calls and the time expended making arrangements, but you can almost always get a better price by negotiating directly with the selected property itself.

Most hotels have both sales and catering departments. The sales office usually handles meetings where sleeping rooms are involved; indeed, they base the meeting room rate on the number of sleeping rooms booked. If you expect out-of-town people, arrange for the sales office to block out a number of rooms, often at lower rates, for your participants and for yourself. Make careful note of the cutoff date for reservations— the date by which the hotel needs to be told exactly how many of the blocked rooms are actually going to be used. If they are not told, you may be stuck with paying for all of your unused rooms which the hotel had reserved. Even if you are not planning on having people spend the night at the hotel, have the sales or catering department book your room, because an in-house booking will often get you a better conference room rate.

Keep in mind that hotels make a large percentage of their money on the sale of food and drinks, so they prefer to sell catered banquets and sleeping rooms along with their meeting rooms. In order of priority, most hotels like to book functions as follows:

1. Conventions with sleeping rooms and catered meals
2. Meetings with sleeping rooms
3. Catered meals, which may include meetings
4. Meetings without catered meals or sleeping rooms

These priorities can present a problem for the seminar promoter with a one-day or partial-day program. Some hotels will not commit space for seminars without meals and/or sleeping rooms until 60 days, six weeks, or even 30 days prior to your seminar date. They hope to snare a more profitable customer for that space and do not want to tie it up until they are sure they can do no better than the no-meal, no-sleeping-room function you are attempting to book.

If an earlier commitment is required because of long-range planning or a direct mail campaign, more than one seminar promoter has responded by being a bit deceitful. Some of my colleagues inform the hotel that they will hold a meal or they block sleeping rooms. Later, say 15 days prior to the meeting, they cancel the lunch or room block. They cannot use this same ploy with a given hotel too often, but the turnover of hotel sales and catering personnel provides more opportunities than you might think to repeat this strategy, should it prove absolutely necessary. A better solution is to book hotels which discourage/don't handle convention business. They are typically smaller, sometimes more "residential."

If a program runs for a single day or a few hours, the catering department usually handles the arrangements. They get the rooms which the sales department does not sell, so if the catering department says that they have no rooms available, try double-checking with the sales department before giving up on the property. If there are no rooms, is it because of a convention which will lock you and your participants out of every hotel in that city, or is it just a busy day for that particular hotel?

The way you ask can have as much impact on the price of a meeting room as whom you ask. Do not call up the hotel and say, "I'm so-and-so from a big-shot seminar company. We do programs all over the world. We are going to do our program in Cincinnati and we've selected your hotel. I need a room that will hold 50 people." They will say to themselves, "Well, this is a big seminar company, they do seminars all over the world, so they're used to paying New York City prices, so . . . ." They will then report to you that they can put you in the Green Room, which will cost $300 and you have now rented the Green Room for $300.

You would do far better to call up and say, "You've never heard of me before, I know, and I don't have any credit with you, but I have been giving these meetings in my living room, and people have been complaining about parking at my house, so would you have a room that would hold 30 or 35 people?" Now they will say to themselves, "It sounds like they've never rented a hotel room before. I don't want to shock them into going somewhere else, so . . . ." They will then report that they can put you in the Green Room for $125 and you have just rented the Green Room for $125. You may, however, be able to rent it for even less if you say to them, "$125!," as if you have just been held up at gunpoint, and then go on to say, "I just wanted to use the room for the day, I didn't want to buy the hotel." They may offer to cut the price even further. Another approach at that point might be to say, "Gee, it sounds lovely, but that's beyond my budget." At that point they'll ask, "What's your budget?" and you'll respond, "I'm not authorized to spend more than $90." They may say, "Just a minute, we'll go talk to the Catering Manager," and perhaps come back with, "I'm sorry we can't rent the room for $90. However, the Catering Manager, in the hopes of getting your future business, would be willing to let the room go for $110." Now you have just rented the Green Room for $110. Keep in mind that everything is negotiable, and how much you pay will be a function of how you ask.

There are, of course, other factors that control the price of facilities and services. You should realize that a hotel has an inventory and the more inventory they have, the more willing they are to dicker with you. If you find yourself in New York City in the middle of the seminar season (fall or spring), when virtually every hotel in town is booked up, and a hotel has one room left while you are still six weeks away from the seminar, they have a very good chance of renting that room at a higher price to someone else, so they aren't going to be easy to bargain with. Your best negotiating stance comes from first finding a property that will book your seminar at a reasonably acceptable price, then continuing to contact other properties to see whether you can make a better deal. Since you can then be far more cavalier, knowing that you have an ace up your sleeve and that if all else fails you still have a place to hold your seminar, you may run into some incredible deal. The more cavalier you are, the better price you are probably going to get, potentially reducing your expenses considerably.

If you discover a hotel or hotel chain with which you are particularly pleased and which you intend to use on a regular basis, it is probably a good idea to establish credit with that hotel or chain. This can be difficult with the first hotel, but once you can list several hotels as references, most of the others will be happy to extend you credit. Be aware that if you don't have credit, most hotels will require a not insubstantial deposit to hold the room, with the balance due on the day of the seminar.

MAKING THE ARRANGEMENTS

Once you have arranged for the price of the room, you will need to make the specific arrangements about setup, schedule, beverage and food service, and other details. Here again you must be careful because many hotels have a tendency to provide and price such services in a way that is financially beneficial for them. For example, you normally save about 30 percent buying coffee by the gallon (approximately 20 cups) instead of by the cup. Be sure that the hotel provides small cups, not 12-ounce soup bowls. Participants who want more can get a refill, while those who don't drink as much won't be wasting coffee. Leave specific instructions about coffee refills. If you are serving coffee when people arrive at 8:30 A.M. and again at the first break at 10:00 A.M., don't let the hotel take away the remaining coffee from the 8:30 break and sell it back to you an hour later. Tell them to *replenish up to the original order.* That way you pay only for coffee actually consumed at the first break.

When you arrange for audiovisual equipment, be very specific. If you order a projector, you probably will not need a separate projection table if you have a speaker's table in front, but unless you tell them not to, many hotels will provide one and charge you for it. If you order an overhead projector, specify that you are bringing your own acetate and pens, or you will end up paying for supplies you did not use.

SHOULD YOU TAKE YOUR PARTICIPANTS TO LUNCH?

Seminar and workshop providers often wonder whether serving lunch (or other meals) at their programs increases participant satisfaction or enrollment levels. Including meals not only has a major impact on program expense but gives most providers an administrative headache. The following research data on the impact of meals may help you make the right decision. With the national average price of catered lunch now running close to $17 per person, making this decision correctly has important economic consequences.

Two-Day Management Seminar for Executives

Using direct mail, the sponsor promoted a two-day, $695 seminar on strategic planning for higher-income executives. Rented mailing lists were combined and split to create two promotionally identical lists of 22,345 each. Half of the prospects received a promotional brochure indicating that the fee included lunch being served both days. The balance received a brochure indicating that lunch would not be served. The lunch-included list produced 36 registrations and the no-lunch brochure yielded 38 registrations. Free lunches apparently had little or no impact on the decision to attend.

A second test, for the same seminar, yielded a different result. Here the lunch-included test indicated that at each luncheon a speaker would be included and the brochure described the attributes of the speaker and benefits to be obtained by hearing the speaker. Each mailing was 28,871 units. The lunch-included mailing produced 47 registrations. The no-lunch mailing resulted in 41 registrations. With a lunch cost of $23 (including tax and tip) and speaker compensation and expenses of $1,432, it was clearly more profitable to include the lunch.

The sponsor concluded that when the lunch is viewed as an integral part of the learning experience, it should be packaged with the seminar. When the lunch is a nonrelated benefit, it does not impact registrations.

One-Day $95 Seminar for Small Business Owners

This university-sponsored seminar, promoted through direct mail, used a controlled, split-run test to assess the marketing pull of a lunch. Half of the mailings (14,543) indicated that lunch would be included at the on-campus event. Half made no mention of lunch. Eighty-three registrations were received from the lunch-included list and 77 were received from the lunch-not-mentioned list. The additional revenue from the lunch-included group equaled $570. At a cost of $8.93 for each lunch served, it would have clearly been more profitable to not serve the lunch. And, were the seminar not held on campus, the lunch would likely have been even more expensive.

An Optional Meal Program

In this test the provider wanted to compare a meal-included package versus an optional meal package. A controlled test of a combined mailing list was used to produce three promotionally equal mailing lists of 22,410. One list received a brochure describing a three-day conference on economics which included five meals and one cocktail party at a fee of $1,250; the second list received the same brochure but was offered the conference at $1,095 and a meal–party package as an optional additional purchase at $155. The last list received only the conference offering at $1,095. The results were interesting.

The $1,250 meals-included offer produced 25 registrations; the $1,095 + $155 meal package offer yielded 32 registrations (with 17 taking the meal package), and the $1,095 offer with no mention of meals resulted in 20 registrations. Those not taking the meal package in the group that produced the 32 registrations received a follow-up promotion for the meal package. Six more signed up. The group that was not offered the meal package at all received a similar follow-up promotion. Only eight of the 20 upgraded to the meal plan.

Obviously, the marketing impact of serving meals is a function of the preference of the individual participant and the type of program. Programs that involve networking and meal functions as integral parts of the seminar are clearly the ones where meals are most likely to have the greatest promotional benefit.

Participant Satisfaction

Optional meals may be the best bet. That conclusion is supported by a comprehensive customer satisfaction study done by a major seminar provider. The provider undertook a longitudinal study of 1,823 alumni of seminars over a one-year period. Most of the data were collected by mail, but follow-up phone interviews were conducted with 132 of the respondents to gain further insight into the meaning of the findings. The results pointed out that meals may not be all that important from either a marketing or customer satisfaction vantage.

Attitudes of Respondents	Those Who Attended a Seminar Where	
	Lunch Was Served	Lunch Was Not Served
1. The fact that lunch was included as a part of the program was an important inducement in my decision to attend.	39.3%	NA
2. I prefer to attend seminars where there is no group lunch. I would rather eat alone, put together my own group, or use the time to make phone calls, etc.	50.5	54.2%
3. Which would you prefer most?		
Prearranged lunch	32.3	29.6
Coupon that could be exchanged at the hotel coffee shop for a lunch priced at up to $10	24.4	20.8
A $10 reduction in seminar fee and prearranged lunch or coupon	43.3	49.6
4. If lunch had not been included with the seminar would you have attended anyway? (yes)	91.2	NA

The data, of course, reflect the findings of only one provider with respect to alumni. Other providers might have participants with different attitudes—and there may well be a big difference between alumni and prospects. You should test your own programs to determine whether meals are desirable or necessary.

FINAL ARRANGEMENTS

When possible, arrive at the hotel early in the morning on the day of the seminar or stay over the night before, so that you can double-check all of the arrangements. Many hotels run their meetings very poorly and seem to have included Murphy's Law as one of their managerial tenets. Expect to have to do everything yourself and view anything done in advance as a welcome surprise.

Careful communication with the hotel will reduce, although by no means eliminate, mismanagement of your program. The instructions in Figure 10–2 for booking and setting up meeting facilities can be very helpful in this regard, both in making your wishes clearly known to the hotel and providing you with some backup of exactly what you ordered. Fill in as much of the information as you can before you start contacting facilities. When you have chosen one, make sure to record the name of the representative with whom you have made the arrangements. Based on what the representative tells you, fill in the rest of the form and send two copies addressed to the hotel representative, with the request that one copy be signed and returned to you.

When the seminar is over and you get the bill, look it over carefully. Considering the number of affairs with which a hotel has to deal simultaneously, and the fact that many hotels are notorious for their poor bookkeeping, it is hardly surprising that occasionally items which you did not order will show up on your bill. When this happens, call or write the hotel and point out the error, noting that you are prepared to back it up with your signed Setup Instructions. Most hotels, desirous of your repeat business, will be cooperative.

(Letterhead)

MEETING FACILITIES BOOKING AND SETUP:
CONFIRMATION AGREEMENT

To: _____

_____

_____

_____

_____

Attn: _____

Date: _____

Confirms verbal reservation of: _____

Made with: _____

Function date(s): _____

1. Please post meeting as follows:

   _____

2. Please set room for _____ people: ____ theater style ____ school room
   ____ conference ____ other: _____

   _____

   ____ Diagram of setup is attached; please follow.

3. It is our understanding that we will be using the room named:

   _____

4. It is our understanding that this room will hold a maximum of _____
   persons, when set in the style specified above.

5. Please provide the following equipment:
   ____ Head table for _____ people with chairs
   ____ Lectern: ____ Standing ____ Table top
   ____ Microphone(s): ____ Podium ____ Hand-held ____ Lavalier
        Number = _____
   ____ Overhead projector for transparencies
   ____ Slide projector(s); Number = _____
   ____ 16mm movie projector(s); Number = _____
   ____ Opaque projector(s); Number = _____
   ____ Video monitor(s); Number = _____ Size = _____
   ____ Audio recorder(s); Number = ____ ____ Cassette ____ Reel-to-reel
   ____ Projection screen(s); Number = _____ Size = _____
   ____ Chalk board(s); Number = _____ Size = _____
   ____ Flip chart(s); Number = _____ Size = _____
   ____ Display table(s); Number = _____ Size = _____
   ____ Registration table(s); Number = _____ Size = _____
   ____ Hat and coat rack
   ____ Other: _____

   _____

Figure 10–2. Form for describing and confirming booking and setup of facilities.

6. This room must be set up and ready for use at _____.

7. If there is a telephone in the room, please inform the Operator that no calls are to be put through to the room after _____. Have messages brought to the meeting room registration table.

8. Please provide ice water and glasses ____ at rear of room ____ on each table ____ on head table. The room will be vacant between the hours of _____ and _____. Please use this time to refresh the water and room.

9. Please provide the following beverage or food and beverage service in the quantities indicated at the times specified below:

Time: _____   Refreshment: _____   Quantity: _____

_____   _____   _____

_____   _____   _____

_____   _____   _____

_____   _____   _____

____ Please do not remove beverage service at end of the break. Leave setup and simply refill as needed for next break.

____ Locate food and beverage service as follows: _____

_____.

10. Please provide _____ standard ____ single ____ double guest rooms for overnight accommodations on _____, at the lowest available rate. Reservation(s) should be ____ guaranteed for late arrival. Reservations should be confirmed in writing and held in the name(s) of: _____.

Checkout date = _____.

11. Terms of payment for charges will be: _____.

It is our understanding that the charges will be:

Room rental	$_____
Food and beverage service	$_____
Audiovisual	$_____
Guest room rental	$_____

12. Special instructions: _____

_____

_____

_____.

Thank you for your attention to these details. Please sign below, acknowledging receipt of this information and return a signed copy for our files. If you have any questions please call me at _____.

Thank you.

Sincerely,

Acknowledged by _____

for _____

Date _____

Figure 10–2. (*continued*)

11

PRICING YOUR PROGRAM

An understanding of appropriate price-setting strategies for seminars and workshops begins with a basic principle of demand: the higher the price (all other things being equal), the lower the sales of the product or service. Having readily grasped this simple concept, some promoters jump to the conclusion that they should set the price for their seminars at the lower end of the scale in order to ensure a maximum turnout.

Setting a price to maximize attendance, while it may have certain side benefits or meet other objectives, will not necessarily ensure higher profits. With maximum profits as the ultimate objective, the seminar promoter should look not only at the relationship between price and volume but also at the impact of a pricing decision on total profitability.

Generally speaking, the price for a seminar or workshop should be set at the highest level participants are willing to pay to attend. Not everyone within the same target market will respond uniformly to a given price. What some consider to be a reasonable figure, others may find too high for the perceived value. Thus, because of the very nature of the marketplace, price setting involves a certain element of subjectivity.

To ascertain the overall price sensitivity of their target market, some promoters conduct market tests. More reliable and usually less expensive than market research, a simple, well-designed test will provide some insight into the market's perception of the value of a given seminar.

Even with the most thorough market testing, promoters cannot determine with absolute certainty the relationship between the price charged and the volume of paid attendance. To further complicate matters, the impact of a volume increase on direct costs must be considered in order to determine overall profitability. For example, a higher price may generate lower attendance, but the profitability per participant may increase due to lower direct costs. A lower price should result in higher attendance, but the increase in direct costs may have a negative impact on profitability. The optimal price is that at which the ratio between price and volume reaches its most profitable level.

RELEVANT VARIABLES

This elusive relationship between the price/volume ratio and profitability is influenced by a number of variables: length of program, quantity and quality of program materials, time of day the seminar is given, location of the seminar, and so on. Testing for each of these variables individually in most cases will not be possible, but the promoter should take them into account in the pricing decision.

Length of Program

People are usually willing to pay more for a program that they perceive as being complete and substantial. A program that lasts a full day rather than a half-day, or two days rather than one, will in most cases be able to support a higher price schedule because prospective participants will be more apt to perceive the program as valuable and worthwhile. This perception of value will be balanced by countervailing concerns, such as the need for cost consciousness. For example, during a recession, a half-day program at a lower price may do better than a longer session. From the promoter's point of view, costs for a half-day and a one-day program could be equal, which may result in higher profitability.

Quantity and Quality of Program Materials

The prospects' perception of value is also affected by the types of materials that will be distributed at the seminar. Providing participants with workbooks, outlines, reports, and other handouts may justify a higher price, provided these materials are perceived as having additional value for the dollars spent. The cost involved in producing these materials must also be taken into account—profits could actually be reduced if the cost is too high.

Time of Day/Day(s) of the Week

Certain times of day and days of the week may be more conducive than others to attendance at a given seminar. Ideally, the program would be scheduled for the day and time perceived as most desirable by the market. But if the program has to be held at some other time, a lower price may be warranted to produce an optimal price/volume ratio.

Location

Even if the price is perceived as reasonable by most prospects, the expense of traveling to the seminar site may induce some otherwise willing prospects not to attend. Some locations, perceived as intrinsically more desirable than others, may be able to support a higher price.

SEMINAR AND WORKSHOP FEES: PSYCHOLOGICAL PRICE BARRIERS DO MAKE A DIFFERENCE

Seminar, workshop, class, and conference providers consistently obtain less registration revenue than they could have because they fail to consider psychological price barriers when setting program fees. A program priced at $85 could have been priced at $95 or $99; a program priced at $155 would have produced higher profit had it been priced at $145. Research has revealed that prospective participants make their enrollment decision, in part, based upon psychological price perceptions. Let's look at three recent research studies.

One-Day First-Line Supervisory Skills Seminar

Sponsored by a major university, this seminar, a consistent winner for five years, was priced during 1988 at $120. The sponsor decided to raise the price for this hot seller to $165 for 1989. The marketing consultant advised that the program would produce a higher total profit at $145 or $149, below the $150 psychological price barrier. Though not convinced, the sponsor agreed to test price.

A total mailing list of 28,212 names, including both in-house and rented names, was subjected to merge/purge and split on an every-other-name basis to create two promotionally identical lists of 14,106. Both groups were sent an 11″ × 17″ self-mailer identical in every respect except for prices listed. Group A received a brochure indicating a fee of $165; group B's had a price of $149.

In Group A, 71 registrants paid $165, producing receipts of $11,715. Total promotion cost for each campaign was $4,090.74, and program conduct/delivery costs were $2,117.30 for the Group A seminar. Thus, the $165 session produced a program profit of $5,506.96. The sponsor was pleased. Average program profit during 1988 had been $4,735.87.

But, would the fee of $149 do even better? In Group B, 87 registered and paid; receipts were $12,963. Marketing expense was the same as the Group A program, but the greater number of participants in the Group B program resulted in a higher conduct/delivery cost: $2,229.16. Total program profit was $6,643.10.

Clearly, the $149 fee was more profitable. Research strongly suggests that pricing just below the $150 psychological price barrier is preferable to pricing at or just above the barrier.

Psychological Price Barriers: What Are They?

When setting program fees, know and make use of psychological price barriers. They can have a strong impact on revenues, profits, and program size. All products and services have psychological price barriers. For seminars, workshops, conferences, and classes, they are: $50, $100, $150, $200, $250, $300, and even hundreds thereafter.

You will secure higher registrations, greater revenue, and higher total program profit by moving up to and backing slightly away from the barrier than by pricing at or above the barrier: set a fee at $95 or $99 rather than $100, at $495 rather than $500. As retailers have known for eons, $399 seems to the buyer to be a great deal less than $400. Conversely, don't rob yourself of valuable revenues by pricing too far below the barrier. Some providers mistakenly think that they will enhance program profit by setting a price such as $85 rather than $95 or $99, or $450 rather than $495. They don't. To the prospective participant, the difference between $650 and $695 either isn't noticed or is so lacking in significance that it does not alter the buying decision, as shown in the next example.

Two-Day Conference on Financing Entrepreneurial Enterprises

Eight sessions of this program, in different geographical locations, were planned by the sponsor. Using random selection, four locations were promoted at a price of $550 and the other four at $595. Although the total number of prospects promoted varied from location to location based on market size, the cost of promotion per 1,000 pieces mailed was equal to $343. The total registration revenue per 1,000 pieces mailed was higher at the $595 fee, although the registrations per 1,000 pieces mailed were about equal.

Session	Fee Charged	Number of Registrants/ 1,000 Pieces Mailed	Total Revenue/ 1,000 Mailed
One	$595	2.3	$1,368.50
Two	595	2.1	1,249.50
Three	595	2.6	1,547.00
Four	595	1.8	1,071.00
Average One–Four	$595	2.3	$1,368.50
Five	$550	2.5	$1,375.00
Six	550	1.9	1,045.00
Seven	550	2.2	1,210.00
Eight	550	2.4	1,320.00
Average Five–Eight	$550	2.2	$1,210.00

The combined mailing for the four $595 programs was 48,301 and produced 111 registrations. Mailings for the $550 programs totaled 43,588 and yielded 96 total registrations. Not only did the higher price produce slightly higher registrations per 1,000 pieces mailed but it also yielded meaningfully greater registration revenues.

Price and Quality: Another Consideration

Psychological price barriers are important for another reason. In a society that tends to equate quality with price, it is sometimes advantageous to price at the higher end of the spectrum to connote an image of quality in the market. A proprietary provider found that a fee of $395 for an eight-session course on interpersonal communications not only produced more revenue than a fee of $195, but also yielded a higher response. In matched mailings of 10,000 packages (letter, brochure, response card) differing only in terms of course fee, the $195 offer produced 32 enrollments for total revenue of $6,240. The $395 offer resulted in 36 registrations and total revenue of $14,220. Excited about the inelasticity of the market, he later tested a mailing at $595. The $595 price resulted in only eight registrations at $4,760.

Experiment with price, using carefully controlled tests. And continue to test. The market changes. Don't pass up added revenues by ignoring the significant impact of psychology on program price.

BREAK-EVEN ANALYSIS: AN EXAMPLE

Suppose a seminar promoter determines a price to charge for a program. How many people will have to attend for the seminar to break even? To calculate this break-even point, the promoter must compare fixed expenses and direct costs against the program fee. Fixed expenses include all promotional and presentational expenses of a program; direct costs are for materials, coffee breaks, and other items provided for participant consumption. The following example shows how to calculate the break-even point:

Fixed expenses	$2,772
Direct costs (per participant)	8
Program fee	150
Less: Direct costs	8
Contribution margin	$ 142

Break-even point = Fixed expenses/contribution margin
    $2,772/142 = 19.52

For this seminar, 20 participants are needed for the program to break even.

INCREASING SEMINAR FEES: SOME EMPIRICAL DATA

Seminar promoters frequently ask: Will an increase in the fee I charge for my seminar/workshop decrease the number of registrations I receive? As noted earlier, the answer to this question will almost invariably be yes. The appropriate question to ask is: By what amount (if any) could I increase my fee to increase the total profitability of my program? Emphasis is on profitability, not on number of participants. Some empirical data, presented in the following studies, illustrate the necessity of focusing on profitability rather than on enrollment.

STUDY 1. ADVERTISING SEMINAR FOR RETAILERS AND SMALL SERVICE BUSINESSES

This pilot-tested seminar on creating effective advertising campaigns was promoted in local/metropolitan daily newspapers, the assumption being that retailers and other small businesspeople tend to scan the papers for advertising ideas and to monitor the competition. Finding it to be a profitable program, the promoter wanted to know how much to charge to maximize profits.

Test Question: What impact would a fee increase from $65 to $95 per person have on the enrollment and profitability of a half-day (four-hour) seminar?

Testing Method: San Diego was selected as the test city, for two reasons: its characteristics were similar to those of the metropolitan areas where the promoter was planning to roll out his seminar, and it has two jointly owned daily newspapers, with a combined Sunday edition. In this test, half of the newspapers would run an advertisement specifying a fee of $65 for the seminar; the other half would run the same ad in the same location, except that the specified fee would be $95. In this perfect A/B split test, every other paper coming off the press would have the alternate ad and would be received (at least theoretically) by every other household, providing a controlled random test environment.

A second variable, day of the week, was introduced into the test, altering its perfectibility. So that participants would not arrive at the seminar expecting to pay different fees, it was decided that the $95 seminar would be held on Tuesday (thought to be the preferred day for most seminars) from 1 to 5 P.M. and the $65 program during the same hours on Monday. Hence, the lower-priced program was scheduled on what was felt to be the less desirable day.

The need for two separate seminars could have been avoided had the advertisements required preregistration. The additional $30 paid by some of the participants could have been refunded with an explanation that a market test was being conducted.

Moreover, the test could have been conducted as an imperfect test, with all homes on the north side of town receiving the $65 ad and all south-side homes, the $95 ad. Such a test may have produced unreliable results, however, in that the variable of income would have been introduced. A more affluent north side, for example, may have enrolled for the more expensive seminar in greater numbers than otherwise would have been the case.

The split-run A/B advertisement was run in the combined Sunday edition of the newspaper on the day before the first seminar. While probably not the optimal promotional schedule for a seminar, it served the needs of this test, which were to measure the impact of a fee increase on enrollment and profitability.

Test Results

	Monday/$65	Tuesday/$95
Participants	27	9
Total gross receipts	$1,755	$855
Expenses:		
Advertising	$ 341	$341
Materials	54	18
Room rental	100	100
Coffee service	52	31
On-site clerical	43	43
Other	156	156
Total expenses	$ 746	$689
Total Profit	$1,009	$166

In this test, an increase of 46 percent in the fee charged produced a 67 percent decline in enrollment and an 83 percent decline in profitability. The results did not eliminate a fee increase as a viable strategy; they merely indicated that the $95 fee would have an adverse impact on both enrollment and profit. A lower increase, say of $15, or a $95 fee for a full-day seminar may have produced slightly higher enrollments and a greater profit margin.

STUDY 2. SEMINAR ON SKILLS FOR EFFECTIVE FULFILLMENT OF CORPORATE AND PROFESSIONAL RESPONSIBILITIES

The impact of a fee increase on a full-day seminar was examined in this study. A technically oriented seminar, designed for corporate personnel and independent professionals, had been successfully conducted in major U.S. markets for two years. A fee of $95 was charged for the one-day program. Promotional costs had increased from 22.6 percent of registration fees to 42.8 percent, which the promoter attributed to the economic recession then being experienced.

The promoter's initial inclination was to decrease the seminar fee in order to stimulate business, but he was advised to increase it substantially. An analysis of his program revealed that the falloff in enrollment probably resulted from the loss of marginal participants who could defer attending the program during the recession.

The principal means of promotion was a four-page, $8\frac{1}{2}'' \times 11''$ brochure sent via bulk mail to names on a rented business list, which was split on an every-other-name basis. While some magazine and newspaper promotion was done, it was found to be less effective than direct mail promotion.

Test Question: Would a fee increase from $95 to $195 produce a higher profit margin for a full-day (seven-hour) seminar?

Testing Method: Dallas, Denver, and Chicago were selected for the test market, providing a broad sampling of geographical locations to enhance the quality of the results. Two versions of the brochure were created, identical in every respect except for the fee; 18,114 of each brochure was mailed to the random split lists.

Registrations were to be made in advance by mail or phone, though a small percentage of walk-ins was expected. To avoid any problems that might result from the fee differential, those who registered at the $195 fee were to be informed that the fee was a misprint and that it would be necessary to pay only $95. Paid registrations were received as follows:

Test Results

Fee Paid	Dallas	Denver	Chicago	Total
$ 95	51	44	68	163
$195	27	24	40	91
Decline	47%	45%	41%	44%

In this test, an increase of 205 percent in the fee produced a 44 percent decline in enrollment and a 35 percent increase in profitability. A decrease in the fee to $65 was also tested; it produced a 22 percent increase in enrollment but a 56 percent decline in profit. Thus, the substantial fee increase appeared to be warranted for this particular seminar.

The cost and profit breakdown follows:

Cost/Profit Breakdown

	$95 Seminar	*$195 Seminar*
Participants	163	91
Total gross receipts	$15,485	$17,745
Expenses:		
Promotion	$ 4,256	$ 4,256
Materials	1,141	637
Room rental	525	360
Coffee service	489	273
On-site clerical	360	180
Other	2,100	1,850
Total expenses	$ 8,871	$ 7,556
Total Profit	$ 6,614	$10,189

Other factors must be considered before a final determination can be made. Some promoters may choose to sacrifice registration profits in order to achieve a higher enrollment. The most common motivation for pursuing this strategy is to enhance back-of-room sales of books, tapes, and other materials. For the seminar studied, the lower enrollment at the higher fee, while producing higher gross receipts, had an adverse effect on total profits from back-of-room sales. While the average profit per participant increased to $23.54, compared to the previous average of $20.11, total profit on back-of-room sales declined because of the lower number of participants. Thus, the overall profit margin for the $195 seminar was up only 31 percent as opposed to 35 percent.

PAYMENT OPTIONS

There are several different methods of participant payment for seminars and workshops. Some allow for convenience to the participant and some protect your investment in the program. You can require payment via a single method, several alternatives, or all of them.

Checks

The risk of bad checks is low in the seminar and workshop business, and most promoters willingly take the slight risk since accepting checks will increase enrollment. Indeed, most checks that bounce are simply the result of sloppy bookkeeping and their issuers will usually make good on their payment. To decrease the chances of getting bad checks, you can request identification and check-guarantee cards when you take on-site payment. If a check-guarantee card is required for on-site registration, indicate the requirement in your promotional materials. On preregistrations via mail, checks will normally have cleared prior to the date of the seminar.

Credit Cards

Accepting credit cards can significantly increase both enrollment (from 12 to 28 percent) and back-of-the-room or post-seminar sales because participants can attend the program and make purchases now, and pay later. The small expense for setting up the account with your bank and the charge on all money collected this way can yield very worthwhile results.

To protect your interest, always take the time—even in the heat of on-site registration—to call in for approval and check the credit card companies' "hot sheets" of unacceptable card numbers. If you don't check credit cards on site, there is a good chance that the credit card company will charge you for being over the floor limit—the amount of money that can be charged on a card without calling for approval. Some providers have handled this by dividing the total amount of the charge by the floor limit and processing the charge as two or more charges for amounts under the floor limit. When the total dollar amount is sizable, some promoters spread out their deposits over a several-day period. They write or stamp "signature on file" on the signature line of the vouchers (referring to the original voucher that the participant signed).

Cash

You can try to encourage cash payment if you wish, but few participants will pay in this way. If you want to encourage cash payment, have on-site, day-of-the-program registration; people are, wisely, very unwilling to send cash through the mail. You can also provide a cash discount, or you can refuse to accept checks and/or credit cards; however, refusing checks and credit cards will probably hurt enrollment much more than gain increased cash payment.

Extending Credit

Credit can be offered *selectively*, to decrease the risk of nonpayment. Many promoters extend credit to recognized organizations—often by

```
┌─────────────────────────────────────────────────────────────┐
│                         I N V O I C E                         │
│                                                               │
│   Name _____│
│   Company _____│
│   Address _____│
│   _____│
│   City/State/Zip _____│
│                                                               │
│                            Date:                              │
│                            Number of Attendees:               │
│                            Terms:                             │
│   - - - - - - - - - - - - - - - - - - - - - - - - - - - - - - │
│                                                               │
│   Seminar registration                             $          │
│   Less: Deposit/Advance payment received           $_____  │
│   TOTAL DUE AND PAYABLE ON OR BEFORE _____       $_____  │
│                                                               │
│                                                               │
│   Payment may be made by ____ check ____ credit card ____ money order │
│   Authorized signature _____│
│                                                               │
│   Please return a copy of this invoice with payment or indicate invoice number │
│   on check or check stub.                                     │
│                                                               │
│   Thank you.                                                  │
│                                                               │
└─────────────────────────────────────────────────────────────┘
```

Figure 11–1. Sample invoice.

accepting their purchase orders—but not to individuals. However, credit can be extended to individuals at low promoter risk if payment is due prior to or on the day of the program. For example, if someone registers for a February 4 seminar on January 5, and you acknowledge registration and send an invoice on January 8, then the fee is due prior to or during registration on February 4. Terms for credit should be simple and consistent: net 10 days, no offset. If you expect a substantial number of your participants to have their fees paid by their employers, you should almost certainly consider invoicing the employer organization for the seminar fee (though with a particularly large and/or well-known creditworthy company you may decide not to insist on payment prior to or at the time of the program). Figure 11–1 shows a sample invoice form.

Whatever your payment policies, indicate them in your promotional materials so that participants are forewarned.

FREE AND NOT SO FREE PROGRAMS

A great number of seminars are conducted without charge to the participants. Most of these seminars are sponsored by commercial entities interested in using seminars to market a product or service such as accounting services, software, insurance, and so on. Many seminar providers use "free" lectures, usually lasting one to two hours, to promote registration in more expensive, longer seminars or classes. Some mistakenly think that offering a free program will solve all of their marketing problems. They believe that they can be sloppy in all other aspects of marketing since a turnaway crowd will be ensured by the lack of a fee. Ten years ago they may have been right; today, just being free isn't a sufficient inducement. There are many free seminars and lectures to choose from and people's time is of great value. Indeed, much research shows that charging some fee, even if small, will produce more qualified prospects, though usually in smaller numbers.

One promoter advertised in newspapers a 90-minute free lecture on buying small business equities; the results were one attendee for each $9.37 spent on advertising. When he charged $10 for the lecture, fewer attended and his advertising expenses rose to $14.74 per head. But his conversion rate from free lecture to paid-for weekend seminar at $595 increased from 4.5 to 6.1 percent and his costs of conducting the free seminar declined. In one test he found the following:

	Free	*$10 Charge*
Advertising cost	$2,051	$2,113
Number of participants	216	137
Conduct cost	$836	$579
Number of sales at $595	10	8
Number of sales at $10	0	137
Total revenue	$5,950	$6,130
Total contribution to profit	$3,063	$3,438

Even in "free" seminars, price is a variable to be played with.

CAPTIVE PROGRAMS

Thus far, the fee-setting information has pertained primarily to public seminars and workshops; captive programs—seminars, workshops, or training programs conducted for a specific client—also have several different fee-setting options. The same fee options can be used if you hire an outside presenter to conduct your seminar. Whatever fee option you choose, whether you are working for a sponsor or hiring an outside presenter, you should always work under some form of written agreement. (Chapter 13 contains sample agreements—for sponsor and presenter and/

or for program developer/promoter and presenter.) Among the options for negotiating a fee satisfactory to both you and your client are the following:

1. *Fixed Fee.* You present the client with a fixed fee which includes the value of the labor of the seminar developers, the seminar presenters, and any additional personnel, plus overhead, an estimate of expenses, and your expected profit.

2. *Fixed Fee Plus Expenses.* Fixed fee plus expenses is the same as fixed fee; however, it excludes an estimate of direct expenses, which are billed to the client in their exact amount.

3. *Per-Participant Charge.* You (the seminar developer) charge your client a fee for each participant attending the seminar. With this method, you take all of the risks, so use it only when you have control over the promotion of the program.

4. *Per-Participant Charge with Guarantee.* With this widely used fee option, the promoter and client share the risks. The promoter is paid a flat fee per participant, with a guaranteed minimum of participants.

5. *Performance Contract.* The seminar developer or promoter is paid after the program is conducted, according to the number of participants who meet agreed-upon criteria—such as passing a test, skill sessions, or evaluations—after the training session.

PRICE IN-HOUSE PROGRAMS LIKE AIRFRAMES

Research on 111 providers of in-house (contract) training has revealed that the majority set program prices in a fashion that prevents them from getting as many signed contracts as they could. An understanding of how in-house training fees should be established and how such pricing differs from the pricing of public (open enrollment) seminars is vital to success.

Too many providers, because of either risk aversion or greed, attempt to charge the in-house training program client for the full cost of program development. This is not only unfair but it makes the provider noncompetitive. When Boeing develops a new airframe for the commercial market, it does not attempt to charge each airline for the full cost of development. Doing so would price Boeing out of the market for commercial airframes.

DIFFERENT APPROACHES TO THE BID

Consider the experience of a major corporation with two university continuing-education providers. The corporation contacted both universities and requested that they present proposals for the training of 150–175 technical managers on the subject of project-based managerial accounting. Both providers had a track record for public seminars on subjects related to the training need. Each university proposed a three-day, on-site training program to be conducted at four different locations to support the training of 30 to 45 managers per program. Both had attractive proposals and well-received technical plans. But their fixed price quotations for the provision of services differed greatly. One provider proposed to conduct the project for a fee of $68,823, the other for $39,300. The low bidder won the contract. The corporation felt both programs would meet their objective; this was not a case of a client buying less training than would do the job. An analysis of the budgets and the pricing strategies behind the budgets explains why the higher priced provider did not get the contract. Compare the two bids shown below.

Item	$39,300 Bid	$68,823 Bid
Program development	$ 4,700	$23,613
Program conduct	9,500	10,120
Direct expenses	3,900	3,745
Overhead	13,700	24,100
Fee (profit)	7,500	7,245

Program conduct costs, direct expenses, and fee are roughly equivalent, with no meaningful differences to explain the disparity in fixed price fees. Both institutions calculated overhead as a percentage of direct expenses. Thus, although the high bidder's overhead seems to be a great deal higher, it really isn't. The important difference is development cost. The actual number of hours of faculty/staff time devoted to the program development phase for the two providers was not significantly different, but the accounting methods used to cover development costs were.

Amortization

The high bidder charged the full development cost for the program to the project. The low bidder did not, reasoning that a well-developed program could be resold to other corporations in the future. The total development cost was actually $28,200, but the low bidder elected to amortize the development cost over six potential contracts, calculating that during the next two years the program could be sold at least five more times. Given reasonable capability in the marketing arena, the calculation was probably correct. After all, the low bidder is delivering high-quality training at a per-participant, per-day cost of about $81 (compared to $141 for the high bidder).

Not all in-house contracts should be priced in such a fashion, of course. Some are so specialized and specific to the client's needs that they are not likely to have resale value. An aerospace contractor recognizes this when pricing for the military market—the government is charged the full development cost on the first contract. But most in-house training programs, or at least components or modules of them, can be sold again to others. Amortizing development cost over the life of the training program is good business. It makes the provider more competitive. Program managers need to adapt three pricing strategies: one for pure services such as highly customized, unique training programs; one for pure products such as public seminars; and one for replicable services such as the training program described above.

Some Guidelines

Pure services should be priced in one of two ways. The traditional approach, and still the most widely used, is to calculate direct labor and direct expense and add overhead and desired profit or fee. In the second, increasingly popular approach, providers use the traditional approach to set a price floor but then charge on the basis of what the market will bear. One proprietary provider's recent contract with a trade association serves as an example:

Direct labor	$ 3,101
Direct expense	1,893
Total	4,994
Overhead (73%)	3,646
Total	8,640
Profit (20%)	1,728
Total	$10,368

If the client is unwilling to pay $10,368, the provider should be unwilling to deliver the service. That is, $10,368 is either the fee that should be charged or the floor, the minimum to be charged. In this case, the provider was training an estimated 180 people and had ascertained that the association was willing to pay about $75 per head for training. Rather than proposing $10,368, the provider bid $12,983 ($72.13 per head).

Pure products such as seminars should be priced like any product. The sponsor should charge a price that will produce the highest total dollar profit. The only relationship between price and cost should be that cost is less than price. Determining the price that will produce maximum profit is an inexact science and no easy task. But market testing will allow you to come quite close to the ideal price.

Perhaps the simplest way to understand how a fee is calculated, for either a public or a captive program, is to review the pricing sheet that a seminar developer usually prepares for his own benefit and purposes, not

Sample Pricing Sheet

Direct labor:	
Program development	
Senior professional (10 days × $250)	$ 2,500
Staff associates (15 days × $150)	2,250
Drafting (5 days × $80)	400
Secretarial (12 days × $90)	1,080
Program development subtotal	$ 6,230
Program conduct	
Senior professional (4 days × $250)	$ 1,000
Staff associates (12 days × $150)	1,800
Program conduct subtotal	$ 2,800
Total direct labor	$ 9,030
Overhead (at 90% of direct labor)	$ 8,127
Direct expenses:	
Survey instrumentation	$ 158
Telephone	200
Per diem (16 days × $150)	2,400
Air service (4 × $188)	752
Rental cars	225
Printing and photocopying	1,220
Other expenses	600
Total direct expenses	$ 5,555
Subtotal (Direct labor + Overhead + Direct expenses)	$22,712
Profit (20% of subtotal)	4,542
Total fixed price	$27,254

for the client. Included in the pricing sheet are the following expenses for developing and conducting a seminar:

- **Direct labor.** The cost of direct labor includes the cost of labor for senior staff member, staff associates, and secretarial staff for both developing and conducting the program.

- **Overhead.** Overhead equals the cost of being in business, including the expense of items such as office expenses, taxes, licenses, marketing, stationery, supplies, and so on. The overhead does not change for each seminar conducted; rather, it is a relatively constant cost, capable of being expressed as a percentage of the direct labor cost, which varies accordingly for different seminar developers.

- **Direct expenses.** These are the expenses generated for a specific seminar or workshop.

- □ **Subtotal**. Direct labor plus overhead plus direct expenses = subtotal. If the program is a session offered by the training department of a corporation (i.e., a captive program) and does not need to make a profit, then this subtotal would be the total cost of the program.
- □ **Profit**. The profit is the percentage of the subtotal—usually between 10 and 25 percent—which you require in order to make money from the program. If you are working for a client on a captive training program, you must keep in mind how much organizations are willing to pay for training when you decide on the profit percentage.

RECESSION STRATEGIES FOR SEMINAR PROMOTERS

During a recession, enrollment for most seminars will likely go down, but you can take preventive measures to ensure that your profitability doesn't go down with enrollment and the economy. Many seminar and workshop promoters' first reaction is to lower prices, believing that this will solve all of their recessionary problems; however, such a strategy is often not the solution.

Many find that a decision to raise fees during a recession is best. Enrollment will go down, but if you have the right increase—which you will have to test for—profits will remain stable or even increase. You may not gain as many new participants or client organizations during this time, but the old ones will keep attending your programs even if there is a moderate price increase.

When you raise your fee, there are other ways in which you can make your program less expensive overall for the participants—particularly lower-level participants. For instance, offer discounts for multiple registrations. Advertise the incentive in your brochure and restate the offer by phone or by mail after the registration. Consider locations that offer better price packages for you and your participants, and if hotel prices are particularly low, advertise that fact. People who attend during a recession are serious about your program and are probably not as interested in fringe benefits; most will greatly appreciate lower hotel costs, less expensive meals, and fewer frills. Try starting late enough on the first day to save a night's hotel bill for traveling attendees. Consider ending early on the last day for the same reason; if a lunch is involved, consider ending the session before lunch; at 12:30 or 1:00 P.M. Particularly for programs that appeal to lower-income participants, consider using local scheduling and advertising; during a recession most people cannot or feel they cannot afford to fly to another state or even to travel to a nearby city for a seminar or workshop. Try evening and Saturday programs so that people need not take time off from work to attend.

Think about promoting and marketing more to higher-level/higher-income audiences who will probably still be willing and wanting to attend seminars and workshops. For such participant groups, consider lengthening your programs to increase the perceived (and real) value of your program among those who can afford the extra time away from the office. Seek out in-house business also: many organizations will still perceive captive programs as cost-efficient solutions to problems or needs they might have.

Select programs that are likely to do well in a weak economy: "Increasing Job Satisfaction" and "Creativity Enhancement" will not do as well as "Improving Sales Performance" or "Cost Reduction." Recession-tone your promotional copy, pointing out cost-saving rationales and motivations for program participation.

To lessen your own costs, cut program frills like lunches, pens, handouts, and so on. *Never cut the quality of your actual program.* Reduce your overhead whenever possible. Do not make large purchases, or take on new space, or hire new personnel (if you must hire, get consultants, part-time help, or one-time services, not full-time employees). Test-market as little as possible during a recession because if a program fails you will not know if the program is truly unsuccessful and unprofitable or is a casualty of the recession. Don't invest heavily in new programs unless you feel particularly positive about them or they are specifically targeted to recession circumstances. In the same vein, be absolutely scrupulous about mailing list and media selections; a recession is not the time to test new lists. Analyze past attendance and list performance and select the most successful lists aimed at the targets most likely to respond (past participants can be particularly responsive).

This may be the time to expend effort in marketing and promoting other services or products, particularly audio cassettes or videotapes of your program, and books or manuals pertaining to the seminar topic. In your brochure, stress the fact that even if people cannot attend your program, they can obtain relevant tapes or books at a lower cost.

In the event of a recession, don't get hooked into a permanent recession mentality. Be ready to change—the recession will likely be over sooner than you think.

STRATEGIES FOR AN ECONOMIC UPTURN

When the economic tide turns, moving toward an improved economy, you can use proven strategies to make sure that your seminar (and your profit) keeps up with the changes.

Broaden your mailing list. This is the time to test new lists and resurrect older lists that were less productive in the past. In an improved economy, response rates will go up.

Raise your prices; don't underprice your program. This is a time when people will be ready to spend more and travel farther. Include fringe benefits and incentives—special reports, extra days, alumni programs, meals, and so on; when times are good, people want more and will pay more for special options.

Retitle programs (where appropriate), tone your copy, and redesign your mailing pieces to suit the upturn. Be positive, optimistic, enthusiastic, realistic, and specific. Convince your audience that, by attending your program, they can profit from the improving economy and tell them how they *will* profit.

Try new programs, new promotions, new audiences and industries. This is the time to be bold, creative, and innovative. But test everything so that you know what is working and what isn't.

Don't overexpand. Your profits may be up along with the economy, and you want to keep it that way. Pay for quality but do not add unnecessarily to your overhead and fixed costs.

Deliver quality and insist on it. Quality costs more but your participants will know it when they see it and they will be willing to pay for it.

Act quickly! Don't let the good times pass you by.

SUMMARY

The information and examples in this chapter illustrated several basic principles regarding fee setting:

1. A fee increase in most cases will result in a decline in enrollment.
2. The impact of a fee increase on total profitability is a function of a number of interrelated factors specific to a particular seminar.
3. In some instances, it may be appropriate to sacrifice some increase in profitability in order to generate higher enrollments.

An arbitrary decision to increase (or decrease) the seminar fee may not result in the desired increase in profitability. Fee changes must be evaluated on a case-by-case basis, keeping in mind an important but often overlooked dictum: It is impossible to know with certainty the impact of a fee change on the profitability of a seminar or workshop. This uncertainty, which keeps many seminar promoters awake at night, can be reduced somewhat by conducting a market test. The market-test method of determining the impact of a fee change is both more reliable and less expensive than market research. Of course, the test must be properly designed. All variables except the fee must be held constant and tested with controlled and unbiased samples. If these conditions are adhered to, the results should provide a reliable basis for determining the impact of a fee change on the seminar's profitability.

12

ADDED PROFITS: SUCCESSFUL BACK-OF-THE-ROOM SELLING

Your seminar or workshop is a fund of knowledge and information which is of value to others—perhaps sufficient value that they will part with hard dollars to obtain that information. Some people cannot afford the monetary expense of your program, and others cannot afford the time away from work. But many others will attend your seminar and will want or become convinced that they need additional information to reiterate and reinforce what they learned in the program and/or to enhance and supplement its coverage. People's need and desire for such information can be very profitable for you, particularly if you provide information products and make them available before, during (back-of-the-room sales), and after the seminar. An endless variety of means can be used to package and market such knowledge and information. One of the most popular is the audio cassette.

SHOULD YOU PACKAGE YOUR KNOWLEDGE AND INFORMATION AS AUDIO CASSETTES?

For most readers, the answer is probably yes! Cassettes have become a highly popular and very effective medium for enabling others to obtain access to your knowledge and information. The world is in the middle of a knowledge explosion. As countless pundits have pointed out, the amount of knowledge available in the world is growing far faster than the ability of the individual to grasp it. Along with this explosion of knowledge has come a growth in our understanding of the different ways in which people assimilate knowledge. Studies of the differing functions of the left and right sides of the brain, for example, have taught us that people differ in the ways in which they can most easily understand information and the ways in which they prefer to learn.

    The popularity of cassettes has been assisted too by the fact that great numbers of people prefer learning via the spoken word because they have either a difficulty with reading or a functional disability that precludes them from reading with a sufficient level of understanding. Audio cassettes, video tapes, computer programs, and other new forms of communication technology are giving people new methods of obtaining information which until now had been available only in books.

The market made up of people who have no reading difficulty, but prefer to learn via audio cassettes is even more extensive.

The decision to develop and market audio cassettes to make your knowledge and information available to others involves complex considerations beyond a preference for the medium. In the following sections I shall attempt to explore the nature of these considerations and provide some practical information on packaging your knowledge in the form of audio cassettes and selling them and other information products profitably through back-of-the-room sales.

WILL MARKETING AUDIO CASSETTES HURT FUTURE BUSINESS OPPORTUNITIES AND SALES?

Many individuals who could profitably market their knowledge and information through the medium of cassettes fail to do so because they are concerned that making their know-how available in this form will hurt future sales of seminars and professional services.

Field research has revealed that this is not usually a valid concern. You must remember that the market buys information in many forms and many buyers will obtain similar information in a variety of forms.

For example, I have been serving in the capacity of a marketing consultant to those involved in the seminar business for some 17 years. To what extent did the publication of my books, the conduct of my seminars, the introduction of my audio cassette learning packages, and the writing of my newsletter on this subject hinder my sales of consulting services? Not at all. Instead, they have been beneficial to that effort. The demand for my consulting services on the marketing of seminars and workshops has increased with the introduction of each of these information products. More importantly, from the perspective of the headline question, the availability of my books and audio cassettes has stimulated the demand for my seminars on seminar and workshop promotion.

You must keep an important point in mind. Many prospects cannot afford to pay several hundred to several thousand dollars a day for professional services but they can afford a few hundred dollars to attend a seminar. Other people cannot afford to pay a few hundred dollars for a seminar but they can afford to pay $100 or $200 for audio cassettes. Finally, there are those who cannot afford a few hundred dollars for cassettes but they can afford $30 to $70 for a book.

Each time you develop an information product you create access to your knowledge and information for a new segment of the market. People will want to obtain your insights in different forms, even though some of the information (or at least the philosophical approach) remains the same.

Individuals who buy your audio cassettes may call you to determine your availability as a consultant or to learn if you have scheduled a seminar. The creation of information products *produces* business.

There is no reason why you should not be a beneficiary of the audio cassette revolution. If you have information to impart, it is well worth your while to consider marketing it in many differing forms, including cassettes.

ARE AUDIO CASSETTES RIGHT FOR YOUR KNOWLEDGE AND INFORMATION?

How can you tell whether the information you have to offer would sell well as an audio cassette program? There are several variables to consider. As with every issue having to do with marketing, the first question you must ask yourself is: Who is your market? Who are the people who are most likely to be interested in buying what you have to sell? In this case, you are specifically asking: Can I identify and reach them? It makes little difference how wonderful your product is if you are unable to identify and reach your market with efficiency and effectiveness. With audio cassettes you might also wish to ask yourself: Are these people more likely to be readers or listeners? In every market there are going to be some of both. If you put out your information in book form, even people who don't like to read will buy the book if they need the information. If you put it out in cassette form, people who detest cassettes will still buy your cassette if they have to have the information. What you really want to know is: In what form are people most likely to buy my information? Even this is not the whole question. Most marketers of both cassettes and books will be the first to tell you that marketing cassettes is more profitable because they command a higher market price—the market price of cassettes does not exactly reflect the higher cost of their manufacture. However, in terms of number of units sold, books generally far outsell audio cassettes and video tapes.

It is important to remember, however, that your audience will be mixed, and you may find it impossible to determine its exact preferences. Your best approach to your market, at least in terms of your long-range plans, may be to plan to market your information in all forms that are appropriate for the needs of the marketplace. Obviously, you will need to begin with one form; choose the form that is easiest for you. For example, it may be easiest for you to record your words onto an audio cassette, but nothing precludes you from then having a professional editor turn the cassette into a well-written piece of prose.

PRICES AND COSTS

How much is your intended audience willing to pay for your seminar's information? Knowledge of your market will help you deal with this question. As discussed above, audio cassettes generally retail for more than books and, while they cost somewhat more to produce than do books, the retail price for cassettes is usually greater than would be indicated by their increased production cost.

Increased quantities bring about cost reductions, but the savings as a result of quantity buying of cassettes are not as spectacular as for other products. For example, a client of mine recently received the following bids for production of his "knowledge and information" as both a six-hour cassette program and a 300-page perfect-bound book:

| | *Per Unit Delivered Price* | |
| | | *Cassettes/Labels/* |
Quantity	*Books*	*Album/Cover Card*
100	$12.97	$15.34
500	9.36	13.10
1,000	6.49	11.42
5,000	3.23	9.71

The price you establish for the sale of your information product should use cost data like these to establish a floor, but the price should reflect what the market will pay vis-à-vis cost. If you are planning, for example, to market via direct mail, keep in mind a mail order "rule of thumb": In order to be profitable, the selling price should be equal to five times the cost of production.

Using the above cost data, a set of cassettes retailing at five times the cost of production would be priced at $48.95–$76.95, depending on the size of the production run. The client's planned market price for his program is $129. His analysis of the market suggests that this is the most profitable price to charge. (This belief could and probably should be tested through a controlled market test of price.)

Some readers may be concerned that such a high selling price will likely result in undue ("monopoly") profits for the seller. A specialized product, which this set of cassettes is, generally sells at a higher price than more generic products. Marketing costs of specialized products are higher and a lower number of units of product is likely to be sold.

The bottom line, of course, is to establish a price that allows you to obtain the greatest profit. Often, price testing is a good way to determine the optimal price.

The majority of seminar providers find that developing audio cassettes is a profitable undertaking. Individuals who attend seminars are receptive to additional information in a format that is "like attending a seminar." A package containing recorded information accompanied by a printed manual offers a learning experience which is very close to a seminar. In addition to packaging information that supplements your seminar, you should consider offering a presentation of your seminar in this medium to accommodate those unable to attend in person. The product will be popular even with those who do attend; they may desire to experience the seminar again, perhaps for review or reinforcement. A recording of your seminar, sold with a manual that contains the participant handout materials, can be promoted along with the seminar. Some people will attend; others will buy the package; if you price properly, some will opt for both. And you multiply the selling power of your seminar promotional materials.

Research has suggested that the price of the audio cassette version of the seminar should be close to the fee charged for the live seminar. If the cassette version is significantly less costly, you will lose seminar enrollments in favor of cassette purchases. If the cassette price is significantly higher, you will hinder cassette sales. One provider did extensive market research and established the following price points for the several seminars marketed:

Seminar Fee	Audio Seminar Price
$ 95	$ 89.95
125	119.95
150	139.95
195	179.95

For this provider (and others) the time and money spent to develop the cassette product were low. The manual already existed for the seminar and a professional recording firm was retained to record a live seminar and produce production masters for a charge of under $1,000.

Seminar attendees are usually provided with an opportunity to purchase the cassette version at a discounted price equal to about 40–50 percent of the regular retail price.

ARE AUDIO CASSETTES AN APPROPRIATE MEDIUM?

Another factor you will need to consider is the type of information you are dealing with: some information is best communicated, or perhaps can *only* be communicated, in certain media. If visual awareness—presentation of examples—is crucial to your topic, audio cassettes alone will not be sufficient. It would be foolish, for example, to attempt to teach people about Gauguin and Renoir without resorting to a visual medium. You may decide to run a videotape or, if your topic has a large visual component and little information content that needs to be expressed orally, you may feel that a book is far more appropriate. If you feel that your data definitely need the support of visual materials and you don't want to go to the expense of videotaping, another approach might be to include a book (your visual component) along with audio cassettes. The dual package may be more attractive to purchasers, who may feel that they are getting more for their investment.

You should also investigate what your competitors are doing. If they have so far failed to bring out their information using media which you think would be attractive to your market, it may be possible to get the jump on them by packaging the same information in a new medium. It also pays to watch out for failures. If the competition has already tried a new medium and abandoned it, don't foolishly waste this free test-marketing information. Just because the competition has failed, however, does not mean that you will fail. Effective marketing of any product, audio cassettes included, depends on the favorable interaction of many variables. A small adjustment in marketing strategy by one promoter can produce great successes where others have failed.

PACKAGING SEMINARS ON CASSETTES

Seminars are one of the most common data bases of information to be turned into tape packages. The marketing of the taped materials can be piggybacked onto the marketing for the seminar, and the people who attend a seminar have already stated their interest in its subject and are extremely good candidates for purchasers. There is very strong reason to believe that if a subject has sold successfully as a seminar, a taped version of it will probably sell well. People who find it too inconvenient, too expensive, or too difficult to attend a live program will purchase it to benefit from the information.

In some situations, people who could greatly benefit from the information offered at a seminar don't want to attend. One of the best examples of this is the reluctance of many individuals to attend seminars on the subject of how to get a job (most of these seminars are unsuccessful). The seminars typically include information on résumé writing, interviewing skills, and other advice that is useful for job seekers. The programs can be extremely useful, but people may not want others to know that they are having difficulty getting a job or that they do not have the requisite skills to get a particular job. While these programs tend to be unsuccessful as seminars and workshops, they often sell quite well as taped programs. People can get them in "a plain brown wrapper" and listen to them in the privacy of their home or car.

RECORDING AND PRODUCTION

If you are considering taping a seminar, you will need to decide whether to tape it in a studio, reading from the notes you use in your seminar as if you were in front of an audience, or to tape an actual, live seminar. Both have advantages. Studio recordings sound more professional. There will be fewer "um's" and "ah's," and grammar and usage will be more correct, particularly if the program is carefully scripted. The sound quality is also likely to be better. On the other hand, seminars that are recorded live give the listener a much better feel for what took place during the seminar and you can include the input of the seminar attendees, if you think their comments were important. Your choice is largely a judgment based on your taste and working style.

Some people are very good at studio work. They can say what they want to say, make use of an outline, and even read a short script as a radio announcer might, making it sound natural—as though they were conversing, not reading. Others find working in a studio very difficult. They constantly want to stop and correct what they have said and find that the motivation of a live audience makes them much more effective and dynamic in that setting. They realize that there will be some errors and poorer sound quality in a tape of a live seminar but are willing to live with them. You will likely discover that your market is willing to live with the few imperfections that come from live work, but quite intolerant of imperfections in a studio product.

Can you make this decision based on the market? Unfortunately the market is divided. Some people like a very tightly structured, neatly organized, consistent body of knowledge which is better achieved in studio work than it would be in most seminars. Others would prefer to have the dynamic excitement and spontaneity of a live seminar.

Unless you have some hard data on your market's preferences, which is difficult to come by, you should probably make the decision based on what is easier for you to do. If you go into a studio and discover that you need to stop every two minutes because you don't like what you said and you want to say it differently or because you don't like the emphasis you used, your costs are going to be much higher and you are going to be much less satisfied with the end product.

When recording your presentation live, remember that if you are using audio tape and will not be including any written materials in your package, there is no visual medium for your listeners; don't say "Look at this chart" or "Look at the blackboard." When seminar participants ask questions or make comments, be sure to repeat each one for the benefit of the listening audience.

When taping your seminar, whether live or in a studio, aside from a consciousness of some limitations in terms of visual media, try to forget that you are taping. Avoid becoming self-conscious; simply give the best program you possibly can and let it be captured.

From a technical standpoint, it is always best to use people who are experienced in professional recording, but it can be perilous to assume that because they have done professional recording in the past they are necessarily aware of all the pitfalls that can occur while taping a presentation, particularly in the field. To at least increase your chances of getting someone who has recorded seminars before, use a company that specializes in recording seminars. Such companies come in, set up, record the seminar, and in some instances bring duplicating equipment with them, so that participants can purchase tapes of the seminar they have just attended and take them home! You may prefer to have the tape edited to improve the sound quality, remove the "dead air" and coughs, and perhaps cut that one question which you were unable to answer right on the spot. Recording companies usually work on a straight fee basis, but some will undertake all of the risk themselves, returning a percentage of the sales of the tapes to you. Under the latter arrangement, most often the tape company retains the rights to the tapes, although they will allow you to buy the tapes at wholesale, to sell. You should give careful consideration to your long-range goals for the product before entering into any agreement with the taping company.

Unless you have worked with a specific recording engineer before, be aware of what he is doing, particularly if he has never recorded a seminar before. Try to make sure that the engineer is adequately backed up and able to deal with tapes breaking, power failure, and so on. If possible and practical, run two recorders so that you never lose anything. Make sure that the engineer places the microphones properly, to avoid picking up sidetalk and rustling from the audience. If you expect audience participation to play an important part in the seminar, have microphones placed in locations where you can record the audience's comments. Remote microphones should be switched to "off" and activitated only when needed to pick up audience comments or questions.

It is advisable to get a signed release form from anyone whose voice or image is recorded on tape. The release should state that you have the right to record and resell the person's voice or image and essentially owe him nothing—or $1—for participation. This is particularly important with video recording, because proving that someone was actually present is easier than with audio recording. Figure 12–1, a sample letter to accompany the release form shown in Figure 12–2, can be adapted as you

(Letterhead)

Good Morning and Welcome!

You are about to participate in a most exceptional seminar
entitled: _____.

So that this information will be readily available in
video cassette format, we are videotaping this seminar
today. If for any reason you do not wish to be included in
any "pan" shots of the class, please sit in the special
section which will be avoided in all camera shots.

Otherwise, we need to ask for your signature on this
"Release Form," in exchange for which we will pay you the
customary one dollar "value received" amount as well as send
you, without charge, a copy of the two video cassettes which
will be produced as a result of this session.

Thank you for your assistance.

        Sincerely,

        _____

Figure 12–1. Sample letter to accompany release for videotaping.

SUBJECT: Consulting Seminar   Date:

In consideration of value received, I hereby grant
_____ permission to copyright and use videotape
recordings of me in connection with the subject production
in any manner or form for any lawful purpose at any time. I
waive any right that I may have to inspect or approve the
finished product. I release and discharge _____
from any liability to me by virtue of any alteration that
may occur in the making or editing of said videotape
recordings.

I have read this agreement before signing below and warrant
that I fully understand its contents.

                    Signed:_____

                    Address:_____

                            _____

                            _____

Date: _____ Witness:_____

Figure 12–2. Sample release form to authorize videotaping.

develop your own form. (In the letter shown, attendees received the tapes for no additional payment.)

PRODUCTION

Once you have an edited master that you like, you will need to decide how many copies to make. One nice thing about tapes is that there is no great advantage to long production runs.

If you decide to retain a company to make an on-site audio recording of your seminar, what can you expect to pay? In general terms, in a large metropolitan area you should expect to pay about $350–$500 for the recording of a six-hour seminar. This can usually be edited down to make four one-hour dub master tapes for approximately $300–$500. Duplicating these masters onto cassettes costs about $0.90–$1.50 per tape in runs of 500 (the cost of the cassette is included), plus another $90–$150 for the labels on the cassettes. An album that will hold four cassettes, with your name silk-screened on the front, costs about $2.75–$4.75 each. The total cost for 500 sets of four one-hour cassettes in an album would be approximately $3,265 to $5,500, an average of $8.77 per unit. When you consider that a tape set such as this can easily retail for $60–$80, the profit margins are substantial.

The copy you prepare for the printed labels on the cassettes should include both ownership and marketing statements. The ownership line is the protective equivalent of a copyright line on published material. Put it on every label you print and use this format:

℗ 19___ by [your name or your company's name]

Give the full program title, in easily readable type, followed by a descriptive subtitle, in a less prominent size. The full name, address, and telephone number of the seller/publisher should appear on the label; you can preface the information with "Additional copies available from" if you are doing order fulfillment. The user directions should include a numbering of the tapes as Side 1 and Side 2 or Side 1 and Duplicate of Side 1, and should give the topics of the content on each side.

AUDIO VS. VIDEO

Should you be recording your information on audio cassette or videotape? As you have probably guessed, there is no automatic answer to this question. The most important factor to consider is the cost; a videotape is many, many times more expensive to produce than an audio tape because technicians are more highly paid, the work is more complex, and so on. The cost of producing copies of the tape is also significantly greater. On the plus side, however, some videotapes sell for a great deal more than audio tapes and their per-unit profit can be much higher. Obviously, the first question to ask about your market is: How much are they willing to pay for the information? There is, however, another, more subtle point.

Let us say, for example, that you are doing a $895, two-day seminar and you would like to make that seminar available on tape to people who cannot attend. You will have a very difficult time justifying to those people the notion of spending $700–$800 for a set of audio tapes. Most are aware that audio tapes don't cost that much to produce. In such a situation it might be necessary, and in your interest, to sell a videotape. Their awareness of the high production costs of videotape will make purchasers more likely to be willing to pay several hundred dollars for a videotape.

BACK-OF-THE-ROOM SELLING

Now you have a warehouse full of tapes—or other products—ready to sell. What do you do with them? You can use them as an adjunct to your seminar marketing, offering a free set of tapes to the first x-number of people who register for the program; however, it is usually to your benefit to offer a somewhat less expensive (but still valuable to your registrants) early registration gift, such as a book or manual related to the program topic, and keep the tapes and other information products for back-of-the-room (BOR) selling during breaks and before and after the seminar.

Back-of-the-room sales of tapes, books, newsletter subscriptions, and so on can be extremely lucrative and valuable—to you and your participants. These sales are beneficial to your participants because:

1. They will remember by the end of the day only a small percentage of the vast amount of information you presented in the program; by several days/weeks/months after the program, they will remember very little. Tapes and books that reproduce or relate to the program will reinforce their learning experience and refresh their memory, allowing them to make the best possible use of the information.

2. Time limits will rarely allow you to cover all of the information on a subject in one intensive day or even several days. Tapes and books can fill in the details and provide additional valuable information for the participants.

3. Even if you can cover the primary, essential information on a topic, there are always individuals who want more information and in greater depth; others want information on additional, related topics.

These people can find such information in the other products and/or services you provide.

4. Some people will want to but will be unable to attend your program for any of a number of reasons; however, they can still obtain (by contacting you) tapes and/or books of your seminar or workshop, thus garnering your wealth of knowledge.

Such sales are beneficial for you because:

1. They can be extremely profitable, as you have seen earlier in the chapter. Back-of-the-room sales can often make up for low registration, particularly when you are first starting out in the business, and can turn a financially unsuccessful program into a successful one.

2. Satisfied participants tend to talk about the seminar or workshop and proudly show off their new learning materials to friends and colleagues—potential new participants and/or sales for you.

To facilitate BOR sales, you can take several measures:

□ Set up a table-display of your products near the registration table at the back of the meeting room or just outside the room, where your participants will see the products.

□ If you don't bring your inventory with you, have handsomely packaged samples on display, since people are more likely to buy products they can see and touch.

□ Have catalogs, brochures, and information cards readily visible and available so that even if people do not buy anything on-site, they can think it over and order material from you days or weeks after the seminar. Participants can also pass such brochures/information cards on to others who might be interested in your program and products.

□ If you are not using your own staff members, hire reliable and experienced (in marketing or convention/trade show work) temporary help from local temporary employment agencies to help with sales and registration.

□ Accept credit cards. Many participants will not have checks or cash on hand to buy your products but will have credit cards. You can substantially increase sales and your overall profits by accepting credit cards.

□ Be aware of sales tax requirements. Technically, you are required to charge sales tax and pay it to the state in which you sell the products; however, knowing the laws and rates and paying sales tax in 40+ states (or the number of states in which you conduct

seminars) is rather difficult. Most seminar and workshop promoters don't charge sales-tax except in their state of domicile and
don't worry about the other states until they are asked. You should
know that Congress is considering requiring all direct mail marketers (of a certain size/sales level) to charge and pay sales tax in
all taxing states.

▫ Test various product prices to ascertain the optimum price to
charge—the highest price participants are willing to pay for the
perceived value of the product.

▫ Stimulate sales by providing incentives for participants to make
purchases while at the seminar—discounted prices, free gifts, special packages or combinations, and so on.

The development, marketing, and sale of information products as
supplements to your seminar can be highly lucrative and successful;
with thought, planning, and creativity, you should enjoy both profits
and success.

Although those new to the seminar business rarely have **BOR** or after-
seminar products to sell when they start, they quickly learn that selling
products is profitable. On the average, those with substantial **BOR** sales
operations derive about ⅓ of their total seminar profit from these sales. A
provider of a one-day, $195 seminar, conducted 40 times a year in the
United States and Canada, found that BOR sales had a profitable impact:

Before Back-of-the-Room Selling	
Gross registration receipts (40 × $195)	$7,800
Less: Cost of promotion	2,900
Gross margin	4,900
Program delivery and conduct	2,050
Seminar net profit	$2,850
After Back-of-the-Room Selling	
Gross registration receipts (40 × $195)	$7,800
Less: Cost of promotion	2,900
Gross margin	4,900
Program delivery and conduct	2,100*
Seminar net profit	2,800
Back-of-the-room sales (14 × $168)	2,352
Balance	5,152
Less: Cost of product sold BOR	718
Total program profit	$4,434

*Increased costs due to sale of products = $50

Sales will be greatly stimulated if you are willing to deliver products on site. Participants like to take delivery of a product at the time of purchase. With a sufficient number of participants in the room you can stimulate a buying psychology. Don't set out your entire inventory in view of participants; display two or three of each item being sold. Fear of scarcity stimulates sales. You can replenish items as they are sold.

Use refreshment and meal breaks to provide an opportunity for participants to buy. Position the refreshments adjacent to the product display and just prior to the break judiciously mention the value of having one of the products. Encourage participants to take time during the break to look at an example of what you are talking about. Pay close attention to the selling strategies used each time the seminar is conducted and note the impact on profits. Test different offers, packages, and combinations and keep track of results, perhaps using a sales analysis form such as is shown in Figure 12–3.

For most seminars that appeal to business executives and professionals, a soft sell produces the best results. Remember, your participants paid for a seminar, not a commercial. Subtle mention of the availability of the products will generally be best. Avoid selling too early during the seminar; don't start the seminar with your sales pitch. Wait for the participants to become comfortable with you, to gain confidence in your professionalism.

If you do not have products to sell and lack time to create and produce them, consider selling the products of others. Although not as profitable as selling your own products, most book and cassette publishers will be happy to sell you their products at wholesale.

IMPACT OF BACK-OF-THE-ROOM SALES ON PROFIT AND IMAGE

Seminar, workshop, class, and conference providers expend considerable time and effort trying to assess the impact on program profit of engaging in BOR selling of information products such as books, tapes, software, newsletter subscriptions, and the like. Some, particularly nonprofit sponsors, worry too about the impact that BOR selling will have on their image as an educational provider. To shed some light on these questions, the following research may be of value.

In a carefully controlled study of nine seminars on business-related subjects, the sponsor attempted to determine the extent to which BOR sales impacted profits. Each of the nine seminars was conducted five times without BOR sales and five times with BOR sales. The seminars were conducted in different geographical locations. Dollar profit at the BOR sales seminars averaged 32.5 percent more—not an unexpected finding. But, how did BOR selling impact image? The following survey data from 1,567 participants, collected prior to the participants' departure from

BACK-OF-THE-ROOM SALES ANALYSIS FORM

Seminar: _____

Location: _____

Date: _____

No. of participants _____

Participant Name	BOR Order ($)	How Paid*	Items Purchased							Comments
			A	B	C	D	E	F	G	

Total BOR sales $_____

Less: Cost of goods sold $_____

Profit $_____

Profit per order $_____

Profit per participant $_____

Notes: Analyze sales and methods used and record pertinent information which may impact future selling strategies.

_____

_____

_____

* C = Check; V = VISA; M = MasterCard; A = American Express; X = Cash.

Figure 12–3. Sample form for analyzing back-of-the-room sales.

the seminars, indicate that participants rate seminars that include BOR sales less favorably.

Question Topic	BOR Sales	No BOR Sales
1. Overall satisfaction with the program	8.4°	8.8°
2. Professionalism of the speaker	8.1	8.6
3. Adequacy of the written materials both within the seminar and as a resource for future use	7.2	7.7
4. Recommendation of this seminar to others	7.7	8.0
5. Attendance at another seminar sponsored by _____	8.2	8.4
6. Expectations met	8.3	8.5

° Scale = 1 (low) to 10 (high)

A total of 2,984 participants attended the seminars. Over an 18-month period following their participation in the seminars they were contacted by direct mail six times for the purpose of encouraging them to attend another seminar and/or to elicit provision of referrals of those who might be interested in attending one of the sponsor's seminars. Additional seminar registrations were received from 5.7 percent of those who attended BOR-selling seminars and 5.4 percent of those who attended non-BOR-selling seminars. With respect to referrals, 5.1 percent of those who attended non-BOR-selling seminars provided one or more referrals, compared to only 4.3 percent of those who attended BOR-selling seminars.

The provider concluded that it was more profitable, in general, to engage in BOR selling of information products.

In a second research effort on BOR selling style and methods, a provider determined that, for business and professional participants, a very low-key, indirect selling approach not only produced higher sales but met with fewer participants' complaints and greater total program satisfaction as measured by both immediate and longer term participant satisfaction surveys. Low-key and indirect selling methods resulted in 36.4 percent of the participants making a purchase at the seminars compared to 24.1 percent of those experiencing what was rated as a direct, more high-pressure selling strategy. A total of 81.2 percent of the participants rated the soft sell seminars at 9 or 10 (highest) on overall satisfaction (1 to 10 scale), but only 68.9 percent of those experiencing the hard sell did so. The benefits of the soft sell for business and professional participants have been confirmed in other studies.

For most business and professional seminars, research been determined that adopting the following strategies will increase total sales and total profits and will minimize any participant dissatisfaction that might be associated with **BOR** selling:

1. Display items being sold throughout the on-site registration period and during the entire seminar.
2. Be able to deliver all or most orders on the spot.
3. Do not sell from the podium too early during the seminar. Participants need to establish confidence in and gain trust in the presenter before they are receptive to buying.
4. Minimize time spent selling. Participants dislike commercials when they have paid a fee to attend.
5. Sell indirectly. Weave into the presentation short comments about the value of items being sold. Suggest that participants take a look at a product (on display in the back of the room) to gain a better understanding of an idea being presented.
6. Accept credit cards as a means of payment.
7. Create packages. Participants prefer to buy **BOR** products in groups of three, four, five, seven, and so on.
8. Discount prices for purchases made during the seminar. Participants need an incentive for buying during the seminar. Discounts, bonuses, or gifts work well.
9. Do not display all available inventory. Scarcity encourages earlier purchases and higher total sales. As inventory moves, replenish from back stock to create an appearance that there may only be two or three of a given item remaining.

A number of providers have found that **BOR** selling is responsible for as much as half of a program's total profits. If done correctly and tastefully it will have a favorable economic impact on revenues and profits. Participant dissatisfaction, if any, can be minimized with careful monitoring of selling methods and styles. You should consider testing **BOR** selling in your programs and experiment repeatedly on different offers and selling approaches.

TURNING SEMINAR PARTICIPANTS INTO CONSULTING CLIENTS

While BOR sales can be very profitable, sales of services can be much more so, and seminars provide an excellent avenue for promoting your consulting services. Research reveals that one out of every nine seminar attendees becomes a client for consulting services, if the seminar leader/consultant is sufficiently skilled at deriving the more lucrative follow-on consulting opportunities from seminar and speaking engagements. The following are proven tips on how to turn seminar participants into consulting clients:

1. *Never solicit consulting business directly.* Feel free to allude to the fact that you do consulting, even tell anecdotes of consulting experiences (without revealing names or proprietary information) if they are relevant to and/or illustrate points in your seminar, but never solicit. No one wants to do business with someone they feel needs the business or is hungry.

2. *Encourage participants to phone or write to you after the seminar, to ask quick questions.* To obtain consulting opportunities, your objective in conducting the seminar is to be seen as both knowledgeable and accessible.

3. *Do a fantastic job.* Nothing sells like success. If you put on an informative, entertaining, quality seminar, the consulting business will follow.

4. *Put your name, address, and phone number on every piece of material (ideally on every page) you hand out or sell.* This will make it easier for participants and others who see the material to contact you.

5. *Send your participants a follow-up letter after the seminar.* Thank them for their participation, give them your evaluation of how the day went, and encourage them to communicate with you in terms of future needs and their evaluation of the program.

6. *Consider clipping an interesting article and sending it, along with a personal note, to your seminar participants several days or weeks after the seminar has been completed.* This serves to keep you in relevant contact with those who are potential clients or referral sources.

7. *In a casual and indirect way, let your participants know that referrals are valuable to you.* Perhaps tell an interesting story of how a past seminar participant put you in touch with someone who could benefit from your services. Let the participants know that the opportunity was advantageous for both: you received a client and the client obtained valuable advice, assistance, or information. But be subtle; remember not to solicit business directly.

8. *Be visible and accessible to participants during breaks and before and after the seminar.* The more available you are for questions, conversation, brief chats, and short discussion of problems, the better your chances of demonstrating your knowledge and expertise, mentioning the services you provide, and subtly promoting your availability for consulting assignments.

9. *Never hold back on information during a program.* Don't lead participants to believe that they must pay for your services as a consultant

to obtain the information they feel they are entitled to (and *are* entitled to) by paying the seminar fee. One of consultants' greatest mistakes is withholding information; this frustrates and angers participants and hurts future consulting—and seminar—opportunities. Show off your knowledge, skills, and expertise to best advantage, expounding on as much information as possible in the given time, leaving the impression that much more can and should be said on the subject.

10. *Develop a systematic means of following up with your past participants.* For example, a newsletter, even if only quarterly, is an excellent way of maintaining contact with those who could provide future business and/or referrals, letting them know that you are still active in their area of interest, needs and problems.

11. *Make sure that any biographical information which participants receive mentions the fact that you do consulting.* Such information should stress your accomplishments (without disclosing names or proprietary information), particularly those achieved for others.

12. *Dress and act in a fashion appropriate for you in your consulting role.* Even though the seminar or workshop setting may be casual, you should avoid being too casual in clothing or behavior. But also avoid being too formal. Dress and behave as you would expect a serious professional consultant to, if you were a participant in the seminar.

13. *Demonstrate that your knowledge and expertise are state-of-the-art.* Cite current research, up-to-date articles, and new information. Whenever possible, report on your own research and studies to demonstrate that you are a contributor, on the topics you are discussing, to the state of the art in your field.

These simple but highly effective strategies can help you take advantage of the marketing potential of your seminar and turn program participants into consulting clients. In addition to gaining you clients, such tactics should increase seminar enrollments as satisfied participants refer others to your excellent program.

13

PROMOTER, PRESENTER, AND PARTICIPANT

While the success of a seminar or workshop may be more a function of marketing and promotion than a result of program design, materials development, and instructional competency, the people involved in your program—the presenters and their knowledge and skill, the participants and their satisfaction—are of tantamount importance. They will have a great impact on word of mouth and referrals and, for some providers, referrals account for 10 to 20 percent of total seminar registrations.

THE PRESENTERS

Conducting your seminar or workshop yourself, particularly on a subject near to your heart and for which you have a fund of knowledge and information, can be an exciting, rewarding, and very profitable venture. Moreover, presenting the program yourself can be the most cost-effective option, especially if you are just starting out, because you avoid the salary, extra overhead, and travel expenses necessitated by hiring an outside presenter. However, there are circumstances and reasons which can warrant the services of an outside presenter; among these are:

1. You understand and excel at the development, promotion, and marketing aspects of the seminar and workshop business but don't know where to begin to conduct the program yourself, or you don't have the necessary knowledge and understanding of the seminar topic to present it yourself.

2. You want to break up into smaller groups during the program and need additional personnel to facilitate (conduct and direct) the smaller groups.

3. Your program is too long and extensive for you to do all of the presenting without putting a severe strain on yourself but building participant self-study materials, skill exercises, and task activities into the agenda to give yourself a rest is insufficient or inappropriate for your program; or, your presentation needs more diversity to keep your participants interested.

4. Your program is structured as a panel or forum, requiring the presence of experts in the field or in various fields.

5. You want to increase the exposure of your program without spreading yourself too thin; thus, you hire someone who will travel to cities to which you would rather not travel or who is a resident in an area you want covered.

6. The drawing power of the name or reputation of the outside speaker is so great that you will garner many additional participants and much greater profit.

Once you decide to hire a presenter, you must select the type of presenter you need. If your agenda and seminar materials are highly detailed, developed, and structured and your program is carefully outlined, with all of the necessary information and resources at the presenter's fingertips, then your presenter need not be an absolute authority on the subject—an experienced speaker working from your prepared material can conduct a good seminar. Indeed, if your program will be conducted many times with many different presenters, your best assurance of consistent quality is to develop a detailed and explicit set of notes that can be adapted to many individual styles of presentation. However, if your seminar or workshop has a short market life, will only be current and pertinent for a short period, or is aimed at a very limited audience for a limited amount of time, then instead of putting your money into in-depth program and material development, you might best spend your money on hiring the best presenter you can find—an expert on the subject, a dynamic speaker who is capable of fielding questions or handling unexpected situations and is able to work from limited material. Figure 13–1 illustrates this principle. Low presenter knowledge and skill requires highly developed program materials and higher development cost. High presenter knowledge and skill requires less structured and less detailed materials, lower development cost, and higher presenter cost.

FINDING PRESENTERS

Once you choose the type of person needed to conduct your program, you must seek out the individual. There are many sources of qualified speakers; you need only look into some of them to find your speaker.

1. *People You Know.* Friends, colleagues, and professional acquaintances may be qualified and happy to conduct your seminar themselves. Or they may know personally or professionally (or know of) talented people in the subject field. Ask them. You may be pleasantly surprised with the successful results.

THE PRESENTER AND THE MATERIALS

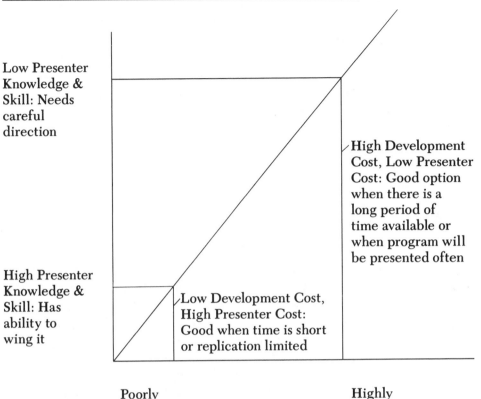

Low Presenter
Knowledge &
Skill: Needs
careful
direction

High Development
Cost, Low Presenter
Cost: Good option
when there is a
long period of
time available or
when program will
be presented often

High Presenter
Knowledge &
Skill: Has
ability to
wing it

Low Development Cost,
High Presenter Cost:
Good when time is short
or replication limited

Poorly
Developed
Unstructured
Materials

Highly
Developed
Structured
Materials

Figure 13–1. Interrelationships of presenter, materials, and costs.

2. *Universities and Colleges.* Educational institutions can be valuable sources of speakers. People in educational environments usually have excellent language and teaching skills along with expertise and the ability to communicate and dialog on ideas about their field of knowledge in a classroom situation. Moreover, the academic environment is, in general, sufficiently flexible so that the availability of academics' time is quite good. With little trouble, you might be able to retain a full- or part-time professor, teacher, instructor, or researcher to conduct your program during university breaks or extracurricular hours.

3. *Business and Government.* Qualified experts and authorities on a myriad of subjects can be found in business and government; many of them hold prominent positions or have written books or articles on your topic and are good candidates to present your program.

4. *Advertisements.* By running ads in appropriate publications (newspapers, magazines, trade and professional journals) and specifying the qualifications and expertise you are seeking, you can generate responses from highly viable candidates. Be as straightforward and specific as possible in your advertisement, to immediately eliminate unsuitable individuals.

5. *Speakers' Bureaus.* Speakers' bureaus are organizations that provide speakers from various backgrounds for seminars and lectures. Such speakers can be expensive, but a bureau is a quick track to finding sophisticated, seasoned professionals to conduct your program.

6. *The Competition.* You can tap the skills of other seminar and workshop developers and promoters whose programs and styles of presentation you are already familiar with, although this is obviously not a possibility with programs that are directly in competition with yours.

Before hiring a presenter, you should be aware of a few cautions and precautions. Often, the drawing power of prominent names and reputations is considerably less than you might expect it to be. Individuals may occasionally attend a seminar because of the reputation of the speaker but more often the content of the program will determine a decision to attend. Thus, your very qualified presenter need not be a world-renowned expert on the subject.

Knowledge, however, is not enough! Because a person has information to convey does not guarantee the skills needed for a seminar or workshop setting. It is wise, if you have an opportunity, to hear the prospective presenter speak in an environment similar to that of your program. You can then evaluate his presentation skills and knowledgeability before you make a commitment.

You can often obtain competent outside speakers free or for very little expense. The opportunity for public exposure and potential contacts is often sufficient reward for presenters, particularly professional practitioners who regard the exposure as an opportunity to find new clients. Indeed, there are few situations where it is necessary to spend great sums of money to acquire a qualified seminar leader/presenter.

Beware of egos. A major disadvantage to using outside speakers is that their egos and their interests may clash with your own. You don't need to benefit others at the expense of yourself and your interests.

Figure 13–2 shows a sample form that will help you to screen potential presenters for your seminar or workshop.

PROFITABILITY OF SPONSORED PROGRAMS

Research has revealed that it may well be to the benefit of proprietary providers and entrepreneurial program developers to link up with colleges,

SEMINAR PRESENTER INFORMATION SHEET

1. Name _____

2. Mailing address _____

   _____

   _____

3. Telephone: Home: _____   Business: _____

4. Best time of day/evening to reach you: _____

5. Present position _____

6. Name & address _____
   of present
   employer   _____

                  _____

7. To what professional organizations do you belong?

   _____

   _____

8. Have you conducted this or similar programs for professional groups?

   Locally: ____ No ____ Yes: For _____   On _____

   Regionally: ____ No ____ Yes: For _____   On _____

   Nationally: ____ No ____ Yes: For _____   On _____

9. Have you conducted this or similar presentations for other public or
   private groups?

   ____ No ____ Yes: For whom and when: _____

   _____

10. Please list the names and phone numbers of three persons who could
    discuss your ability to make this presentation.

    Name   Phone #

    _____

    _____

    _____

Figure 13–2. Presenter screening form.

Part II

1. Listed below are topics that are of interest to us and our audience. Please check the ones you have presented on or would like to present on.

   Topic   Have Presented   Would Like To

   _____   _____   _____

   _____   _____   _____

   _____   _____   _____

   _____   _____   _____

   _____   _____   _____

2. What is the proposed title of your session?

3. Briefly describe your session: its purpose, objectives, and format; the skills, knowledge, or attitudes it addresses, etc.:

4. Briefly outline the major points you will cover:

Figure 13–2. (*continued*)

universities, associations, and other high-profile providers who will sponsor their seminars and workshops. The advantage can be mutual. Many continuing-education providers incur high costs to develop and bring to market new, highly demanded, state-of-the-art programs. The lack of an entrepreneurial environment within institutional organizations often makes creation of programs difficult.

Given the difficulty that so many institutional providers experience in bringing "hot" programs to market, it is surprising that so few have taken time to sell their services as a sponsor to proprietary and entrepreneurial developers/providers. In addition, the majority of proprietary providers report that when they initiate contact with potential institutional sponsors they frequently encounter a lack of interest and understanding and a barrier of bureaucracy. If both sponsor and developer/presenter could recognize how smooth their working together could be, all (including participants) would benefit.

These suggestions are directed toward both sponsors and developers/presenters:

1. Sponsors should inform developers/presenters about the financial and public relations benefits of having their programs sponsored. A 1988 study of 23 different proprietary seminars presented by 18 different institutional sponsors indicated that for 19 of the programs the marketing expense was lower per registration received than when the programs were offered by the developer. On the average, marketing expense was 17.2 percent less. In a perfect A/B split-run, controlled test using two identical newspaper ads for a management seminar, one ad prominently indicated that a major university was the sponsor. Being sponsored paid off: 39 registrations were secured from the sponsor-indicated ad, but only 25 were secured from the other ad.

2. Developers/presenters need to understand that they must give up some profit for the benefit of being sponsored. After all, the sponsor is not in business for nothing. On the other hand, sponsors need to be realistic about what they expect the developer to give up. One successful proprietary developer consistently earned a program profit (including instructor compensation, but not expenses) of $3,400. Seeing the advantage of sponsorship with a local college he was surprised to learn that the college would pay only $500 for his services—despite substantial data about his successful track record. Even when he expressed a willingness to work on a profit split, he discovered that the sponsor's offer was unlikely to yield him more than $1,100. One professional association consistently cuts deals with proprietary providers on a share-the-risk/share-the-profit basis. It works well for both. The parties agree to a budget for all expenses and split both the expenses and the profits fifty-fifty. During 1987 and 1988 the association sponsored 14 programs.

The average profit earned per program equalled $3,410. The association's management likes the risk-sharing formula. The program director believes that such an arrangement is fair to both and the marketing support of the proprietary partner enlists someone just as interested in the program's success as the association is.

3. Both parties should realize that proprietary developed programs may be the best sellers. One major university compared profitability on outside developed/conducted programs with its in-house developed offerings. In a comparison of 27 outside and 52 inside programs, the profit margin on outside programs was 22.6 percent higher. Program area managers now have an added job responsibility—scouring the country for proprietary programs that show strong promise. The dean of continuing education notes, "These entrepreneurs are teaching us a lot about marketing. We used to tell them how to market. Now we have come to understand that they know a great deal about how to get the right participants into their programs. What we are learning is having an impact on how we promote our internal programs too."

AGREEMENTS

If you decide that it is necessary and beneficial for you to retain outside presenters (or if you are conducting a captive program for a sponsor), you should always work under a written agreement or contract. Written documents provide you (and your speaker or sponsor) with some measure of security and also serve to clarify the business relationship by spelling out terms in a straightforward manner. Whatever the nature of your agreement—be it an informal letter or a formally drafted contract—include provisions for the following:

1. *Compensation.* Terms for payment should be clear and concise. Your obligations to the presenter should not be contingent on the success of your program or payment from clients, or open to responsibility for unforeseen program costs, unless agreed on in writing beforehand.

2. *Nature and Extent of Services.* The parties involved, whether corporations or individuals, and the program(s) to be presented should be clearly defined. Your responsibilities and the presenter's should be specified.

3. *Period of Service.* The duration of the business relationship should be established, and provisions (and penalties) for termination should be included.

4. *Protection.* The copyright of your materials should be protected by you. You should also set clear liability limits.

5. *Control and Authority.* You should specify who (you or the presenter) has control and authority over what—press releases, requests for refunds, and so on—and under what circumstances.

The following documents are sample written agreements for your review. The first two are letters of agreement—the first is between a sponsor and seminar developer/presenter (Figure 13–3), and the second, between a seminar promoter and outside presenter/developer (Figure 13–4). These are not formal contracts; however, they are designed to illustrate a commonly used form of agreement and to show you what sorts of information can be—and typically are—included in a written agreement of this type. Figure 13–5 is a typical (and more formal) contract which could be used for a sponsored or in-house training program.

If you retain outside presenters to conduct your seminar, take the following measures to ensure that the experience will be successful:

□ Always test out presenters before turning them loose on your participants.

□ Train your presenters and orient them to the participant group.

□ Ensure that presenters complement, not duplicate, one another.

□ Schedule and conduct a meeting for the presenters in advance of the program, to review materials and policies, discuss problems, and so on.

□ Have backup presenters available in case planned presenters cannot conduct the program.

Under certain circumstances, and with careful research and precautions, retaining outside presenters can be an expremently helpful, relieving, and profitable experience for you.

THE PARTICIPANTS

Understanding people's motivation to attend your seminar or workshop can help you to make the most of the program—for your participants and yourself. By knowing some of the prospective participants' reasons for attending, you can target their desires and needs, thus attracting them to the seminar. And once they have registered, you can better ensure that the information and agenda of the program will fulfill those needs and

```
                          (Letterhead)

Date


Name
Company
Address
City/State/Zip

Dear


This letter shall serve as an agreement between _____,
hereinafter the "Sponsor," and _____, hereinafter the
"Consultant," governing the development and conduct of _____
_____ for _____ on _____.

The Consultant  shall supply camera-ready masters of materials
to be provided to participants for duplication by the Sponsor and
distribution to participants on or before _____.

The Sponsor  shall supply a head table, speakers podium, hand
held microphone and overhead projector for transparencies.

The Sponsor agrees to provide the Consultant with the names,
addresses and telephone numbers (when available) of all
participants.

The Sponsor shall compensate the Consultant in an amount equal to
_____.   This compensation shall be for professional services
and travel expenses and shall be paid as follows:

     . Upon acceptance of this agreement............._____
     . On or before _____ ...................._____

If this agreement is not signed and returned along with the
initial payment due at the time of execution on or before _____
it shall be voidable at the option of the Consultant.

If the terms of this agreement meet with your acceptance, please
return a signed copy of the agreement along with your check.


Sincerely,


_____

               Accepted for _____

                       By_____

                       Date_____
```

Figure 13–3. Sample letter of agreement between sponsor and seminar provider.

```
                              (Letterhead)

Date

Name
Company
Address
City/State/Zip

Dear

1. This letter shall serve as an agreement between _____,
hereinafter the "Client," and _____, hereinafter the
"Consultant," governing services to be provided by the
Consultant in connection with the development and/or conduct of
seminars, workshops and training programs and related services
for the Client as herein specified.

2. The Consultant shall provide services as determined necessary
and appropriate for the general benefit of the Client, including
but not limited to: _____.

3. All services will be provided with the highest and best state
of the art known to the Consultant.  The Consultant reserves full
control of his or her activities as to the manner and selection
of methods used with respect to rendering his or her services.

4. The Consultant is an independent contractor and shall provide
workmen's compensation insurance or self-insure his or her
services.  The Consultant is not an employee of the Client and
shall be personally responsible for the payment of any and all
United States, state and local income taxes.  The Consultant
shall also hold and keep blameless the Client, its officers,
agents and employees from all damages, costs or expenses in law
or equity that may at any time arise due to injury to, death of
persons or damages to property, including Client property,
arising by reason of, or in the course of performance of this
agreement.  Accordingly, the Client shall not be liable or
responsible for any accident, loss or damage, and the Consultant
at his or her own expense, cost and risk, shall defend any and
all actions, suits or legal proceedings that may be brought or
instituted against the Client, its officers or agents thereof on
any claim or demand, and pay or satisfy any judgment that may be
rendered against the Client, its officers or agents in any such
action, suit or legal proceeding.

5. The period of service by the Consultant under this agreement
shall be from _____ through _____ and may be renewed
upon the mutual agreement of the parties hereto.  Either the
Client or the Consultant may terminate this agreement by giving
the other party _____ days written notice of intent to
terminate.
```

Figure 13-4. Sample letter of agreement between seminar promoter and outside
presenter.

```
Name
Company
Letter of Agreement
Date
Page 2 of 4
```

6. The Client reserves the right to halt or terminate the conduct of any seminar, workshop, training program, lecture or presentation by the Consultant without prior notice or claim for additional compensation should the Client determine that the conduct of such activity by the Consultant is not in the best interest of the Client.

7. Upon the Consultant's acceptance hereof, the Client agrees to compensate the Consultant for services provided under this agreement as follows: _____ .

8. Client agrees to notify the Consultant, in writing, of an engagement of the Consultant's services for the conduct of a specific seminar, workshop, training program or presentation as far in advance of the scheduled date of such services as practicable, but in no case in less than _____ days in advance of such activity.

9. The Consultant, as an independent contractor, shall be responsible for any expenses incurred in the performance of this agreement, except as otherwise agreed to in writing prior to such expense being incurred. The Client agrees to reimburse the Consultant for reasonable travel expenses incurred as follows: _____ .

10. Payment to the Consultant by the Client for fees due and reimbursement of authorized expenses shall be as follows: _____ _____ .

11. The Consultant agrees that the Client shall determine the disposition of the title to and the rights under any copyright secured by the Consultant or his or her employee on copyrightable material first produced or composed and delivered to the Client under this agreement. The Consultant hereby grants to the Client a royalty free, nonexclusive, irrevocable license to reproduce, translate, publish, use and dispose of, and to authorize others to do so, all copyrighted or copyrightable work not first produced by the Consultant in the performance of this agreement but which is incorporated into any materials furnished under this agreement, provided that such license shall be only to the extent that the Consultant now has or prior to the completion of the final settlement of this agreement may acquire the right to grant such license without becoming liable to pay compensation to others solely because of such grant.

12. The Consultant agrees that he or she will not knowingly include any copyrighted material in any written or copyrightable material furnished or delivered under this agreement without a

Figure 13–4. (*continued*)

license as provided in paragraph 11 hereof or without the consent of the copyright owner, unless specific written approval of the Client allowing the inclusion of such copyrighted material is secured. The Consultant agrees to report in writing to the Client promptly and in reasonable detail any notice or claim of copyright infringement received by the Consultant with respect to any material delivered under this agreement.

13. Any and all drawings, sketches, designs, design data, specifications, notebooks, technical and scientific data, photographs, negatives, reports, findings, recommendations, data and memoranda of every description including preliminary working papers in any media, including computer media, of every description relating thereto, as well as copies of the foregoing relating to work performed under this agreement shall be subject to inspection of the Client at all reasonable times; and the Consultant or his or her employees shall afford the Client proper facilities for such inspection; and further shall be the property of the Client and may be used by the Client for any purpose whatsoever without any claim on the part of the Consultant and his or her employees for additional compensation, and subject to the right of the Consultant to retain a copy of such materials shall be delivered to the Client or otherwise disposed of as the Client may direct during the progress of the work, upon its completion or at time of termination of this agreement.

14. This agreement is binding upon and enures to the benefit of the parties hereto and their respective heirs, assigns, successors, executors, administrators and personal representatives and shall be governed by the laws of the state of
_____.

15. In the event of a dispute relative to this agreement, either party may request and require that such dispute be resolved by arbitration under the procedures established by the American Arbitration Association, with the site of such arbitration being _____ or such other location as the parties may mutually agree.

16. This agreement is the entire and complete agreement between the parties and no reliance is made by either party regarding any warranties or representations not included within this agreement and this agreement may be extended in duration and/or scope by mutual written agreement.

17. No waiver of any provision herein shall be deemed or shall constitute a waiver of any other provision of this agreement. In the event that any provision of this agreement shall be

Figure 13-4. (continued)

determined to be unenforceable or voidable, all other provisions of this agreement shall remain in full force.

18. If any legal action or other proceeding is brought for the enforcement of this agreement, or because of an alleged dispute, breach, default or misrepresentation in connection with any of the provisions of this agreement, the successful or prevailing party or parties shall be entitled to recover reasonable attorneys' fees and other costs incurred in that action or proceeding, in addition to any other relief to which it or they may be entitled.

19. The Client reserves the right to assign all or any part of its interest in and to this agreement. The Consultant may not assign or transfer his or her responsibilities under this agreement without prior written approval of the Client.

20. If a signed copy of this agreement is not returned to the Client by the Consultant on or before _____ it shall be voidable at the option of the Client.

If the terms and conditions of this agreement meet with your approval please sign and return a copy of this agreement for my files.

I look forward to a long and mutually beneficial working arrangement between us.

Sincerely,

_____

Accepted for _____

By _____

Date _____

Figure 13–4. (*continued*)

[Letterhead]

AGREEMENT

THIS AGREEMENT is made, this _____ day of _____, 19___
by and between _____ and _____, hereinafter referred
to as the "University" and "Contractor."

WITNESSETH:

WHEREAS, the University desires to develop and conduct a training program for
its personnel and the personnel of such other eligible education agencies as may
become participants in this program, and

WHEREAS, the purposes of said training program are to:

Upgrade the managerial and technical skills of career counseling and placement personnel and increase the professional stature of career counseling and
placement personnel and provide a cadre of trained professionals and appropriate materials to continue further training as required with minimum funding support needed, and provide a vehicle for the ongoing assessment of
in-service training needs of career counseling and placement personnel.

WHEREAS, the Contractor is particularly skilled and competent to conduct such
a management training program, and

WHEREAS, funds for this contract are budgeted for and included in a federal
project plan approved under _____, and as described in the
program prospectus identified as Grant _____, which is hereinafter referred to as the "Project," and

WHEREAS, said Project was approved [date] and project expenditures approved
on [date]

NOW, THEREFORE, it is mutually agreed as follows:

1. The term of this Agreement shall be for the period commencing [date], continuing to and until [date].
2. The Contractor agrees to develop and conduct a training program consisting
   in part of a series of three workshop session presentations. Each of said
   workshop presentations shall be of eight hours' duration and shall be conducted at [place]. The aforesaid training program shall be developed and
   conducted by the Contractor in accordance with the project prospectus sub-
   mitted by the University for funding under _____ and in particular
   with the "attachment" to said program prospectus, which is marked Exhibit
   "A," attached hereto and by reference incorporated herein.
3. The aforesaid workshop presentations shall include three days of intensive
   training using an approach which has demonstrated considerable success

Figure 13–5. Sample contract for sponsored or in-house training program.

working with career counseling and placement personnel of this type. Specific workshop topic coverage shall include the following:

    a.

    b.

    c.

4. The aforesaid training workshop will be conducted during the contract term in accordance with a schedule mutually agreed upon by the University and the Contractor.

5. In connection with the conducting and development of the aforesaid training program, the Contractor agrees as follows:

    a. The Contractor will plan for and prepare such necessary materials as are needed to conduct the various program sessions as described. Such material preparation and development will include the preparation of participant resource material, development of work sheets, orientation materials, participant guides and handbooks. All materials developed will reflect the highest standards of quality applicable to educational material development state of the art.

    b. The Contractor will provide expert session facilitation staff as follows:

    A minimum of one (1) expert staff for the first twelve (12) participants in attendance at each session, further the Contractor will provide one (1) additional expert staff for each additional twelve (12) participants in attendance at each session to a maximum of 48 total participants per session.

    c. The Contractor will regularly consult with designated personnel of the University for the purpose of monitoring program progress and planned activities so as to improve and strengthen the overall program.

6. The Contractor further agrees to:

    a. Furnish the University on or before [date] with a final report. This report will describe all relevant aspects of program activity and will be in such style and format as to comply with the requirements of the enabling grant.

    b. Prepare appropriate pre-session and post-session participant testing materials to enable the ongoing assessment of the overall program activities. The Contractor shall collect, analyze, and interpret these findings as an integral part of the program development and conduct activity.

    c. Conduct, within 4 to 6 months after the conclusion of the workshop presentations, a post-test follow-up survey which will seek to discover what difficulties, if any, the participants in the program have encountered in applying the principles developed in the workshop training activity to career counseling and placement problems. A component of the follow-up survey will probe for participant attitude and individual assessment of the relevancy of the workshop training activity and the topic material in the context of program administration experience during the intervening period.

    d. Furnish the University with copies of all written and visual materials produced for distribution to the workshop participants. The Contractor will retain no proprietary rights to such materials, said rights being vested to the University.

Figure 13–5. (*continued*)

7. The University agrees as follows:

   a. To designate one of its staff members as Project Director to represent the University in all technical matters pertaining to this program.

   b. To arrange the necessary pre-program advertisement and participant notification so as to encourage participation.

   c. To provide or otherwise arrange for facilities which are adequate to conduct the workshop sessions.

   d. To limit session attendance, exclusive of Contractor staff, to the maximum eligible number of participants _____ plus up to three (3) additional non-participating persons.

   e. To make the necessary arrangements with the participating educational agencies to make personnel available as participants in all specified training activities.

   f. To arrange for the use on an as-available basis of University instructional equipment including 16mm sound projectors, overhead transparency projectors, 35mm slide projectors, tape recorders, and/or related audiovisual equipment, as requested by the Contractor in response to program requirements.

      The University agrees to provide competent personnel to operate all such equipment. The University will provide adequate maintenance and care of such equipment and will provide operational assistance to the Contractor as requested.

   g. To distribute to the program participants at the request of the Contractor, various project materials which are relevant to the program. Such materials may include training session handout material, descriptive information, questionnaires, and announcements.

   h. To provide or arrange for assistance to the Contractor at training session locations as mutually agreed in connection with facility arrangements, scheduling, and other matters pertaining to the successful conduct of the program.

8. It is expressly understood and agreed by both parties hereto that the Contractor while engaging in carrying out and complying with any of the terms and conditions of this contract is an independent Contractor and is not an office, agent, or employee of the University.

9. The Contractor shall provide workers' compensation insurance or self-insure his services. He shall also hold and keep harmless the University and all officers, agents and employees thereof from all damages, costs or expenses in law or equity that may at any time arise or be set up because of injury to or death of persons or damage to property, including University property, arising by reason of, or in the course of the performance of this contract, nor shall the University be liable or responsible for any accident, loss or damage, and the Contractor, at his own expense, cost and risk, shall defend any and all actions, suits or other legal proceedings that may be brought or instituted against the University or officers or agents thereof on any claim or demand, and pay or satisfy any judgment that may be rendered against the University or officers or agents thereof in any such action, suit or legal proceeding.

Figure 13–5. (*continued*)

10. In consideration of the satisfactory performance of the Contractor, the University agrees to reimburse the Contractor in the amount of Fifteen Thousand Dollars ($15,000) in accordance with the following schedule:

30 May 19____	$ 6,000.00
30 June 19____	$ 5,000.00
30 July 19____	$ 4,000.00
	$15,000.00

IN WITNESS WHEREOF, each party has caused this agreement to be executed by its duly authorized representative on the date first mentioned above.

CONTRACTOR   UNIVERSITY

_____   _____
Name   Name
Title   Title

Figure 13–5. (*continued*)

desires to the best of your abilities. The following motivations are among the most prevalent reasons that individuals attend seminars or workshops:

1. *The Desire to Learn.* Personal interests and/or professional ambitions can motivate an individual to want to learn more about a topic.

2. *The Desire to Make More Money.* Almost everyone wants to learn how to increase profits and/or save or maintain accumulated wealth.

3. *Self-Recognition of Limitations.* Some people register for a program as a means of overcoming self-perceived limitations.

4. *Desire for Self-Improvement.* Many individuals seek physical (appearance, personal style, public image), mental (education, philosophy, psychology, influencing others), and/or spiritual self-improvement through seminars and workshops.

5. *Change of Organizational or Personal Priorities.* Career and life events can lead to a need or desire to expand one's horizons.

6. *Change in Job Description or Working Conditions.* The dynamic nature of the workplace often requires individuals to expand their career roles or change professions entirely.

7. *New or Added Personnel.* Expansion and restaffing can create a need for training, which may be as casual as on-the-job training or as formal as a degree program at a college or university (captive program).

8. *Ineffective or Inefficient Procedures.* A poor efficiency level can lead to a need for training, although, depending on its nature, the problem can also be handled by better management, increased proceduralization, or reduction of the human element. Training is often the preferable solution because it reaches the root of the problem and develops human resources within an organization.

9. *Mandates of Government or Trade and Professional Associations.* To respond adequately to new regulations can require additional knowledge or understanding.

SUCCESSFUL PARTICIPANT–PRESENTER RELATIONS

Potential participants' first contact with you is through your brochure or advertisement. Your promotion should convey a favorable impression of you and your program and should answer all of the readers' typical questions. Review your marketing promotion against the following checklist for promotions:

1. Motivational message
2. Cost, registration, and payment procedures

3. Your address and phone number
4. Background information on presenters
5. Information about seminar materials
6. Options if participants cannot attend
7. Business reply mechanism
8. An "act-now" kicker
9. Endorsements, testimonials, sponsors, or any other kind of accreditation
10. Tax-deductible status
11. Cancellation policy
12. Whom to contact for further information

When prospective participants call or write for further information, the favorable impression conveyed by your promotion should be confirmed. Telephone calls should be answered promptly, courteously, and competently by someone who can provide the desired information and answer questions or can direct and/or transfer the caller elsewhere for information. Reservations or requests for further information—by mail or by phone—should be responded to with a letter of confirmation, notice of pertinent details, and another brochure; quick response will heighten your image of professionalism and thoroughness. Sample letters of confirmation are given at the end of the chapter.

AT THE SEMINAR

When your participants arrive at the seminar site, they should be able to find you easily. The program should be posted on the meeting board in the hotel lobby; however, if it is not or if it is incorrect and you cannot get the hotel to change it, set up your own sign (which you should have with you for just such an occasion) with the name of the program, room number, date, and time.

Whenever possible, you should be on hand to meet your participants, ensure that they are relaxed and comfortable (have coffee/tea/decaffeinated coffee or suitable refreshments available at this time), answer questions, and verify that the registration process, for which you may have hired local temporary help, is going smoothly.

Before you begin the program, you should firmly establish your policy regarding dissatisfied participants and your policy regarding the use of tape recorders during the session. In fact, your policies on these issues should often be stated in your promotion and should always appear in your program materials so that registrants know ahead of time what to expect. However, you may not wish to advertise a very liberal money-back guarantee—even if you have one—because it tends to make people skeptical about the quality of your program. A good guarantee policy that protects the participant and avoids the provider's being taken advantage of is to offer a money-back guarantee for any person not satisfied with the program by the first coffee break (or about 75 to 90 minutes into the program). Tailor your policy according to what you feel is fair and appropriate for your program.

The same is true of your tape recording policy. If you sell live recordings of your program, you may not wish to allow any taping because you will lose sales; moreover, the clicking and fumbling that go along with taping can be distracting to the participants and the presenter. On the other hand, allowing participants to record your program provides them with an excellent resource for continued learning after the session, and while you may lose some potential participants because people will share the tapes with friends and colleagues, you may also gain new participants through the resulting word-of-mouth advertising (at no cost to you). Establishing these policies at the beginning of the program will eliminate most misunderstandings, avoid hasty or last-minute decisions on your part, and leave you free to concentrate on your presentation.

If you sell tapes and/or other information products relating to your program topic or related topics (to capture the lucrative BOR selling discussed earlier), you may wish to use a dual pricing structure: a slightly lower fee for the seminar and outline, and a higher fee for a complete seminar package—seminar, outline, cassette tapes, handbook, follow-up consultation, and so on. When preregistering, participants will often pay the lower price; however, once at the seminar, or following the seminar, many attendees will upgrade their order to the complete seminar package.

Stick to the planned schedule. Research has clearly demonstrated that seminar participants become dissatisfied with sloppy in-seminar time management. Start on time, end on time, begin and end refreshment and meal breaks when you say you will, and cover the topics in accordance with your promised schedule.

DEALING WITH QUESTIONS

Most seminar presenters are happy to answer questions and even encourage them—at convenient and appropriate times in the program. However, there will be times when you will be asked a question that you don't want to answer, particularly because you were about to answer the question in a few moments, or later in the program, or because it interrupts your train of thought and a specific point you were about to make.

If you were planning to address the question/issue later on, it is often best to provide some sort of partial or short answer to appease the questioner and some assurance that you will be answering the question in greater detail at a later time. If you can, be specific as to when it will be answered. If you had planned to answer the question within the next three to five minutes, you can avoid an immediate answer by indicating that it will be addressed in a moment or that it is included under the next heading in your outline or notes. If possible, answer the question immediately even if you have to alter your outline slightly or present your topics a little out of order, but don't do so at the expense of the point you were about to make.

Do not allow one or a few individuals to take over your seminar or workshop; it is your program, and people are paying to hear you conduct it. Some participants like to make speeches and/or want to turn your program into their program. To deal with such people, provide a short answer and, without pausing, go on with your planned remarks. Use their questions or comments as a bridge to the next point you were about to make.

If you really don't want to answer a question at a particular time, develop the skill of looking right through the questioner as if you don't notice the raised hand. If your peripheral vision is average or above, and if the meeting room is of normal width, you can look slightly to the left or right of the questioner and pretend that you do not see the waving hand. This at least allows you to complete your sentence and the particular point you are making without being interrupted. Most participants will not suspect that you are purposefully ignoring the questioner. It is also permissible for you to ignore questions blurted out or shouted out in the middle of your program without the courtesy of a raised hand and subsequent acknowledgment from the presenter. If you continue your program without stopping, most participants will realize that a raised hand is much more courteous, appropriate, and productive in receiving an answer.

However, don't make a practice of ignoring or putting off questions. By answering questions when they are asked, you acknowledge the right of the participants to take an active role in the learning process, instead of sitting back as passive recipients while you speak. In addition to responding to questions as they arise, you should plan specific times—twice a day, perhaps before lunch and again at the end of the day, or, if time allows, every hour or so—for question-and-answer or discussion sessions. Once the participants are aware that your agenda allows ample opportunity to ask questions or make comments, they may ask fewer questions in the middle of your presentation.

When the program has been conducted several times, the presenter will come to recognize the questions that are asked repeatedly and can incorporate their answers into the presentation, in anticipation of the question's reappearance. Guard against overdoing this; it tends to make the program less interesting and less spontaneous.

EVALUATING THE SUCCESS OF THE PROGRAM

While you are conducting your seminar or workshop, it is often beneficial to be aware of the response, attitude, and receptivity of your participants. Body language often communicates more than words (your participants are not likely to tell you that they are bored or enthused) and can reveal quite a lot about the moods and feelings of your audience. By understanding what messages some common body actions may be communicating from your participants, you will be better able to tune your presentation to their moods, attitudes, and feelings. You can then switch to an audiovisual presentation or an exercise if they are bored, or hold a question-and-answer session or review previously given information if they seem confused. Knowing the meanings or possible interpretations of common body actions and/or positions is important to any presenter:

1. Folded arms: Very defensive. *Prove it to me.*
2. Crossed legs: Bored and defensive.
3. Hand stroking the chin: Thinking about it. *I haven't reached a decision.*
4. Putting things (pencil/pen) in the mouth: *Give me more information. What's in it for me?*
5. Touching or rubbing the nose: *I doubt it. I don't believe you. Doesn't make sense.*
6. Rubbing eyes: *Convince me. I really don't know. Tell me what I should do.*
7. Sitting on the edge of the chair: *I'm interested. I'm cooperative.*
8. Unbuttoning of coat/jacket: *I'm opening up to you. I believe you.*
9. Tilted head: *I'm still interested.*
10. Short in and out breaths: Frustration and disgust. *Get out of here now.*
11. Tightly clenched hands: *I'm tense, not relaxed. I'm getting hostile.*
12. Palm to the back of the neck: Defensive. *Are you through yet?*
13. Clearing throat: Uncertain and apprehensive.
14. Fingers positioned to make a church steeple: Confident. *I'm very sure of what you are saying.*
15. Tugging at ear: *I want to say something. I want to talk.*

Program Evaluations and Follow-Ups

Program evaluations and follow-up communications will establish your eagerness to elicit feedback from participants and will illustrate your desire to maintain and improve the quality of your program and the satisfaction of your participants. (Two sample program evaluation forms— one designed for a public program and one for an in-house program—are shown in Figures 13–13 and 13–14, at the end of the chapter.) In a captive program, evaluations can reveal how much the trainees have learned from the session and help ascertain whether they need additional information that could have been incorporated into the program or can be supplied by other services you may provide. Feedback is valuable in public programs as well; however, a formal follow-up is often unnecessary because on-site comments about the program and future phone calls, letters, and visits to you from participants (or friends and colleagues of participants) will indicate the response to and the degree of success of your seminar or workshop.

Even if you do not conduct some sort of follow-up or evaluation, you should always be available directly after the seminar to talk with your participants and answer questions. Your time and your obvious concern for their needs and desires will contribute to their satisfaction with the program and their favorable impression of you. If you don't plan to con- duct a formal follow-up, you should write brief notes to your participants, thanking them for their participation in your program. If possible, be as personal as you can—comment on suggestions, questions, or compliments made by the participant; however, don't invent incidents which didn't take place or attribute comments that were not made by the participant. A follow-up letter can be the ideal way to ask for the names of friends and colleagues of the participant who might be interested in your program or to advise the participant of your other services or products which he might find helpful.

Figures 13–6 through 13–12 are sample follow-up and referral let- ters, letters to potential participants, and letters of confirmation for regis- tration. Figures 13–13 and 13–14 are sample program evaluation forms for your review. You can pattern your own letters and evaluation forms after these samples, adapting them as necessary.

```
Date


Name
Company
Address
City/State/Zip


Dear


It was my pleasure to meet you at _____ on _____
and I thank you for your thoughtful comments regarding my
remarks.  They are much appreciated.

My remarks were drawn from material which I use in my seminar
entitled _____.

I would welcome your participation in the seminar and have
enclosed a brochure which describes the many benefits of
participation.  The next session of the seminar will be conducted
on _____.

I look forward to our continuing interactions.  Please feel free
to give me a call if I may be of assistance to you with
registration for the seminar.


Sincerely,


_____


Enclosure
```

Figure 13–6. Sample letter seeking participant registration, sent to audience member at speaking engagement.

```
Date

Name
Company
Address
City/State/Zip

Dear

I am writing to confirm your registration for _____

_____.

The seminar will begin at _____.

You should plan on arriving at _____.  Please bring this
letter with you.

I look forward to working with you at the Seminar and if I may
provide further information or otherwise be of assistance prior
to the Seminar please don't hesitate to contact me.


Sincerely,


_____
```

Figure 13–7. Sample letter confirming registration.

```
Date

Name
Company
Address
City/State/Zip

Dear

Thank you for your registration for _____.

We have an excellent program planned and you will be particularly
pleased to know that the Seminar will _____.

The Seminar will be conducted on:  _____.

It will begin at _____ and conclude at _____.

The Seminar will be held at:  _____.


I look forward to working with you and if I may provide further
information or otherwise be of assistance prior to the Seminar
please don't hesitate to let me know.


Sincerely,


_____
```

Figure 13–8. Sample acknowledgment of registration.

```
Date


Name
Company
Address
City/State/Zip


Dear


Just a short note to thank you for your participation in _____
_____.

I enjoyed having the opportunity to work with you and wish to
thank you for your meaningful contributions which made the
seminar a more beneficial experience for both me and the other
participants.

It has been my experience that participants in the Seminar
usually know of one or more individuals that would benefit from
participation in this program.  I would appreciate your providing
me with the names and addresses of any friends or associates that
would profit from participation.  I have enclosed a pre-
addressed, postage-paid form for this purpose.

Again, my thanks for your participation and please don't hesitate
to contact me should you have any questions or if I may be of
assistance in any fashion.


Sincerely,


_____
```

Figure 13–9. Sample follow-up letter.

```
Date

Dear Participant:

If you have benefited from this Seminar, I would appreciate your
providing me with the names of other individuals whom you feel we
should notify about the next session of the Seminar.

Space is provided below for you to indicate the names of friends,
associates, colleagues.

Thank you!

Sincerely,


------------------------
------------------------------------------------------------------


Your Name_____

Please list the names of those we should contact:

Name_____ __Mr.  __Ms  __Dr.  __Mrs.

Firm/Org._____Title_____

Address_____

City_____State_____Zip_____Phone_____/_____-_____


Name_____  __Mr.  __Ms  __Dr.  __Mrs.

Firm/Org._____Title_____

Address_____

City_____State_____Zip_____Phone_____/_____-_____


Name_____  __Mr.  __Ms  __Dr.  __Mrs.

Firm/Org._____Title_____

Address_____

City_____State_____Zip_____Phone_____/_____-_____
```

Figure 13–10. Sample follow-up letter and referral form.

241

```
Date


Name
Company
Address
City/State/Zip


Dear


Just a short note to express my thanks for recommending that
_____ contact me.

As you know, referrals are a vital part of successful marketing of
my seminars.  Your support and confidence is greatly appreciated.


Sincerely,


_____
```

Figure 13–11. Sample response to referral.

```
Date

Name
Company
Address
City/State/Zip

Dear


_____ has requested that I provide you with
information about _____.

Enclosed please find a copy of _____, which is designed
to provide you with information about _____.  I am
hopeful that you will find this information to be of value.

If I may answer any questions, provide further information or
otherwise be of assistance please don't hesitate to contact me.


Sincerely,


_____
```

Figure 13–12. Sample letter to a referral.

Name _____

Title _____

Organization _____

Mailing Address _____

City _____ State _____ Zip _____ Phone _____/___-_____

What is your overall evaluation of the program?

( ) Excellent   ( ) Good   ( ) Satisfactory   ( ) Unsatisfactory

What would you most like to see changed for future programs?

_____

What did you find most valuable in the program?

_____

_____

Which newspapers and/or professional or trade periodicals do you read?

_____   _____

_____   _____

To which trade or professional associations do you belong?

_____   _____

_____   _____

How did you first learn about this program?

( ) Brochure   ( ) Advertisement in _____

( ) Friend/colleague (name) _____

( ) Personal call from _____ ( ) Other _____

Please list the names of others in your organization and/or other friends
and colleagues who might be interested in this program and should receive
advance notice of meetings.

_____

_____

Figure 13–13. Program evaluation.

Name _____ Phone No. _____/_____-_____

Title _____ Organization _____

Address _____

City _____ State _____ Zip _____

1. Overall Evaluation

Excellent	Very Good	Good	Fair	Poor
10 9	8 7	6 5	4 3	2 1 0

2. Facilities

Excellent	Very Good	Good	Fair	Poor
10 9	8 7	6 5	4 3	2 1 0

3. Planned Meals

Excellent	Very Good	Good	Fair	Poor
10 9	8 7	6 5	4 3	2 1 0

4. Instructor's Presentation

Excellent	Very Good	Good	Fair	Poor
10 9	8 7	6 5	4 3	2 1 0

5. Instructor's Knowledge of Subject

Excellent	Very Good	Good	Fair	Poor
10 9	8 7	6 5	4 3	2 1 0

6. Usefulness of Content

Very useful	Somewhat useful	Not very useful	Useless
10 9 8	7 6 5	4 3 2	1 0

7. Usefulness of Program Materials

Very useful	Somewhat useful	Not very useful	Useless
10 9 8	7 6 5	4 3 2	1 0

8. Time Spent in Program

Well used	Sometimes wasted	Often wasted	Almost entirely wasted
10 9 8	7 6 5	4 3 2	1 0

9. How knowledgeable on the program subject do you feel you were before the program?

Very	Somewhat	Not very	Not at all
10 9 8	7 6 5	4 3 2	1 0

10. How knowledgeable on the subject do you feel you are after the program?

Very	Somewhat	Not very	Not at all
10 9 8	7 6 5	4 3 2	1 0

11. Should the speaker:

_____ Be asked again soon

_____ Be asked sometime in the future

_____ Never be asked again

Figure 13–14. Captive program evaluation.

12. Please check or suggest topics on which you would be interested in gaining more information through attendance at another program.

_____ Stress _____ Time management _____ Goal setting
_____ Motivation _____ Organizational effectiveness
_____ Team building _____ Problem solving and decision making
_____ Fundamentals of management _____ Other _____

_____

_____

13. What was the least valuable aspect of the program for you? What would you have liked to be different? What would you like to see changed?

_____

_____

_____

14. What was the most valuable aspect of the program for you?

_____

_____

_____

Figure 13–14. (*continued*)

14

THE WINNING PROGRAM

Your seminar, workshop, or whatever form your program takes, is part of a training cycle that begins with your recognition that people need the information you have to offer and your potential participants' recognition of and desire for the value of that information. The cycle ends when your participants learn, assimilate, and utilize knowledge, skill, and training from your program.

THE TRAINING CYCLE

The training cycle consists of several stages:

1. *Recognition of the Need for Training or Assistance.* A seminar developer identifies public need or demand for a particular type of knowledge or information, or an organizational client (in a captive program) or individuals who will ultimately attend the program, recognize the need for specific training, and convey that need to a seminar developer.

2. *Determination of the Need.* The general need identified in the first stage is analyzed, defined, and refined to establish and clarify what information must be conveyed to fulfill the need.

3. *Development of Learning Objectives.* The new knowledge, experience, or skill that participants will acquire as a direct result of the training program is specified by the learning objectives.

4. *Establishment of Information Requirements.* By thoroughly researching and analyzing the topic subject, the seminar developer establishes the course content that will meet the specified learning objectives.

5. *Establishment of Material Requirements.* Practical exercises are incorporated into the program agenda in order to allow participants to practice some tangible skill during the session.

6. *Establishment of an Agenda.* The seminar developer establishes the agenda for the program, determining how long each part of the program will be and planning for question-and-answer sessions.

7. *Development of Participant and Trainer Materials.* The seminar developer decides upon participant materials that will fulfill two objectives: first, they will aid the participant in the learning process, and second, they will assist in selling the program to others who will see the materials. Written materials are created to provide tangible, straightforward information that will reinforce the verbal presentation. Their layout provides enough space, either in the margins or throughout the outline of the text, for note taking. (People are less likely to lend or give away materials that include their personal notes. Their interested friends or colleagues must contact the seminar developer for further information.)

8. *Design of an Evaluation System.* An evaluation system that will be valuable and useful in assessing the effectiveness and success of the program and in making changes for future presentations is created in advance. After the presentation, participants will be asked to evaluate, anonymously if they prefer, the program elements and presenter skills. Questions focus on specific information pertinent to the program and on participants' reactions.

9. *Conduct of the Program.* The seminar developer conducts the seminar or workshop, working according to the established agenda and keeping in mind the specified needs, objectives, and requirements for the program.

10. *Report of Results.* A summary report is written after the presentation to keep track of the rejection or acceptance of the ideas tested. Such a report helps the developer to trace and direct the progress and changes of a seminar or workshop; in a captive program, a summary report may be part of the contractual obligations of the presenter.

11. *Follow-Up.* After a suitable length of time (neither too soon after the program—participants have not had time to assimilate their new knowledge and information—nor too long after—participants have forgotten that they even attended the session and certainly cannot remember its particulars), the seminar developer decides whether to conduct a follow-up evaluation. Its purposes would be to: test the long-term efficacy of the training program and consider changes, according to the results; and determine whether the need and demand for further information are sufficient to warrant additional programs, materials, or products marketed to the individual participants or client organization.

Figure 14–1 illustrates the training objective. The shaded area shows the difference between where a participant is at the start and at the end and thus equals the training requirement.

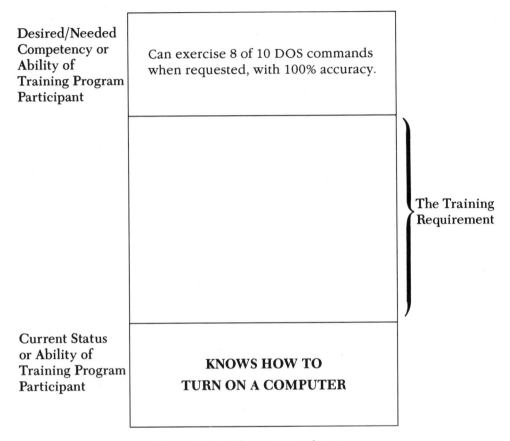

Figure 14-1. The training objective.

SEMINAR, WORKSHOP, OR WHAT?

"Seminar" or "workshop" may not be the most motivating title for your program; the two words tend to be overused. Look at what the competition is doing, research the expectations of your participants, and select the most appropriate/marketable description for your session; the nature of the interaction during a program often determines what it should be called. Among the major training models/program descriptions are the following:

Audience Reaction Team. A team of trainees who are expected to interrupt the trainer during the program to seek immediate clarification of unclear points and to otherwise help the trainer meet the particular needs of the trainees.

Brainstorming. A stream-of-consciousness technique in which creative thinking, rather than practical thinking, is encouraged. Participants spontaneously suggest ideas—any ideas—on a topic, the seminar presenter writes the ideas on a chalkboard or flip pad, and then the presenter and participants edit the list of ideas. The atmosphere must be comfortable enough for the trainees to be uninhibited about presenting ideas.

Buzz Session. A discussion method that encourages or requires all attendees to participate. The larger group is divided into three-person discussion groups for about five minutes and each individual contributes ideas.

Case Method. Narrations and discussions of actual situations (case studies) given in order to identify underlying principles. The identified principles are used to diagnose and solve problems. This training model encourages participants to develop problem-solving abilities; variations of the case method include the Harvard Method, the Incident Process Method, and the Abbreviated Case.

Clinic. A meeting or series of meetings which involve analysis and treatment of specific conditions or problems.

Colloquy. A modified version of the *Panel* in which participants express opinions, raise issues, and ask questions to be responded to by the resource person.

Conference. A group of presentations offering several different programs for participants to choose from. Many authorities may present information in a variety of training models in each of the individual programs that make up a conference agenda.

Consultation. A deliberation—via telephone conversations, personal letters, or on-the-job visits—between a trainer and one or more people.

Correspondence Course. A self-instructional course using print and/or nonprint materials as the educational medium. Such a course may include tutorial or small group sessions, consultation with a trainer, written assignments, examinations, and grades or other evaluations.

Critical Incidents. Dramatized educational experiences in written, audio, and/or visual form, exemplifying actual events. Often, trainees must make decisions and perform actions in a "laboratory" setting that simulates critical moments in behavioral situations.

Demonstration (Method). A visual presentation, accompanied by oral discussion, showing how to use a procedure or perform an act.

Demonstration (Result). Shows by example the outcome of some practice that can be seen, heard, or felt. A demonstration often deals with operational costs, production procedures, or the quality of a product. This method generally requires a considerable period of time to complete.

Discussion Group. An informal meeting of two or more people who discuss a topic of mutual concern and interest; usually based on a common background achieved through assigned readings or shared educational experiences.

Exchange Study. Trainees' examination of a situation from a point of view different from their usual point of view.

Exhibits. Collections of related items displayed to assist in the learning process or to carry an educational, informational, or inspirational message.

Field Trip or Tour. Events in which a training group visits a place of educational interest for direct observation and study. Field trips usually take less than four hours; tours include visits to many points of interest and require from one day to several weeks to complete.

Forum. Discussion of a topic by attendees after the topic has been introduced by a speaker, panel, film, or other technique. A moderator functions to give everyone a chance to speak in an orderly manner.

Information Sheets (Handouts). Learning aids—often trainer-made or copied from published materials—given to participants to support and/or supplement a presentation.

Interview. An informal presentation in which one or more trainees question one or more resource persons, to explore a topic in depth.

Leaderless Discussion. Discussion in which the trainer does not participate and no formal leader is designated; instead, spontaneous participation is encouraged. Facilitates participant involvement, introduction of issues or problems, and exchange of ideas, while overcoming the inherent formalities of large classes and lectures.

Lecture (or Speech). An often formal and carefully prepared oral presentation by an expert on a topic.

Lecture Series. A sequence of speeches delivered by either a single speaker or many speakers, extended over a period of several days or as intermittently as one day a week or month for several weeks or months.

Letters, Circular. Printed or duplicated letters that carry announcements, reports, and training information. They tend to be less personal than newsletters.

Listening Team. Method of interaction between a speaker and trainees. A small group listens, takes notes, asks questions, and/or summarizes a training session (particularly useful in a captive program where a speaker is not very knowledgeable about an organization's special problems).

Newsletters. Bulletins usually mailed to many people—subscribers, interested individuals, program participants, and so on—conveying announcements, news, events, or reports. Newsletters often carry training information and are the trainers' way of personally communicating with many people.

On-the-Job Training. A learning experience, conducted normally under the guidance or direction of an experienced person, in which trainees learn some job, act, skill, or procedure by doing it.

Panel. A discussion among four to eight experts on an assigned topic in front of a group of participants. A moderator ensures that each resource person gets equal time, that the topic is covered adequately, and that order is maintained.

Programmed Instruction. Similar to a correspondence course; a method of instruction using a self-teaching format through print and/or nonprint materials. The trainer exerts influence indirectly through programmed textbooks, teaching machines, computer-assisted instruction, dial-access information retrieval systems, and so on.

Question Period. An organized follow-up session to a lecture or speech, in which the audience asks the lecturer questions, asks for clarification of points made in the presentation, and requests any other information.

Seminar. A presentation format used for a group of participants who are engaged/interested in some specialized area or topic. A leader opens the seminar with brief remarks and then guides a discussion in which all attendees participate.

Simulation. Contrived educational experiences which have the characteristics of a real-life situation. Simulations allow trainees to make decisions or perform actions in a "laboratory" setting before actually interacting with people and things. Examples are driver training simulators, educational games such as Monopoly, Blacks and Whites, or CLUG (Community Land Use Games), all of which require actions and decisions from the participants.

Skit. A short, rehearsed, dramatic presentation performed by participants. Working from a prepared script, the participants act out an event or incident, dramatizing and/or exemplifying a situation taken from on-the-job experience.

Symposium. A series of lectures on a singular subject, given by two to five resource people, in which each speaker presents one aspect of the topic. The presentations are brief and straightforward.

Workshop. A training method that permits extensive study of a specific topic; usually gathers about 15 to 30 people together to improve their proficiency in some area and to collectively develop new operating procedures while solving problems.

MAKING THE MOST OF YOUR PROGRAM

Once you have chosen your seminar or workshop topic, established your program format and agenda, selected the locations, decided on a fee, conducted your marketing, and registered participants for the session, you are in a position to make the most of your program—to prepare and conduct it, to the best of your abilities, profitably and successfully.

Characteristics/Attributes of a Good Program

1. *Provides Necessary and Useful Information to the Participants.* Because participants want to make the most of their valuable time and money, a program that presents superfluous, incorrect, or easily obtained information will not last long.

2. *Provides Practical, How-To, and Specific Information Rather than Conceptual and Theoretical Knowledge.* Participants' time and money are valuable (to them and to you), and they will insist them only to gain practical knowledge and skill which will measurably improve their productivity, capability, or expertise in some specified area.

3. *Minimizes Time Required to Obtain Information.* Seminar and workshop attendees generally want to acquire a thorough understanding of a subject in a short period of intensive learning. A good program enables participants to get all necessary information in the shortest possible time.

4. *Provides Support Materials That Enhance Learning During and After the Program.* Materials should be designed to help participants organize new information during the presentation and access and review it easily afterward.

5. *Provides an Avenue for Further Learning or a Means by Which Questions Can Be Answered.* Participants should be able to acquire more information after the program through their own research (with the help of starting points provided in the session), through resources (bibliographies or other supplementary information supplied in program materials), or through contacting the presenter directly by mail or telephone or at a in the future meeting.

6. *Entertains as Well as Informs and Educates.* A lively and interesting presentation, with humor judiciously used in the context of the topic being discussed, will contribute to a comfortable atmosphere and will enhance the learning process. Participants will be relaxed, satisfied, and enthusiastic (rather than dissatisfied and bored).

7. *Provides Regular "Status Reports" to Participants, Informing Them of Where They Are Headed and Reminding Them of Where They Have Been in the Session.* Periodic summaries of topics covered and brief previews of upcoming information will help participants to organize their new knowledge; question-and-answer sessions will actively engage the attendees in the learning process, instead of allowing them to slip into "passive recipient" mode.

8. *Provides an Opportunity for Presentation of Ideas and Practice of Learned Skills.* As time, agenda, and type of program permit,

participants are allowed time to express ideas, opinions, and questions and to apply practically the skills learned in the session.

9. *Provides for Participant Comfort.* Seminar location, setup, and format should create an atmosphere comfortable for participants and conducive to their learning. Regularly scheduled breaks and changes in training technique—alternating from lecture to audiovisual presentation to exercise to discussion, for example—will alleviate restlessness and boredom. Alternating training techniques should assist greater numbers of participants in learning, because different people are receptive to different modes of presentation.

Length of the Program

To determine the ideal length of a seminar or workshop, you must consider the amount of time needed to cover the subject in sufficient depth. Participants' time and money are valuable and, for the most part, they want to learn as much as possible in the shortest amount of time, without sacrificing detail or quality of information. However, while some subjects can be adequately covered in an intensive afternoon, other topics require several days of training to address all of their complexities.

You must also consider the cost to the participant. In addition to the program fee, there are other quite costly expenses. A multiple-day public program, with the added costs of hotel rooms, meals, and transportation, will be much more expensive to the participant than a one-day seminar. Busy professionals or business executives—attorneys, doctors, or consultants, for example—may lose hundreds or thousands of dollars a day in lost time or lost billings resulting from their participation in an extended program. However, if your client is a corporation or other organization that is willing to give people time off from their jobs and pay their expenses, then a two- or three-day seminar might be more practical and lucrative: your participants will have more time to better absorb new information, and you will make more money. Thus, you should consider your potential audience and how much time and money, above and beyond your fee, they are willing to spend, when deciding the length of the program.

The burdens placed on you, the seminar developer/presenter, should not be minimized. In a single-day program, one individual can most likely handle the entire presentation; however, in a longer program extending over several days, either more presenters will probably be necessary or more participant activity must be scheduled to ease the pressure on the presenter. The hospitality requirement on the part of the provider grows as the program's time is increased. Providing suitable and sufficient beverages and snacks and making sure that there are ample hotel, restaurant, entertainment, and transportation facilities nearby both complicate management and increase costs, when the session extends beyond a single day. The cost of renting the room where you will hold the seminar can be particularly expensive as the program's length increases. Hotels try to rent conference or meeting rooms for several uses each day; if your meeting will last an entire day, or more than a day, the hotel will charge you for the lost opportunities to rent the room. However, this additional cost can often be absorbed by the higher price people are willing to pay for a full-day program rather than one that is several hours long, or for a two-day rather than a one-day program. If you schedule your meeting for 10 A.M. to 5 P.M., instead of from 8 A.M. to 6 P.M., your rental fee may be lower because the hotel will have the opportunity to rent the room for an early breakfast and an evening function. Your participants will still perceive the program as a full day and will pay accordingly.

Planning Ahead

A little advance planning can go a long way toward making your program run smoothly, alleviating last-minute problems, and averting potential disaster.

Try to have all of your seminar materials ready to ship several weeks before the program date, so you can ship them ahead inexpensively and can confirm their arrival at the hotel/conference facility before you leave your home city. If time does not permit, or if your programs are scheduled close together, your only option may be to take the materials on the plane with you. The airlines' excess-luggage charge for extra baggage can be quite high; often, a generous tip to a skycap will send your luggage through free of charge.

An essential part of planning ahead, and a much less expensive solution than bringing people with you and paying their salary and travel expenses, is to hire reliable, local, temporary help to run the registration table at your seminar or workshop. If you need two or more registrars, it is always wise to request help from two different temporary employment agencies and confirm the day before the program; thus, you can be relatively certain that at least one person will show up and you will not end up handling registrations yourself. Request employees with top marketing skills and experience dealing with people. Indicate your willingness to pay a little extra to guarantee that the temporary help will be qualified, competent, and prompt; registration will provide participants with their first impressions of your presentation, and you want to establish a comfortable, professional environment to start off your program.

Make sure that you arrive at the seminar site sufficiently early to handle any problems that might arise. This is the time to check out the meeting room to make sure everything is as you requested: the room is the right size, heating or air conditioning is working properly, and all supplies you asked for (overhead projector, blackboard, slide projector, and so on) are present. During this preseminar time, you can also review your materials and meet your participants.

Checklist for Preparing Effective Presentations

1. Practice your presentation aloud once or twice before friends, family, or colleagues.

2. Don't practice too much, and never try to memorize your presentation; it will sound too rehearsed and unnatural. And, don't try to read it verbatim.

3. In developing an outline, forget the rules of formal outline procedure. Use what works for you. Many seminar leaders find that a list of key points—memory joggers telling the speaker when to move on to the next topic—is ideal.

4. Put times alongside items on the outline so that you can occasionally check your progress relative to the clock, to ensure that you don't reach the end of the session having covered only half of what you have to say.

5. Keep your mind on what you are saying. Don't allow your mind to wander; if you do, you will forget what you have already said. This is particularly important if you are giving the same presentation over and over again. Force yourself to stay with the here and now and don't think about what you will do the next time you give the seminar or what you have planned for the next day.

6. Try to limit unnecessary distractions. Keep the door to the room closed, and if there is a telephone in the room, instruct the operator to hold calls during the seminar. If possible, assign a registrar to stay in the back of the room to ensure that you are not bothered by drop-in visitors or late walk-ins.

7. Place your emphasis on meaningful communication to your participants and not on being the world's greatest orator. Aristotle once said, "Think as wise men do, but speak as the common people do."

8. Remember that you know your topic better than the participants do. In a seminar, unlike a book, the participant cannot go back to obtain clarification of a point that he or she has slept through. Provide your participants with a road map: from time to time tell them where they are going and remind them of where they have been. Many seminar leaders treat each subject/content area in this sequence: first they inform the participants about the information to be presented, then they provide the promised information, and finally they explain the information just provided.

9. Remind participants to pay attention, by saying things like, "Here is a crucial definition," "You may wish to make a note of this," or "I regard this next point as being of particular importance for you."

10. Make note taking easy for your participants. Provide detailed information such as addresses, phone numbers, precise citations on publications, and so on in their seminar materials so that they don't have to spend their time on minute details. If you don't do this, you will never meet your set schedule because slow or late note takers will repeatedly be asking you for such details.

11. Learn the techniques of dealing with questions that you do not wish to answer at a particular time.

12. Start strong and finish strong. Your opening and your closing should be the high points of your presentation.

13. People learn best in seminars when they have both visual and audio stimuli to assist them. Try to provide visuals and outlines or notes which will help the learning process and will provide relevance after the seminar for a participant who is attempting to remember information.

14. A story is worth a thousand facts. A simple story or anecdote which clearly makes a point is far easier for your participants to remember than long, complicated theories and facts. Stories add color to your remarks and communicate much more meaningfully than factual exposition.

Seminar Materials

The seminar materials you provide are essential both as learning aids for the participants—reinforcing information during the presentation and supplementing information afterward—and as marketing devices—giving the participant a reminder of you, your seminar, and your knowledge. The participant may contact you for further information, advice, and information products and may show the materials to colleagues and friends who might be interested in your program. There are many possible ways in which to obtain or develop successful seminar materials; with a little creativity and imagination, you should have no trouble finding your optimal selections.

One of the best ways to obtain seminar materials is to develop your own; although this may take some time, it is well worth the effort because the material will be specific to your needs and will follow your program outline. Book extracts and magazine and professional journal articles can be excellent sources of supplemental material. Publishers are usually generous with their permissions and low-cost reprints when the information is used for educational purposes. Full credit should be given to the original source. In addition, products of the Government Printing Office, which publishes vast amounts of free or low-cost information, can be good sources for seminar materials; government publications are in the public domain and can be reproduced without permission (credit should still be given to the source). You can also inquire for assistance and information from government experts on almost any topic. These people are not going to create your seminar materials for you, but they should be able to point you in the right direction and provide some additional resources and information sources. Trade and professional associations, banks, and insurance companies typically produce a wealth of undiscovered written information that may be just what you are looking for. Many companies are in the business of creating and producing training materials, sometimes even free or at low cost for educational programs. And, of course, library reference sections can direct you to a myriad of possible sources in encyclopedias, directories, and reference books.

Guidelines for Preparing and Packaging Participant Materials

1. Place all materials, including advertising and promotional materials which you will give participants, in one binder or bound volume. Loose items are likely to be lost during or after the seminar or workshop. Tabbed dividers used to separate sections are recommended.

2. When your materials contain forms which the participants are likely to copy or modify for their own use, provide a duplicate within their materials. They can then make notes on the first copy and use the second to reproduce.

3. Include a welcome letter at the start of your materials. Participants often arrive early and this letter will welcome them to the seminar and provide some direction relative to what they can expect during the day. The letter can cover "housekeeping" information and agenda, to reduce the questions you are asked while you are busy preparing to start the seminar or managing the on-site registration.

4. Be sure to include biographical information on the speakers, presenters, or staff conducting the program. Stress their practical, real-world experience and accomplishments.

5. Consider enclosing background information on the city, particularly at a multiple-day program with participants from outside the immediate area. Information on restaurants, entertainment, local attractions, and transportation services can be very helpful, and providing such tips demonstrates a concern for the well-being of the participants and enhances their favorable impression of you and your program.

6. Give serious thought to providing participants with copies of all visuals used during the program. They will need to take fewer notes, they will be able to follow the visual presentation even if they are seated in the back of the room, and they will have a convenient way to remember points you have made in the program.

7. Provide participants with background reading information and/or a bibliography for their further study. Some will want to study the content you are presenting in much greater detail.

8. If your program contains a great deal of new and different (particularly technical) information and terminology, provide definitions, in one specific place, of the words and concepts being used.

9. Include your name, address, phone number, and copyright information, if appropriate, on every page. Seminar materials often become separated and photocopied, and it will be to your long-run marketing benefit for every page to be identified as having come from you and your seminar.

10. Structure your materials so as to encourage participants to write in them, particularly to record personal and proprietary information. This approach reduces the likelihood that people will copy your materials and give them to others, and increases the prospect that more people will attend your program later.

11. Consider including other information that might be appropriate for your program:

    □ A checklist that participants can actually use on their job

    □ A summary of key points that will be fully or partially covered but that would require extensive note taking to record in full

    □ Schematics of a technical process, systems flow charts, graphs, and formulas (all of which are usually projected on an overhead as well)

    □ Reprints of articles, sample correspondence, and case studies

    □ Photographs, which should typically also be projected

Audiovisuals

Appropriate audiovisual aids—particularly visual aids—that complement and supplement your presentation can greatly enhance the participants' learning and the effectiveness of your seminar or workshop. Many people learn best visually; thus, visual aids help the seminar leader to control the meeting and maintain the group's attention. We retain 10 percent of what we hear, but with added visual aids, retention increases to approximately 50 percent. The combined use of sight (the visual aid) and sound (the presenter explaining the visual material) allows the participants to understand information easily and quickly. Many seminar developers and presenters choose inappropriate audiovisual materials or use them ineffectively, particularly because they tend to believe that elaborate, state-of-the-art technology is their best option. Proper use determines the value of an audiovisual aid. Simplicity is often preferable to high technology.

Many seminar leaders use slide projectors or even video recorders and television screens instead of overhead projectors. Slide projectors produce a sharp image and can be operated by remote control but they require a dark room; note taking becomes difficult and turning lights on and off can be extremely distracting and make participants uncomfortable.

In small programs with a very limited number of participants, TVs and video recorders can be appropriate additions to your presentation; however, even big-screen TVs are designed for small groups and should not be used in large group settings.

Advantages of Overhead Projectors

Research has revealed that overhead projectors continue to be the most effective audiovisual aid for most seminar providers, for several reasons:

1. You can present to any size group in a fully lighted room.
2. You face the audience.
3. You are using a very personal presentation tool because you can create your own transparencies.
4. You can switch the machine on and off easily and quietly, directing attention to you or the screen, as you wish.
5. You can reveal material point by point.
6. The participants are not distracted by the machine or a change in lighting conditions.
7. Anyone can operate the equipment and, compared with other audiovisual equipment, the cost is usually low, whether you buy or rent.
8. Overhead transparencies can be made quickly and inexpensively.

Use of overhead projectors can be highly beneficial and effective, but only if used properly. The following hints should help you obtain the maximum impact with your overhead projector:

1. *Keep Your Transparencies Simple.* Present one idea per transparency. Have a maximum of six or seven lines of copy on each, with the fewest words possible to convey your idea. Select a highly visible typeface and keep the size between 18 and 24 points—or larger, if your room and group require greater visibility.
2. *Use the On/Off Switch.* Never leave the projector on without showing a transparency; it will distract the viewers. Switching the overhead on and off allows you to focus attention where you want it—either on the screen or on yourself—when you want it.
3. *Make Use of the Write-On Technique.* With a water-based pen, you can write on a blank transparency or add to a previously prepared

visual; later, the information can be easily wiped off if you want. In this way, you can tailor a general transparency to a specific audience.

4. *Use the Pointer Technique.* Pointing to an item (even with a pen or pencil) is very effective for drawing attention to major information in your presentation because participants can see the pointer moving around on the screen.

5. *Reveal Material Point by Point.* Keep the bottom of the transparency covered with a plain piece of paper so that participants concentrate on the particular point being made, instead of reading ahead. Slide the paper down as you reach each new point.

6. *Use Color Effectively.* Transparencies with colored backgrounds can reduce eyestrain and fatigue, but don't select colors just for the sake of having color. Light, pastel colors work best because they do not diminish the clarity of the material you are presenting. Avoid dark backgrounds; they tend to overshadow the material and inhibit learning.

Keeping these tips in mind should contribute to the success of your program and the overall learning of your participants.

FINE-TUNING

Quality seminars are those that meet the desired educational and marketing objectives. To be successful, they require substantial attention to detail. This chapter has offered valuable insight based on experience in conducting programs. However, it is easy to forget or overlook some of the most important details that produce a quality result. Figure 14–2 is a checklist of essential details, to help ensure the quality and success of your seminar or workshop.

No matter what unforeseen problems or difficulties arise at the last minute, stay cool, calm, and professional. Even if you cannot solve the problem, your participants will be impressed with your composure and, if you remain confident and proceed with the program, many attendees will not even notice that there is a problem.

Figure 14–3, a more extensive seminar and workshop planning checklist, is provided for your use in future programs. While each program may not require all of the steps outlined, the checklist serves as a useful reminder of action steps you might consider. Awareness of these considerations can make the difference between a substandard or mediocre program and a superlative one.

Speakers/Presenters

_____ The presentation style and the presenters themselves serve to enhance my image, reputation, and market position (and/or that of my firm).

_____ I select speakers with care. I have only one opportunity to make a good first impression. The speakers selected must have a demonstrated ability to meet both the educational and marketing objectives of the seminar.

_____ I test out the presenters before hiring them to speak.

_____ The selected speakers are technically competent, recognized authorities on the subject.

_____ The speakers I select have the ability to relate to the level of the participant group and have an understanding of the group's needs, problems, and concerns.

_____ If I am using technical speakers, the audience is sufficiently technical to ensure quality communication. My speakers will not be over the participants' heads or too remedial.

_____ If there are multiple speakers, they complement—they don't duplicate—each other.

_____ I carefully review the content of the talks that will be given by outside speakers, to ensure that their remarks are consistent with my philosophies and policies (and/or those of my firm) and the objectives of the seminar.

_____ I schedule and conduct for the presenters a meeting in advance of the program, to make sure that they are informed of all information, details, and changes relevant to the seminar.

_____ I have backup speakers available in case planned speakers cannot make the seminar.

Agenda and Materials

_____ The seminar materials used always reflect my professionalism, competence, and image (and/or that of my firm) and are highly beneficial to participants.

_____ I establish an agenda that has variety and interest. Participants are not required to sit and listen to a lecture/series of lectures for long periods of time. I build into the agenda different types of activities and breaks, to ensure that the seminar will be entertaining and productive.

_____ I have extra copies of presentation outlines, visuals, and participant materials in case they are misplaced or lost.

Figure 14–2. Seminar checklist—quality and procedures.

_____ All mail and phone registrations and information requests are acknowledged promptly with written confirmation.

_____ If my materials have been sent to the hotel prior to the seminar, I confirm their arrival and find out exactly where they will be.

_____ I double-check all seminar facilities arrangements (size and setup of the meeting room, refreshments, posting of the program in the lobby, and so on) and registration processes before the participants arrive.

_____ If needed, I obtain temporary help for on-site clerical and registration purposes. If two or more registrars are necessary, I reserve help from at least two different agencies, to ensure that at least one person will show up.

Presentation

_____ I (and/or the speakers) repeat all participants' questions and answers from the podium, to make sure that everyone has heard them.

_____ I make sure prior to the program that participants can see and hear the speaker and all audiovisuals and demonstrations no matter where they are seated.

_____ I (and/or the speakers) adhere to the schedule. The program doesn't run over into scheduled breaks nor do breaks drag on past the scheduled time.

_____ I (and/or the speakers) maintain eye contact with participants. I do not read verbatim.

_____ Audiovisual equipment and information are selected for their usefulness rather than for being artistic or high tech.

_____ The audiovisual presentation is selected based on what will be most effective for the learning and marketing objectives of the seminar.

_____ I am accessible and available to answer questions, provide information, and talk to participants before and after the seminar.

Figure 14–2. (*continued*)

SEMINAR TASK CHECKLIST

Seminar _____

_____

Instructor/Presenter _____

Date of first session _____

Task	Number of Weeks Prior to Program	Person Responsible	To Be Done By	Date Done
Outside Speakers/Presenters				
Determine budget for speakers	____	____	____	____
Identify available speakers	____	____	____	____
Review credentials/references	____	____	____	____
Select & prioritize speakers	____	____	____	____
Invite speakers/presenters	____	____	____	____
Develop speaker/presenter contract	____	____	____	____
Obtain signed speaker contract	____	____	____	____
Obtain biographical/résumé data from speakers & presenters	____	____	____	____
Obtain approval of brochure & materials, including biographic information, from speakers & presenters	____	____	____	____
Communicate logistics & procedures to speakers/presenters	____	____	____	____
Provide speakers with presentation & materials development guidelines	____	____	____	____
Obtain materials for reproduction from speakers/presenters	____	____	____	____
Confirm with speakers/presenters	____	____	____	____
Seminar Facilities & Hospitality				
Select program location(s)	____	____	____	____

Figure 14–3. Seminar checklist—tasks.

Identify available facilities & costs _____ _____ ____ ____

Rate adequacy of facilities _____ _____ ____ ____

Select/Book facilities _____ _____ ____ ____

Obtain guest room block & rates _____ _____ ____ ____

Obtain facility contract/
  confirmation _____ _____ ____ ____

Determine refreshment
  requirements _____ _____ ____ ____

Provide facility with requirements _____ _____ ____ ____

Confirm facility arrangements/
  provide final counts/guarantees _____ _____ ____ ____

Seminar/Workshop Materials

Determine information
  requirements _____ _____ ____ ____

Determine information passing
  requirements _____ _____ ____ ____

Determine exercise/skills practice
  requirements _____ _____ ____ ____

Design participant materials _____ _____ ____ ____

Design trainer/presenter materials _____ _____ ____ ____

Determine published materials
  requirements _____ _____ ____ ____

Pilot-test materials _____ _____ ____ ____

Select packaging _____ _____ ____ ____

Order packaging _____ _____ ____ ____

Schedule printing & binding
  services _____ _____ ____ ____

Prepare camera-ready art _____ _____ ____ ____

Proof materials _____ _____ ____ ____

Produce materials _____ _____ ____ ____

Produce visuals _____ _____ ____ ____

Inspect finished materials _____ _____ ____ ____

Deliver completed materials to
  seminar/workshop site _____ _____ ____ ____

Figure 14–3. (*continued*)

Confirm arrival of materials
   at site   ———— ———— ——— ———

Promotion of Program

Determine promotional objectives ———— ———— ——— ———

Select promotional strategies   ———— ———— ——— ———

Establish promotional schedule   ———— ———— ——— ———

Develop rough promotional
   materials   ———— ———— ——— ———

Test promotional materials for
   readability   ———— ———— ——— ———

Test promotional materials for
   validity   ———— ———— ——— ———

Direct Mail

Identify available mailing lists
   & costs   ———— ———— ——— ———

Determine size of mailing   ———— ———— ——— ———

Select mailing lists   ———— ———— ——— ———

Design promotional brochure   ———— ———— ——— ———

Order mailing lists   ———— ———— ——— ———

Select/schedule printer/mailer   ———— ———— ——— ———

Develop brochure camera-
   ready art   ———— ———— ——— ———

Check mailing lists for accuracy ———— ———— ——— ———

Print brochure   ———— ———— ——— ———

Mail brochure   ———— ———— ——— ———

Space Advertising

Determine available publications & costs   ———— ———— ——— ———

Select publications   ———— ———— ——— ———

Book advertising space   ———— ———— ——— ———

Design advertisements   ———— ———— ——— ———

Produce camera-ready art   ———— ———— ——— ———

Deliver camera-ready art to
   publication   ———— ———— ——— ———

Figure 14–3. (*continued*)

Public Relations

Identify those who will help to
promote your program & the
advance notice they need   _____   _____   ____   ____

Prepare mailing list for those
who will be providing promo-
tional/ publicity assistance   _____   _____   ____   ____

Determine information
requirements   _____   _____   ____   ____

Develop publicity materials   _____   _____   ____   ____

Print publicity materials   _____   _____   ____   ____

Deliver publicity materials   _____   _____   ____   ____

Follow-up Promotions

Determine follow-up marketing
strategies   _____   _____   ____   ____

Implement follow-up strategies   _____   _____   ____   ____

Participant Registration

Develop registration policies &
procedures   _____   _____   ____   ____

Design registration forms   _____   _____   ____   ____

Print registration forms   _____   _____   ____   ____

Confirm participant registration   _____   _____   ____   ____

Set go/no go date and number   _____   _____   ____   ____

Remind participant of seminar   _____   _____   ____   ____

Prepare seminar rosters   _____   _____   ____   ____

Develop participant evaluation
forms   _____   _____   ____   ____

Print evaluation forms   _____   _____   ____   ____

Type name badges   _____   _____   ____   ____

Arrange for on-site clerical
assistance & equipment   _____   _____   ____   ____

Figure 14–3. (*continued*)

CONCLUSION

The seminar and workshop business can be extremely profitable and rewarding for you and your participants, but it is not an easy business. Despite the industry's potential for success, not all providers are successful. Caution and conservatism are key requirements for a program developer or promoter; equally important are creativity and innovation. Overzealousness and greed, usually combined with inadequate market testing, are primary reasons for failure. However, creative thought, tempered with careful testing of *all* aspects of program development, and well-developed promotions can lead you toward success.

Overall success and revenues in the seminar and workshop industry should increase in the next five to 10 years. Conservatively, revenues should grow by an average of about 6 percent annually for the industry as a whole through the late 1990s, and profit margins should maintain their current levels. Renewed emphasis on increasing productivity and on improving the ability of the United States to compete relative to its major trading partners will result in an increase in seminar revenues and profitability of perhaps as much as 50 percent in growth rate and 20 percent in profitability. A growth rate of double the 6 percent forecast could occur if American industry finds it necessary to continue to expend vast sums to compensate for the poor quality of the American public education system. Since I regard both of these trends as likely, it would not be unreasonable to expect an annual growth rate in revenues of 10–12 percent between now and 1995. It would not then be unrealistic to expect that public seminar profitability (as a percentage of sales) would grow to 20 percent.

The greatest growth will no doubt be in public seminars. I would anticipate that public seminar enrollments will grow at about double the rate of contract training enrollments. Traditionally, growth has been associated with emerging technology and trends. There is no reason to anticipate that this will change. The following areas should be particularly strong in growth during the next five to seven years:

- Basic skills training to compensate for the deficiencies of the public education system
- Productivity and motivation
- Entrepreneurship and intrapreneurship, particularly programs that concentrate on identifying entrepreneurial capability and

the building/starting of small businesses should be especially strong as the number of individuals interested in entering private practice or starting consulting-training-information product/service businesses grows)

▫ Programs on coping with increasing governmental regulation

▫ Avocational interests

▫ Computer and data processing, particularly the use of sophisticated software.

Many individuals enjoy satisfaction, profit, and success from the seminar and workshop business and, if these predictions are correct, will continue to do so. With hard work, thorough research, consistent testing, appropriate marketing, innovation, and enthusiasm, you should enjoy equal rewards. If this book has helped you to conceive of an idea for a seminar or workshop, or turn an idea into a viable program, or upgrade a viable program into a thriving one, then it has served its purpose in serving you.

INDEX

ABOUT THE AUTHOR

Howard L. Shenson is a nationally recognized authority on the marketing of seminars, workshops, training programs, conferences, classes, and other educational events. His creative approach to the marketing of seminars and workshops has resulted in the sale of more than one million seminar seats for both his clients and his own proprietary programs.

The author of more than three dozen books, audio/video learning programs, software packages, booklets, assessment instruments, and research reports, he is a frequent contributor to professional magazines and journals. Shenson publishes his own monthly newsletter and serves as a columnist for two professional publications. He has developed a comprehensive seminar marketing and management software program.

More than 100,000 have attended seminars developed and conducted by Shenson and he regularly speaks before national professional societies. His seminars have been sponsored by leading institutions of higher learning and he often conducts training sessions for the continuing education departments of colleges and universities. His consulting clients include proprietary seminar providers, colleges and universities, training companies, professional firms, and speakers/trainers. In addition, he serves commercial organizations that use seminars as a strategy to market products and services.

Shenson is a Certified Management Consultant and has been active in the formation and development of professional organizations serving the consulting and training professions. He and his work have been the subject of more than 400 newspaper and magazine articles and he has appeared on more than 200 radio and television talk and news shows.

Prior to entering full-time consulting in 1971, Shenson served in administrative and teaching positions at both the University of Southern California and The California State University. A native of Seattle, he received his education at Seattle University and the University of Washington. He resides with his wife and three sons in Calabasas, California, and maintains offices in the Los Angeles suburb of Woodland Hills.

658.456
SH546

85562

LINCOLN CHRISTIAN COLLEGE AND SEMINARY